WITHDRAWN

Feminist criticism has not been kind to Charles Dickens, scorning in particular what Orwell referred to as his "legless angels" – good daughters like Little Nell, Agnes Wickfield, Esther Summerson, and all their dutiful ilk. Such critics have turned instead to the dark, angry women whose path seems to cut across the ordered progress of the Dickens novel, but they have ignored the good daughter's own wanderings outside the paternal house. Hilary M. Schor argues that in doing the necessary work of conveying value and meaning – dutifully carrying out her father's will – the good daughter acquires many of the attributes of her dark sister. The more earnestly the good daughter struggles to transcribe her father's story, the more she inscribes her own, overstepping the limits of domestic goodness, and claiming her own secret inheritance as a center of narrative authority in the Dickens novel.

HILARY M. SCHOR is Associate Professor of English at the University of Southern California. She is author of *Scheherezade in the Marketplace: Elizabeth Gaskell and the Victorian Novel* (1992).

CAMBRIDGE STUDIES IN NINETEENTH-CENTURY
LITERATURE AND CULTURE 25

DICKENS AND THE
DAUGHTER OF THE HOUSE

CAMBRIDGE STUDIES IN NINETEENTH-CENTURY
LITERATURE AND CULTURE

General editor
Gillian Beer, *University of Cambridge*

Editorial board
Isobel Armstrong, *Birkbeck College, London*
Terry Eagleton, *University of Oxford*
Leonore Davidoff, *University of Essex*
Catherine Gallagher, *University of California, Berkeley*
D. A. Miller, *Columbia University*
J. Hillis Miller, *University of California, Irvine*
Mary Poovey, *New York University*
Elaine Showalter, *Princeton University*

Nineteenth-century British literature and culture have been rich fields for inter-disciplinary studies. Since the turn of the twentieth century, scholars and critics have tracked the intersections and tensions between Victorian literature and the visual arts, politics, social organization, economic life, technical innovations, scientific thought – in short, culture in its broadest sense. In recent years, theoretical challenges and historiographical shifts have unsettled the assumptions of previous scholarly syntheses and called into question the terms of older debates. Whereas the tendency in much past literary critical interpretation was to use the metaphor of culture as "background," feminist, Foucauldian, and other analyses have employed more dynamic models that raise questions of power and of circulation. Such developments have reanimated the field.

This series aims to accommodate and promote the most interesting work being undertaken on the frontiers of the field of nineteenth-century literary studies: work which intersects fruitfully with other fields of study such as history, or literary theory, or the history of science. Comparative as well as interdisciplinary approaches are welcomed.

A complete list of titles published will be found at the end of the book.

DICKENS AND THE DAUGHTER OF THE HOUSE

HILARY M. SCHOR

CAMBRIDGE
UNIVERSITY PRESS

PUBLISHED BY THE PRESS SYNDICATE OF THE UNIVERSITY OF CAMBRIDGE
The Pitt Building, Trumpington Street, Cambridge, United Kingdom

CAMBRIDGE UNIVERSITY PRESS
The Edinburgh Building, Cambridge CB2 2RU, UK   http://www.cup.cam.ac.uk
40 West 20th Street, New York, NY 10011-4211, USA   http://www.cup.org
10 Stamford Road, Oakleigh, Melbourne 3166, Australia

First published 1999

Printed in the United Kingdom at the University Press, Cambridge

Typeset in Monotype Baskerville 11/12½ [SE]

A catalogue record for this book is available from the British Library

Library of Congress cataloguing in publication data
Schor, Hilary Margo.
Dickens and the daughter of the house / Hilary M. Schor.
p.   cm. – (Cambridge studies in nineteenth-century literature
and culture: 25)
ISBN 0 521 44076 9 (hardback)
1. Dickens, Charles, 1812–1870 – Characters – Daughters.
2. Women and literature – England – History – 19th century.
3. Domestic fiction, English – History and criticism.   4 Dickens, Charles.
1812–1870 – Characters – Women.   5. Fathers and daughters in
literature.   6. Daughters in literature.   I. Title.   II. Series.
PR4592.D27S38   1999
823'.8 – dc21   99-11166   CIP

ISBN 0 521 44076 9 hardback

PR
4592
·D27
S38
1999

010400

Contents

Acknowledgements

To acknowledge the debts I have incurred in the writing of this book would require a preface longer than a Dickens novel, and I only wish I could be as improvident with my thanks as others have been with their support. Fellowship support from the Graves Foundation and the Stanford Humanities Center, and travel money from the American Council of Learned Societies, made both research and writing possible. The University of Southern California also provided support and I wish to thank in particular Deans Marshall Cohen, Richard S. Ide, and Morton O. Schapiro, each of whom also engaged intellectually with this project at key moments. Among the many colleagues who read portions of this book are Rosemarie Bodenheimer, Leo Braudy, Joseph Allen Boone, Janice Carlisle, Edwin Eigner, Stephanie Jed, Donna Landry, Peter Manning, Tania Modleski, Arden Reed, Garrett Stewart, and Peggy Waller. Rob Polhemus in particular illuminated the process of writing. Jim Kincaid, whose intelligence and generosity are as genuine as they are legendary, contributed far more than readings to this book, and to me. Peter Starr and Nomi Stolzenberg, with whom I team-taught and from whom I have learned so much, are owed a deeper acknowledgment. My research assistants, Duncan Faherty, Richard Menke, and particularly Kris Deffenbacher and Ned Schantz, exceeded my vision of assistance by as much as I am sure my demands exceeded their expectations – to them, I owe the thanks due the closest of colleagues. For less material but no less valuable support, I must thank Murray Baumgarten, Joseph Childers, Carolyn Dever, Regenia Gagnier, John Glavin, Gerhard Joseph, Joe Litvak, Robert Patten, Meg Russett, Richard Stein, and with special thanks, Helena Michie and Sylvia Manning. The Dickens Project was a special home in the years I was writing this book, and I owe a particular debt (of labor and of love) to John Jordan. I must also thank Josie Dixon and Kevin Taylor of Cambridge University Press for all their support; my gratitude to Cathy Gallagher, who not only read this manuscript with imagination but inspired its most complicated thinking, goes beyond the rhetoric of any acknowledgment page.

For many gifts of friendship and intellectual community, I must thank Elinor Accampo, Alice Gambrell, Barry Glassner, Peggy Kamuf, Jayne Lewis, David Miller, Ellen Quandahl, and Robyn Warhol. My deepest thanks go, as always, to Eric Mallin, whose loyalty is almost as remarkable as his discernment; to Robert Newsom, whose clarity of thought made my murkiest moments turn bright; and to Laurie Novo, who remains my first, and my best, reader. To my dear family, Arthur Schor, Judith and Sylvan Silberg, and my much-loved sisters Barbara and Renée, I owe much, much more – something, I fear, for which there are not enough words, even in Dickens . . .

Introduction

Shortly before her death in 1929, Kate Perugini, Charles Dickens's second daughter, described her father to her friend Gladys Storey. Kate returned repeatedly to the time after Dickens's separation from his wife Catherine, when all the children (except the oldest, Charley, the only child given a choice) had remained with their father, and Catherine had been forced out of the family house.[1] She recounted how their father would send his daughters to their music lessons across the street from where their mother lived, and Catherine Dickens would watch them from the windows of her house. "They would drive up and drive away," Storey reports, "but never call to see their mother."[2] Haunted by the "recollection of other lost opportunities to be kind to her mother," Kate turned back to those years, and the fear they all felt of their father: "My father was a wicked man – a very wicked man," she said; "We were *all* very wicked not to take her part."

It is tempting to invoke Kate Perugini as one of a series of witnesses against Charles Dickens, those readers (not least among them feminist critics) who have deplored his treatment of women, not only as a sign of the flatness and unrealistic nature of his fiction more generally, but as the signature mark of his inability to confront the complexity of adult (and particularly sexual) relations.[3] The women Orwell referred to as Dickens's "legless angels" – Little Nell, Agnes Wickfield, Esther Summerson, Amy Dorrit, and all of their dutiful ilk – have been conjured repeatedly as evidence against a writer as insidious as his own "Captain Murderer," who marries young virgins only to turn them to pie-making. At the end of their labors, after they have rolled out the crust and deplored the absence of a filling, Captain Murderer leads them to a mirror, shows them their own faces, cries out "*I* see the meat in the glass!" and, after beheading them, bakes and eats them.[4] The Dickens novel has seemed a similar machinery for the entrapment and consumption of gullible girls, and the novelist's wickedness has seemed inarguable. For most critics (and indeed, for me at the beginning of this project) the only answer has been to turn to the dark, angry women who punctuate and disrupt the seemingly calm surface of the Dickens novel, characters like Nancy in *Oliver Twist*, Honoria Dedlock in *Bleak House*, Miss Wade in *Little Dorrit*, who seem to challenge the gender order (and gendered flatness) the fiction proffers.

Kate Perugini, however, tells a more complicated and more compelling story, one in which the role of the good daughter is complexly interwoven with that of her angry double: "My father was a wicked man . . . we were *all* very wicked not to take her part." The daughter, in recounting what is easily read as paternal violence, casts her own regretful look back at the mother's house as she proceeds to walk away from it; she seems to be poised between paternal law and maternal absence, unable entirely to turn away from the father whom she reported she loved "better than any man in the world – in a different way of course," but of whom she said also, "I loved him for his faults." She has constructed a narrative in which her father is at once guilty and helpless ("what could you expect of such an uncanny genius?" she asked Gladys Storey) and in which her guilt and complicity are unmitigated. Yet that sense of complicity hardly seems, in our terms, "realistic." As Storey reports,

Mrs Perugini took her mother's part in-so-far as it was possible to do so. But the situation was a difficult one, since Dickens had sternly impressed upon them that "their father's name was their best possession" – which they knew to be true – and he expected them to act accordingly. (95)

The father's law is crafted explicitly in "the name of the father," and the father's name is, in a narrative of filial inheritance, imagined as the daughter's best (and indeed, at this moment, her only) possession. And as Kate's sister Mamie stressed, "It is a glorious inheritance to have such blood flowing in one's veins"; she was "so glad," Mamie said, "I never changed my name."[5] Kate Dickens Perugini knows how to tell a good story, but we might note that one reason why her tale reverberates so powerfully is its use of novelistic elements – indeed, to be more specific, of "Dickensian" elements. The daughter's story is a melodrama, her position that almost of a spectator, the innocent child torn between parental loyalties, looking back on her own inaction, and condemning it. The story seems to bear the relationship to the Dickens novel of a second order of fiction, almost as if Kate Dickens Perugini had learned story-telling from Amy Dorrit or Esther Summerson, but her story serves as more than a gloss of his. As if she herself were a reader and a reviser of the Dickens novel, the daughter's story (both Kate's, and those of the daughters within the novels themselves) makes necessary a rearrangement of the elements at its heart, pointing out the ways the fairy-tale labor of the daughter in every Dickens text – the work of complicity and regret, of bearing the father's name, of casting the backward glance at the mother's house – is integral to the social and fictional work these novels perform. The hesitations and silences, the pensive retrospection of the daughter, the unexpected critical power of the most passive person within the story: all these are present in every Dickens text, and mark the daughter's story as a central place of narrative authority.

A significant part of that authority comes from the very opacity of the story itself, for the story raises more questions than it, in itself, can answer: Why the daughter? Where is the absent mother? What is the law of the father, and what is the daughter's status before it? In whose name is this story to be told, and whose "part" is it to take? Even my brief account of this biographical material suggests some of the frames we are tempted to put around this story: the daughter's fear of the father's anger; our own psychological readings of the daughter's "seduction"; the difficulty of divorce and custody battles in the mid-nineteenth century; the daughter's powerlessness under law; the power of narratives of inheritance, possession, and self-possession; the necessary absence of the daughter's "proper" name in the realist novel. To account for the story's power is to go beyond its power as a fiction, to locate in it the place where the social, the formal, the legal, and the psychological seem to meet. Kate Perugini's story meets up with other stories of names, daughters, and possessions, where notions of property and women's status before the law (their existence as "legal persons") and their ability to freely plot and narrate (their existence as "characters" and "agents") come together.[6] But it also points to the curious doubleness of the daughter's position "before" the law: as at once under its strictures and prior to it. This doubleness, which stands in for the fixity and the fluidity of both narrative and the law, is at the heart of the daughter's story, and the story I am telling. The seeming inevitability of the Dickens novel (that machinery for turning women into cultural meat pies) was a product of the filial ambivalence it represented; reading with the daughter in mind makes a necessary difference in "the Dickens novel."

But this reading also opens up more general questions about the daughter, the novel, and the law. What the Dickensian daughter shares with larger stories of daughters and culture is her role as the site of value, for daughters in English law are not so much possessors but transmitters, not only of material property, but of ideology, memory, and faith.[7] Indeed, the only narrative William Blackstone imparts about daughters in his *Commentaries on the English Law* is of a "Jew of immense riches," whose "only daughter having embraced Christianity, he turned her out of doors."[8] The story of the daughter *out* of doors is of values gone wandering: with her departure, the transmission of culture is no longer so certain.[9] The daughter bears a similar role in property law, where (only rarely herself the inheritor of value) she guarantees, by her chastity and virtue, the proper progress of property through the inheritance plot. This is again to identify the daughter's legal role as akin to a central narrative function. The daughter must convey the father's message (often in the face of paternal violence) into the new certainties of the closural plot, that is, a plot whose closure promises resolution and an end to conflict; but she must also make her way into the new forms of plot (and of property) that narrative makes possible.

This is one secret of the romance plot: to transmit is also to transform, and when the daughter takes "property" (value, meaning, the father's word) into the streets, she is also in an open space within the laws of genre and inheritance. To move the plot forward, to do the work of narrative and inheritance, the daughter must move outside the father's house: just as narrative can happen only at the crossroads, so the daughter's story depends on leaving the space of domesticity. This displacement built into the daughter's plot displaces narrative perspective as well: as Alison Milbank has noted, daughters in the streets "reveal the private house as itself a market-place." Quoting Ian Ousby, Milbank reminds readers of the origins of the word "detective": to detect, etymologically, is to "take the roof off."[10] This is what the Dickens narrator (in *Dombey and Son* and in *Household Words*) notoriously wants to do; this is what the daughter's wanderings always make possible, the opening up of the paternal roof to the streets and throughways. It is the daughter who reminds us of the real nature of the social: "economics," as Ruskin noted, takes its roots from *oikos*, the household; to set the house (the family, the nation) in order, as Florence Dombey, Esther Summerson, and a host of other good daughters have noted, is to move beyond the father's house into the wider streets, and to set in motion a wider progress. That progress widens the daughter's sphere, setting free various forms of narrative and social possibility, but it is not itself without dangers. And this is the other secret of the romance plot: the daughter must survive the ending, but she will not always survive it intact.

The question of how the daughter enters culture, how she conveys property and value through the closural rituals of the marriage plot, returns us to the question of the daughter and the law, the formal means by which the individual enters the social order. Charles Dickens and Kate Perugini told their stories of daughters under a particular dispensation of the law, one very much under attack in the period of Dickens's great fiction. The debate over the Married Women's Property laws was one of the signal parliamentary concerns of the time, drawing the attention of peers and radicals, pushing towards the rationalizing of the law with which Dickens was in other ways associated, one that separated the law from custom and rendered it (in theory) more purely transparent, less a subject of mystery.[11] And the laws governing female property were nothing if not mysterious. The question of whether a wife maintained her rights over separate property – rights which did not exist under "coverture," in which a "husband and wife are one person, and that person the husband" – cut deeply into questions of what constituted a separate person, and the nature of modern (bourgeois, civic) identity. The daughter holds out the possibility of an individual identity lost within (and needing rescue from) plots of property. Until she enters the state of marriage (and should she legally depart from it) she maintains a perfect, that is, contractual, individualism: she can move as a free agent, maintaining her own property, the right to her earnings, the right to contract debt, the right to sign her name as a legal person. That space of possibility is a space of fiction – indeed, we might note that both property and daughters seem to call out for plot, wandering otherwise in that space of cultural indeterminacy, before the relative worth of property and persons is determined.

But here again the doubleness of the daughter's plot returns to haunt the Dickens novel. For all his support for various forms of legal reform, of demystifying the law, the attraction this story holds for Dickens is the daughter's potential separation from her own agency, her lack of a solid legal identity, her association with fictions. From at least the time of Shylock, daughters and ducats have made for stories of property and dissolution; for Dickens, they carry the additional burden of a modern subjectivity at once enabled and disenfranchised by the law. The law, as Susan Stewart has noted, may be "written and . . . subject to temporality and interpretation," but it has developed as a "a particularly idealized and transcendent form of writing," one that limits the fictions of personality it permits.[12] What Stewart identifies as the ambivalence of "the role of the law in positioning subjectivity [and] the tragedy of one's entry into the domain of the law as an enabling subjection," is an ambivalence at the heart of the Dickens project: to exist purely as a legal subject (to be made "rational") is to lose other versions of subjectivity.

This is linked for Dickens to problems of persons and property, the attendant problem of becoming too much (and too exclusively) a legal person. Models of rational, possessive individualism which drew him on (of people with purchasing power, the power to plot and possess) also disturbed him, suggesting that people might become – for others and for themselves – only objects. The daughter's powerful alienation before the law (that she exists as a token of her father's authority, that success in the marriage plot means the daughter's successful disappearance into the "shadow" of coverture) offered a tool for the fiction, a way of plotting outside a modern, legally determined subjectivity, a way of exploring the other notions of identity the daughter embodied. For in the daughter's enclosure within, and alienation from, the paternal house, we catch a glimpse of the fictionality of the structures we hold most dear: our sense of the family as at once a tribe and a household; of the home as a refuge and a site of patriarchal violence; of the private as at once a sign of personality and individuality, and a sense of loss, of deprivation from the wider world.[13] In the Oxford English Dictionary, the daughter stands for relationship: among the collected definitions of daughter are "the relation of female to her parents . . . (the feminine term corresponding to son)"; "a female descendant; a female member of a family, race, etc."; "a woman in relation to her native country or place"; "a term of affectionate address to a woman or a girl by an older person or one in a superior relation"; "Anything (personified as female) considered in relation to its origin or source." The daughter, in language as in law, is incapable of singularity, is always a term of exchange, conveyance, relatedness. But in order to convey, the daughter must be made foreign; to recount her story, she must depart from her own plot. It is that impossibility of being that Dickens draws on in his fiction – and that presents such telling ambiguities, such productive gaps, in the unfolding of her story. In Kate Perugini's anecdote, as in the Dickens novel, the daughter stands poised between worlds, between houses, unable quite to choose. Her alienation is her fortune; her equipoise is the space of other fictions of subjectivity.

To take on the daughter's separate story is to re-encounter the nineteenth century story of individuals from a different perspective, for the story of Dickens's career in many ways articulates (forming as much as echoing) the history of the modern subject. Indeed, in many ways Dickens gave us the modern subject. In his own ambivalences about individuals and institutions, the growing gloom of his autobiographical fiction, and his somewhat feverish anxiety about the market relationships that danced around his authorship (copyright, public readings, the incredible fanfare of a Dickens publication) we can see the shadows of larger arguments about what it means to write, to own, and to publish in the nineteenth century, and the way Dickens came to represent the author for his culture. For modern critics of the novel, that has been the story of Dickens's own disenfranchisement as a laboring boy at Warren's Blacking Factory, and the way he reassembled his own identity through authorship; the way he wrote himself into the heart of his culture. The story of lost identity and resumed connections is most marked in Dickens's most "autobiographical" novel, *David Copperfield*, which has had a talismanic position in critical accounts of Dickens and his career, and what it meant to be a novelist at mid-century. But *David Copperfield* also tells a complicated story of gender, identity, and writing, one in which coming-to-identity, successfully traversing the marriage plot, and becoming an author are one. One place to begin to question the authority of the Dickens plot and its "proper" dispensations of daughters (its proper "housing" of their alienated stories) is to return to *David Copperfield*, the ur-text for so many readings of Dickens's career, and ask if it tells so certain a story of closure, homecoming, and gendered identity, and consequently, if its inheritance is so clear.

David Copperfield takes as its point of origin not a story so much as an image, which stands as both the central visual icon for the novel and a repeated point of narratorial coherence. We see David making his way along a hot, dusty road towards Dover, orphaned, set upon, robbed, struggling to reach the aunt he hopes will love him. This image recurs throughout the book, returning even at the moment of greatest happiness, when he and Agnes declare their love at the novel's end:

We stood together in the same old-fashioned window at night, when the moon was shining; Agnes with her quiet eyes raised up to it; I following her glance. Long miles of road then opened out before my mind; and, toiling on, I saw a ragged way-worn boy, forsaken and neglected, who should come to call even the heart now beating against mine, his own.[14]

David as narrator begins here to blur again into that young boy, sharing his "toil," the toil of telling the story again and again, offering it in a series of alternate versions, but always seeing that same young boy,

always still being that young boy. The scene raises the saddest of autobiographical questions: does Agnes see only the moon, or the "ragged
way-worn boy" she never met? Does Agnes ever hear the story of
David's progress, or is "even the heart now beating" against hers a
mystery to her? There is little textual evidence to suggest David ever tells
all of his story to anyone – Uriah's threat to reveal David's past is his
greatest hold over David – and we might hear in this almost conclusive
paragraph the autobiographical fragment's assertion, that the middle-
aged Dickens had never met the "one friend" to whom he could tell the
complete story. "Even now," Dickens claims in the fragment, "famous
and caressed and happy, I often forget in my dreams that I have a dear
wife and children; even that I am a man; and wander desolately back to
that time of my life."[15]

The power of this narrative extends not only over the novel or
Dickens's oeuvre, but over the act of novel-reading itself. Long the center
of seminal works on the importance of Dickens's fiction for our understanding of the modern novel and its readers, for recent critics rethink-
ing the Dickens novel, *David Copperfield* has been the entry point for new
stories of identity and reading. D. A. Miller has suggested, in a powerful
rereading of the novel, that there is something in *David Copperfield*'s very
universality ("Davy who?" is the question with which Miller begins) that
makes possible the reading of Victorian fiction. The novel, with its
double obsession with eccentric characters and the boxes they both carry
and are, confirms our own expansive and individual subjectivity, and
offers the comforting assurance that we are *not* characters ourselves.[16]
The various containments of fiction allow us, as readers, to roam free –
to wander.

Something in *Copperfield*'s self-consciousness about fiction lends power
to that effort of consolation. *David Copperfield* (the novelist's "favourite
child," as he called it in its preface) is a novel about a novelist – Dickens's
only novel to make that claim explicitly – and it begs to be read as autobiographical, at the same time that it is notoriously vague on the actual
writing of fiction. Not only, as Mary Poovey has argued, does it work to
domesticate literary labor, it also reflects Dickens's increasing ownership
of his own fictional authority: as Alexander Welsh has suggested, it is the
novel that comes not at the beginning (as most critics read it) but at the
end of a certain crisis in Dickens's authorial self-representation, a representation that has as much to do with copyright as with consciousness.[17]
As Miller might put it, the novel convinces us that we own interesting
versions of ourselves (selves that do not come in small packages); as

Welsh might put it, *David Copperfield* was the novel in which Dickens claimed ownership of himself and his literary "creations."

But both these stories – the story of origins in which the young boy comes to be a hero; the story of creation in which the young boy grows up to be an author – have a great deal also to do with gender, and a series of less orderly narratives of origin, creation, and ownership, all of which are linked in this text to writing, and which have not offered the same point of entry for recent evaluations of the novel. The conventional view of *David Copperfield*, taking much of its tone from Gwendolyn Needham's "The Undisciplined Heart,"[18] has argued that David's recognition that "there can be no disparity in marriage like unsuitability of mind and purpose" (the recognition that will lead him away from the "first choice" of an undisciplined heart, Dora, towards its real and final choice, his "sister" Agnes) is also the recognition that will lead him to write true novels of human endeavor and suffering, and will lead him to "make use" of his painful earlier experience. This trajectory leads David from his flirtatious mother's disastrous marriage to the murderous Mr Murdstone; from his lodgings with the wordy and spendthrift Micawbers to his residence with his gruff, loving Aunt Betsey; from his efforts to shape the character of his child-bride Dora to his recognition that he loves Agnes, the woman who has loved him all along. In this economy, that is, childhood sufferings make art stronger; bad marriages discipline the heart; and you grow up to marry your muse, rather than your mother. At the end of this "progress," which ends with the patently absurd fiction that David has been up all night writing, he turns to the face next to his, and he sees Agnes, pointing "upward, always upward" – towards inspiration, spiritual fiction, and death.[19]

Initially, then, the son's progress is equally towards authorial and sexual maturity, a story in which women can play only a passive role. But David's relation to his muse is more complicated than this. The hero's initiation into narrative not only has a considerable sexual charge to it, but carries with it considerable gender confusion. In the midst of his neglect at the hands of his stepfather, David finds a collection of novels that belonged to his father, which give him precisely that sense of himself as a hero that will allow him to survive his abandonment. When he is sent off to school he wins the affection of the older boys by his ability to retell those stories – though, as he makes clear, his narrative abilities already err on the side of creation rather than copying, for he invents as much as he remembers – a useful talent for the prospective auto-biographer. But it is here that the female story-teller enters the novel. As

David sits in the darkened room telling stories to his hero, the far more senior boy Steerforth, who will represent David's class and sexual ambitions throughout the novel, he says, "it was a tiresome thing to be roused, like the Sultana Scheherazade, and forced into a long story before the getting-up bell rang; but Steerforth was resolute" (145). Here, the blushing, shy David has become "Daisy" for his hero Steerforth – who goes on to wish that David had a sister, for "If you had had one, I should think she would have been a pretty, timid, little, bright-eyed sort of girl. I should have liked to know her" (140). Perhaps, though, he already does; certainly, "Daisy" (to whom Steerforth is a "person of great power," and who goes to stare at him as he sleeps) already connects his story-telling power with passivity: "I admired and loved him, and his approval was return enough."

Story-telling, gender, and power are linked and confused throughout the novel – and David's exclusive control of authorial enterprises seems less than totally secure. To put it most simply, not only David but everyone in the novel wants to be a story-teller. "This is my grumpy, frumpy story" says David's Aunt Betsey (757), when she has told her story of the return of her violent, abusive husband, from whom she was separated before the novel began, and who has been blackmailing her all through the remainder of the novel. In another such self-dramatizing moment,

"I am well aware that I am the umblest person going," said Uriah Heep, modestly; "let the other be where he may. My mother is likewise a very umble person. We live in a numble abode, Master Copperfield, but have much to be thankful for. My father's former calling was umble. He was a sexton."

"What is he now?" I asked.

"He is a partaker of glory at present, Master Copperfield," said Uriah Heep. "But we have much to be thankful for." (291)

Everyone in this novel tells a story of origin and growth, in which even "glory" may be only a road upwards, a temporary ("at present") position, and it is hardly clear why David's carries any particular weight.

But here we rejoin my initial argument about the daughter's story, for women's stories throughout the novel carry a special emotional significance, one that will extend not only to the novel's angry women, but to its eccentrics and its good daughters – and cast a skeptical gaze over David's (and perhaps Dickens's) narrative powers. David's nurse, Peggotty, tells the story of his mother's death, a story marked off as "Peggotty's narration," ending "I put it as she asked; and oh Davy! the time had come when my first parting words to you were true – when she was glad to lay her poor head on her stupid cross old Peggotty's arm –

and she died like a child that had gone to sleep!" (186). Though David claims his own commentary on it ("From the moment of my knowing of the death of my mother, the idea of her as she had been of late had vanished from me . . . In her death she winged her way back to her calm untroubled youth, and cancelled all the rest" [186-187])[20] the exaggeration of David's voice-over only makes more resonant the Wordsworthian simplicity of what is set off from the rest of the text. A similar double vision hangs over Miss Julia Mill's journal from her exile with Dora Spenlow, which contains such passages as:

Thursday. D. certainly improved. Better night. Slight tinge of damask revisiting cheek. Resolved to mention name of D. C. Introduced same, cautiously, in course of airing. D. immediately overcome. "Oh, dear, dear Julia! Oh, I have been a naughty and undutiful child!" Soothed and caressed. Drew ideal picture of D. C. on verge of tomb. D. again overcome. "Oh, what shall I do, what shall I do? Oh, take me somewhere!" Much alarmed. Fainting of D. and glass of water from public-house. (Poetical affinity. Chequered sign on door-post; chequered human life. Alas! J. M.) (624)

It is easy to dismiss Julia's ramblings as sentimental trash, a site of excess in the novel, but what is the difference between that and David's narcissistic rambling (about which he is admittedly ironic – note particularly his desire to shield Dora "I don't exactly know what from. . . . Perhaps from mice, to which she had a great objection" [535]) or between that and the passage above, in which the mother mysteriously wings her way back to her youth? Which romantic autobiographer is being mocked here?

A similar uncertainty underpins the central (indeed, the originary) question of the novel: "whether I shall turn out to be the hero of my own life, or whether that station will be held by anybody else, these pages must show" (49).[21] Dickens may be sure David is his favorite child – and critics may rest comfortably with the centrality of the hero's progress – but the novel is less certain that it belongs to David. It raises repeatedly the question of what to call the hero, who is, in the course of the novel named after him, himself named David Copperfield the younger, called Daisy by Steerforth; Doady, by his child-wife; Mr Copperfull, by his landlady; Brooks of Sheffield by his stepfather; "Trotwood" Copperfield, by his wife and his aunt; and at several points in the original manuscript actually referred to as Charles by his confused creator, who hadn't noticed, until Forster pointed it out, that he had given his hero his own initials. This conundrum turns into the deeper questions of who is a hero; indeed, of what is heroic. Is it the handsome, talented, promising, and damned Steerforth; is it that rebounding father of letters, the comic spirit, Micawber; or is it that man of letters himself, David/Dickens? David's own answer would seem to be clear: the hero of his life is his wife Agnes, who, busily pointing upwards at the end of the novel, represents the highest he can attain, represents the self-sacrifice he must learn, represents his own aspirations *back* to him so that he can pursue them. It is Agnes who has made possible the author's heroism – and his novels – and it is her light, the light of the near-final chapter title ("A Light shines on my Way") by which, not to put it too quaintly, we all read the novel.

But Agnes's story is also the narrative that most completely revises David's, and puts into question his accounting of things; Agnes's account of both their lives suggests the daughter has not only her own story, but her own version of his. And here we return to the question of the daughter's passivity, her goodness, and her lack of erotic interest. It is only in David's (acknowledged, explicit) recounting that she is without passion, without pain, without desire, without interest. Her statement to him at the end of the novel, "I have loved you all my life," along with his aunt's refrain of "blind, blind, blind" that echoes from the moment of his marriage to another woman, and the observation of everyone else in the novel (including Dora, who is forced to participate in her exile from closural bliss) that he should have married Agnes – all this not only revises, and supplements, his novel, but suggests that he has been a lousy narrator, indeed, reader, of his own life; that he is hardly fit to write his own autobiography.

Agnes's gentle admission of her own pain, of the story she has lived while David was off leading his own life, of her labor and dispossession, is one with a series of female narratives throughout the novel: Annie Strong, married to a much older man who comes, wrongly, to suspect her of marrying him for his money and loving her worthless cousin, Jack; Aunt Betsey, divorced since her husband attempted to throw her out a window to get her property; Mr Dick, whose sister was tortured to death by the husband pursuing her fortunes; Mr Creakle, the schoolmaster, who earned his claim to be "a Tartar" by ill-using his wife and making away with her money; the fierce Rosa Dartle, disfigured by the young Steerforth when he throws a hammer at her mouth, left with a scar that will catch fire, like a seam, across her face; even Dora herself, who must live with the knowledge that David thinks he has made a mistake in marrying her. The novel that had initially seemed only David's story now seems a collection of passionate, suffering women, whose property is held only tenuously, whose stories are told only elliptically, and whose anger, like Rosa's, darts out unexpectedly at the hero, much like the dwarf, Miss Mowcher, who, at the end, grabs Steerforth's evil servant Littimer and continues to hold on to him (while he cuts open her face) in order to bring him to justice. Like Aunt Betsey's "pious fraud," the trick she plays on David to bring him to reveal his love for Agnes, the narrative tricks women play are at once signs of powerlessness and of power – most clearly, a sign of authorial anxiety.

To take *David*'s anxiety about female plot and plotting women (does Aunt Betsey know the secret of Agnes's heart – and of his – better than he does?) and return it to Dickens is at once to imply an authorial control (and lack thereof) that goes beyond David's consciousness as a narrating character, and to take that narration back into Victorian culture, into the agitation over women, property, and writing.[22] While the novel frames scenes of female copying (Dora holding David's pens; Sophy Traddles copying Tommy's legal documents), it is David who may be the great copyist. The end of the novel suggests that what David has been writing is Agnes's story all along; it is her conclusion, and her letters, that "inspirit" him. And who is it who is writing? The Sultana Scheherazade may be at work in his novels; or, perhaps, David himself (Dickens himself) may have grown up to be not "David Copperfield the younger," but rather the imaginary child "Betsey Trotwood Copperfield." Both the cultural and the literary plots lead us back to the figure of the woman, and away from the autonomous authority Dickens seemed to be writing – Victorian culture seemed to be writing – in this text, reminding us of the words of the autobiographical fragment, which here echo in a very different way: the successful, "caressed" Dickens forgets "even that I am a man." In the end, David may be his own Scheherazade; he may be a dispossessed daughter; he may be a woman writer; he may, after all, be the heroine of his own life.

Turning back from the seeming authority of the hero's progress to the daughter's more elliptical path makes these questions of authorship and power far more complicated. Our digression through *David Copperfield*, rather like Kate Perugini's autobiographical account, raises questions of identity and writing that make the daughter's story a less comfortable haven for paternal (and patriarchal) authority. But it raises these questions precisely through its indirection: if David's story is more than the simple exchange of one daughter for another, one wife for another, what then are we to make of the daughters-in-motion? Is it enough merely to substitute Agnes Wickfield for David Copperfield at the center of the novel's dizzying turns, and feel we have reread (or even rewritten) Victorian culture? The argument of this book is that it is not, although such readings open up important avenues for other explorations.

To put this another way, Agnes Wickfield may have a secret, but she is no novelist; she is not even, really, a rival autobiographer to David. She does write a series of inspirational and inspiriting letters, culminating in the one that reaches David on his melancholy journey after Dora's and Steerforth's deaths and leads him to become a novelist himself, but David's insistence on their importance can seem merely conventional spousal apotheosis; at any rate, their language reaches us only through his summary, and his descriptions of the power of her writing voice not only must reach us at one remove, but are seen only as an echo of her more powerful personal presence and gentle resonance. The anxiety of Agnes's writing, as it so often is for daughters from *King Lear*'s Cordelia to Bone in Dorothy Allison's *Bastard Out of Carolina*, is how she is to represent, and how we are to read, "nothing." In the same ways that the daughter's relationship to the law was precisely to stand for relationship, and her work for Dickens is to represent a powerful dispossession before the law, so the daughter's story-telling is vexed by the problem of absence.

It would be possible to follow the strand of Agnes's silent and silenced writing through the rest of Dickens's career: to trace out the history of such scribbling women as Miss Wade (author of the "History of a Self-Tormentor"); Amy Dorrit, teller of fairy-tales and travelling correspondent; Esther Summerson, whose "portion of these pages" makes up at least half of *Bleak House*. But there is a danger in reading these novels only for the female counter-narratives they offer. To do so leaves intact the hero's progress, and it fails to account for the shadow the heroine's plot casts across that journey: the daughter's progress cannot follow the son's, any more than Freud, in his own versions of the nineteenth century daughter, can send her travelling tidily through her own Oedipal plot.[23] To read for the counter-narrative is to miss the tension at the heart of the Dickens novel: like the efforts to protect the divisions between the good daughter and her dark double, such readings see the heroine's plot as merely the negative version of the hero's plot, and fail to note the disruptions within both.

But while I do not want to read only for the heroine's plot, I do find myself returning repeatedly to those scenes of the daughter's *plotting*, and particularly, to the moments when she enters the plot through writing. Sigmund Freud, the great theorist of houses and consciousness, brings writing, houses, and women together at the end of *Civilization and its Discontents*: "Writing," he says, "was in its origin the voice of an absent person; and the dwelling-house was a substitute for the mother's womb, the first lodging, for which in all likelihood man still longs, and in which he was safe and felt at ease."[24] The Dickens daughter who turns to writing is similarly uneasy in her house, as Kate Dickens Perugini suggests at the moment when she attempts retrospection, when she goes to gather the disparate pieces of the story. Interestingly, Kate Perugini did not write her own story, but left it for her friend to do; Dickens's other daughter, Mamie, did write a book, but could enter her own book only tangentially: it is called *My Father as I Recall Him*. These two texts, though again not "Dickens novels," raise important questions about the daughter's power to reinscribe her story within that novel: neither daughter, we might argue, was able to write her father out of her life. The question is, was their power only that of memorializing or ghost-writing, or did some other story get told through that "recollection"?

Dianne Sadoff, in her penetrating study of Victorian fathers, *Monsters of Affection*, argues that the daughter can turn to writing only to efface the father's violence; indeed, most studies of the Dickens daughter have seen her as in some way inscribing not her own but her father's story, as if (like the Roman daughter Martin Meisel has so insightfully recreated[25]) all her power were devoted to the father's resurrection. But even in Mamie's adoring book, as the daughter "recalls" the father, it is her power over his story that she reveals; the daughter's text even there holds out the possibility of stepping outside the father's law, of turning away from the father's name, the "daughter's best possession."

Indeed, when the daughter turns to writing she invokes an entirely different order of possession, of self-possession, of property relationships – or so this book will argue. The daughter's ability to "convey," as Alexander Welsh has put it, the "immortality" associated with the English novel, the "denouement [which characteristically linked love with property and marriage with an on-going estate" might turn us back to Kate Dickens Perugini's history with new eyes.[26] For in her story, the tension between "taking the mother's part" and "possessing the father's name" suggests a different kind of both powerlessness and authority before the law. In that story, the ability to comprehend, to gaze retrospectively, and to reshuffle the elements of the "Dickens novel" we have identified, is the daughter's best revenge; in her story-telling are interwoven the law of the father, the absence of the mother, and her coming into her *own* inheritance. At that moment, the daughter stands "before" another legal fiction, for the law must read novels as much as the novel reads the law; their rules exist in complex interplay, and offer stories of resistances and hesitations, engagements and reservations – the daughter's different story. In that story it is the daughter's writing that constitutes the most powerful form of property there is, and the best story-teller might turn out to be "a daughter after all." In spite of her own eclipsed legal presence, and in spite of her own habitual silence, that daughter casts her own shadow over all of Dickens's fiction, and her silhouette is everywhere.[27]

PART ONE

Making fictions

The uncanny daughter: Oliver Twist, Nicholas Nickleby, and the progress of Little Nell

Charles Dickens's early novels are a mess. Where critics have rightly reveled in their comic energy, their linguistic verve, and their anarchic plots, it is impossible not to note the incoherence that is their strongest effect, in particular the battle they seem to stage over realism and the forms the fiction is to take. That passive form is intentional, for the early novels seem to be without much narratorial or narrative control, veering uneasily in style, diction, point of view, and even genre. But these novels do offer one recurrent device that is of particular use to readers of the later fiction, something even Dickens was to note when he reread his earlier novels. When Dickens went back to this body of work to present it to readers in a more definitive form through authorial prefaces, he seized on the figure of a woman to exemplify his fictional method and morals. In virtually every case, and most strikingly in *Oliver Twist* and *The Old Curiosity Shop*, the reader looking for the author is told: *cherchez la femme*.

This authorial habit suggests something powerful at stake for Dickens in the allegorizing of women, but the language of these prefaces, as well as the thematic and narratorial work the figures of women are set to do in the early novels, suggests more than a simple process of allegory: Dickens's obsession with female presence and representation (and, increasingly, with female narrative power) suggests a spectacularizing of women as well, one marked out by the two very different images of women these texts offer, Nancy (the "vicious" and murdered prostitute of *Oliver Twist*) and Nell ("good, gentle, patient, quiet Nell") of *The Old Curiosity Shop*. The obsession with the figure of the woman, and particularly of the uncanny daughter, suggests that Dickens's own icon for his literary art is, from the start, a devious and twisting figure.

The Preface to the 1838 edition of *Oliver Twist* makes enormous claims for the power of its realism and the originality of its perspective: just as "Cervantes laughed Spain's chivalry away," so *Twist* will dim the glitter of the Newgate novel and the tradition of glamorous thieves and their "ladies."[1] To do this, Dickens must assert his own "unattractive and repulsive truth," showing "by words and deeds" the "most debased and vicious kind" of degraded life (36). "In the case of the girl, in particular, I had this intention constantly in view," the author claims, and stresses that he would not abate "one scrap of curl-paper in the girl's dishevelled hair" (36, 35).

A Mrs Massaroni, being a lady in short petticoats and a fancy dress, is a thing to imitate in tableaux and have in lithograph on pretty songs; but a Nancy, being a creature in a cotton gown and cheap shawl, is not to be thought of. (35)

Morality, Dickens seems to be arguing, could be as simple as couture and hairstyle.

But the emphasis on the realism of his tale ("that Sikes is a thief and Fagin a receiver of stolen goods; that the boys are pickpockets, and the girl is a prostitute") gives way to a different problem of verisimilitude: that Nancy's "devotion to the brutal house-breaker does not seem natural" (36). And here Dickens strikes a new tone of indignation:

It is useless to discuss whether the conduct and character of the girl seems natural or unnatural, probable or improbable, right or wrong. IT IS TRUE. Every man who has watched these melancholy shades of life, must know it to be so. Suggested to my mind long ago, but what I often saw and read of, in actual life around me, I have tracked it through many profligate and noisome ways, and found it still the same. From the first introduction of that poor wretch, to her laying her blood-stained head upon the robber's breast, there is not a word exaggerated or over-wrought. It is emphatically God's truth, for it is the truth He leaves in such depraved and miserable breasts . . . it is a contradiction, an anomaly, an apparent impossibility; but it is a truth. I am glad to have had it doubted, for in that circumstance I should find a sufficient assurance (if I wanted any) that it needed to be told. (36)

The passage is a catalogue of realism's alibis: it is useless to discuss; IT IS TRUE; every man must know; it was suggested by what I saw and read of; I have tracked it; not a word is exaggerated or over-wrought; it is God's truth, a contradiction, and it needed to be told. In short, it is true because I said so; it is true because I shout it; everyone knows it's true; I read it in a book; it is true because I am not over-wrought; it is a moral truth; it is true because it makes no sense ("an apparent impossibility") and, most interesting for our purposes, it is true because *no one believes it*. The very fact of its implausibility makes it not only a true story but one that "needed to be told."

For Nancy's realism (and particularly the realism of her passionate loyalty to "the house-breaker") to be doubted is the very condition of Dickens's fiction: the appearance of female exaggeration is what makes fiction both necessary and good. The less likely it seems, the more the novel must represent it. A similar exaggeration clings to the figure of Nell in *The Old Curiosity Shop*, in its own terms "a tale that is told" by the presence of a female icon, one around whom great authorial feeling congregates, and claims of affective power collect. "In reference to the tale itself," says Dickens in the Preface to the 1848 edition, "I desire to say very little," going on to note only the "many friends it has won me, and the many hearts it has turned to me."[2]

> I will merely observe, therefore, that in writing the book, I had it always in my fancy to surround the lonely figure of the child with grotesque and wild, but not impossible companions, and to gather about her innocent face and pure intentions, associates as strange and uncongenial as the grim objects that are about her bed when her history is first foreshadowed. (42)

Here again, in a "strange and uncongenial" world, the text and the female body become one: where Nancy's curl-papers guaranteed the grittiness of realism, the wanderings of the "lonely figure" of Nell ensure the readerly engagement: "I have a mournful pride in one recollection associated with 'little Nell,'" the author recounts: "While she was yet upon her wanderings, not then concluded," an essay appeared "of which she was the principal theme, so earnestly, so eloquently, and tenderly appreciative" that the author could not read it without "an unusual glow of pleasure and encouragement" (42). Praise of little Nell becomes praise of Boz; her peregrinations become the public progress of the novel-in-parts; and author and heroine blur together in a "glow" of pleasure and encouragement.

While both prefatorial presentations are made to *preserve* something about Dickens's representational practices, each turns out to be unsteady in some way essential to the book's plot and thematic concerns. Nancy's very vulgarity disappears, as the dark, angry woman blends into her opposite, the good, gentle woman; Nell's allegory dissipates, as the heroic daughter blends into her freakish opposite. In both texts, the literary terms the prefaces meant to invent and contain, realism and romance, become unsettled. Both prefigure an instability in the *representation* of women which will become, in the later novels, an anxiety about the narrative *place* of women, a refusal of women to sit quietly in their narrative station. What the women share (in their wanderings, in particular) is an anxiety about female propriety that gives way to anxieties about property itself; both women (figured by the text and by the narrator as fictional "goods") show an uncanny willingness to get up and move the property about themselves.

Much of Nancy's power as spectacle comes from a curious absence at the center of *Oliver Twist*: the book offers, in its subtitle, to give us a "parish boy's progress," but it is fairly careless of its boy, in fact, it has a tendency to lose its hero while he is on the road. And while Oliver faints, weeps, and disappears, only rarely does he think, and even more rarely does he act. Not only is he not heroic, he is only marginally, in conventional gender terms, even a "boy." Critical responses to Oliver have ranged from those who view him as no character at all, a cipher, to those who, while allowing him to be a character, believe him an improbable one; these critics either make the excuse (doubtless the right one) that this is an *un*realistic novel, or they take the happy expedient of singling out other heroes for praise.[3] Never, it seems, do they ask if this novel without a hero could, in fact, be a novel with a heroine.

The confusion that runs throughout the novel about its relationship to its new-born author, about a hero the novel can comfortably leave in a ditch for five chapters, even about the gendering of narration, all seem to be related to an alternative pattern of story-telling, one that unites an autobiographical anxiety about the hero's story to an obsession with the heroine's version of that story, and the kind of progress the novel must undergo – a pattern of narrative disruption – to tell that story.[4] The harlot's progress in this novel is one that moves in ways opposite to the forward motions of the parish boy's, and is one that Dickens was repeatedly drawn to in his career; that progress suggests that female wandering (in particular, the way Nancy both occupies and controls the central spectacles of the novel) contains the truth of representation that the "Preface" was so anxious to locate. But it also suggests, as does Dickens's obsessive performance of the murder of Nancy, literally up until the day of his death, that the narrative of female wandering opens up a powerful space of authorial speculation, and of authorial anxiety, that will mark the rest of Dickens's career.

To see Nancy's progress as central is to reverse critical truisms, for her role in the novel has been consistently described as essentially passive: she is there to represent the element of good, to both arrange and suggest Oliver's salvation. But in fact, she dominates the second half of the novel, disrupting the expectations of others, generating new plots of her own. Her primary activity is narrating: as Monks says late in the novel, "but for babbling drabs, I would have finished as I began" (459). But Nancy does more than babble: she opens up the text of Dickens's realism, performing a series of textual transgressions – sneaking, watching, betraying – that mirror the sexual transgressions the text cannot represent. Nancy has lived among – and done – she tells Rose Maylie, "something worse than all" (362) that marks her as finally fallen in the novel, but it is her freedom as a streetwalker that seems to allow her the freedom to walk from plot to plot. No other character chooses to move or even to speak in so many different worlds: Oliver is notably mystified and silent every time he is transported; only Nancy, as it were, is able to translate. Because she can read all these stories, she can act in all of them – and she does.

Significantly, her first verbal activity in the book is to say no, and her first long scene is one of deceptive theatricality. While introduced as one of what Oliver thinks "very nice girls indeed" she is first addressed when Fagin asks her to rescue Oliver from prison. "What do you say," the Jew asks in a soothing manner, and she replies, "That it won't do; so it's no use a-trying it on, Fagin" (139). But after a variety of "threats, promises and bribes" she is persuaded, and she does "a-try it on," literally trying on the dress of a more respectable lower class. She is given a white apron, a straw bonnet, a little basket, and a door-key to carry; she is transformed in front of us into a domestic heroine, and she goes off to perform her own play, acting out a devoted sister rescuing a lost brother – acting out the role Rose Maylie is to play in the second half of the novel.

But Nancy's "trying it on" is itself an oddly transformative moment in the text, for she reenters the novel already a different character, ready to see in Oliver a lost self. When the virginal but illegitimate Rose Maylie first sees Oliver, she exclaims to her guardian,

"Oh! as you love me, and know that I have never felt the want of parents in your goodness and affection, but that I might have done so, and might have been equally helpless and unprotected with this poor child, have pity upon him before it is too late!" (269)

Rose assumes immediately that he is an orphan, that he "may never have known a mother's love, or the comfort of a home." As it turns out, Rose is right, but what Nancy sees of herself in Oliver is even stranger. From the moment she adopts the fiction of a younger brother (she spontaneously rechristens him "Nolly," a name much like her own, and one she continues to use even after the fiction is ended), she sees in him some shadow of what she, too, could have been:

"I shall be glad to have him away from my eyes, and to know that the worst is over. I can't bear to have him about me. The sight of him turns me against myself, and all of you." (240)

This divided Nancy is not only the most complex character in the novel, the one most capable of fictions for the benefit of others, she is the one who most consciously articulates a self – a self she can create through the blank space of Oliver, that she can act out through rescuing him; she is the character who tells the most complicated story.

But it is not her own story that she tells. Nancy's narrative is one in which she disappears: like the crime "worse than all" she cannot name, her actions consist in not being observed, in not being narrated. And she has good reason to disappear. Every action she takes to save Oliver leads to more violence against her: in one of the novel's most poignant moments, she reminds Oliver, "every word from you is a blow for me" (199).

"I have saved you from being ill-used once, and I will again, and I do now. . . . I have promised for your being quiet and silent; if you are not, you will only do harm to yourself and me too, and perhaps be my death. See here! I have borne all this for you already, as true as God sees me show it."

She pointed, hastily, to some livid bruises on her neck and arms; and continued, with great rapidity. (198–199)

The pattern of violence against women is one that runs through the novel, as through so much of Dickens, but it is linked most often to *Nancy's* being quiet and silent, and it is quietly, silently, that she will commandeer the novel's plot.

She does so by, as she ironically claims to Fagin, being "stupid." After she delivers Oliver to Sikes, only to have him disappear into the "ditch" of narrative, Fagin comes to the Three Cripples and seeing her, seemingly drunk, stops to "test" her docility. He is still fearful after her initial outbursts in protection of Oliver, and she baits him till she provokes from him enough of the story of Monks to lead her to follow Fagin through the streets. But to baffle him, she retreats into the drunken "disorder" in which he found her, saying "You put me up for a minute, but now I'm stupid again" (241). Her pursuit of Fagin requires that she be more than "stupid" – or rather, less, for in the next chapter, she becomes a shadow, an image of a woman in a bonnet and cloak, sneaking into a locked house, crouching on a dark stairway, then escaping, again through locked rooms, again without a trace. But she must disappear for the narrator as well, in order to maintain any sense of mystery: all the narrator tells us is that "a listener might easily have perceived" (243) some portions of their conversation. It is not for many chapters that we learn it was Nancy rather than, as seemed equally probable, a figment of Monks's melodramatic imagination; it is not until after Nancy is dead that her "voice" repeats what she heard, and then, only as it is reported to Monks by Mr. Brownlow. "Shadows on the wall," Brownlow says, "have caught your whispers" (440), but Nancy will soon be a shadow again, lost to the novel. We are kept in the dark to keep us reading; but Nancy is kept in the dark so she can become a narrator.

The only real mystery in this novel is who will solve the mystery, not what it is. As it turns out, the most significant evidence is Oliver's resemblance to a picture on Brownlow's wall, so that it is only the "chance" of his turning up in that living room that can solve the mystery at all. In part, the novel substitutes Nancy for Oliver – her murder for his inheritance – as a central plot, only to provide something to hunt for; though I cannot assert with any conviction that there is much mystery there, either. Nancy achieves heroic stature, one might argue, by allowing herself to be killed in Oliver's place. If the novel's real suspense is if Oliver will "twist" or not, it maintains and releases that suspense, as many critics have noticed, by "twisting" a number of surrogates instead. When Nancy goes to Rose Maylie to betray Monks, she initiates not only the solution of Oliver's identity crisis, but her own self-destruction; in speaking up for Oliver, she has insured that "blows" will fall on her.

But Nancy does not just become another Oliver; rather, her story displaces the progressive, heroic model, and reveals a series of *re*gressive and open-ended narratives that begin to suggest an alternative plot. This plot is one of female masochism and sexual obsession, and its patterns are closer to those of the harlot's than of the parish boy's progress. They involve the uncovering of a series of seduced girls, dead mothers, and angry women: they are the "babbling drabs" whose story Nancy begins to set free with her crossing of that magic boundary, taking her unrespectable, almost literally unrepresentable self into the Maylies' hotel, and the darkness of her story into what had been the angelic light of Rose Maylie's pure girlhood.

The contrast between Rose and Nancy is what the novelist thought of as his best idea for the book: at first, it seems to do both narrative and ideological work by presenting the question of the social formation of character, the neglect of children, the initial equality of all humanity. It does so, tidily for the novel, at a moment when the revelation of Oliver's good birth might be likely to *undo* any social message at all: it has begun to look as if Oliver might be incorruptible simply because he is not lower class – or, in the novel's terms, because he is not ungrammatical. But the Rose/Nancy opposition suggests once more that it is the *neglect* of Nancy that makes her a prostitute; unfortunately, the Maylies ask her too late, and she can no longer begin again, but for others, not in love with house-breakers, presumably social change may not come tardily. Nancy can still become Rose.

But the opposition is beginning to break down in the opposite direction: it is now Rose, it seems, who sees herself in Nancy; Rose's desire and obsessive love for Harry Maylie that creates the womanly bond between them. Most readers have taken her rejection of her (adopted) cousin's love as pure Victorian selflessness, taking their cue from the narrator's unpalatable introduction of Rose:

The younger lady was in the lovely bloom and spring-time of womanhood; at that age, when, if ever angels be for God's good purposes enthroned in mortal forms, they may be, without impiety, supposed to abide in such as hers. (264)

She is "not past seventeen," slight and of an exquisite mold, full of intelligence; her face has "no shadow," and her "smile, the cheerful, happy smile, [was] made for Home, and fireside peace and happiness" (264).[5] Nothing, presumably, could be farther from Nancy – except that Nancy spends much of the novel by the fire, staring into it, saying nothing, the first of Dickens's fire-gazing women.[6]

If we do not look for Rose's "fireside peace and happiness" in Nancy, no more do we look for Nancy's firm resistance in Rose. Yet it is there, for Rose's reasons for not marrying Harry Maylie are not entirely the shame and ignominy to *him* of marrying an illegitimate, penniless girl:

"I owe it to myself, that I, a friendless, portionless girl with a blight upon my name, should not give your friends reason to suspect that I had sordidly yielded to your first passion, and fastened myself, a clog, on all your hopes and projects. I owe it to you and yours, to prevent you from opposing, in the warmth of your generous nature, this great obstacle to your progress in the world." (316)

And more than her refusal to be a "clog," "fastened" to his hopes, she will not "mingle with such as may hold in scorn the mother who gave me life; nor bring disgrace or failure on the son of her who has so well supplied that mother's place" (317). It is Rose's mothers (her own dead mother, and Harry's, the woman who raised her) whose "name" she imagines here; like Oliver, prompted to his only violent act by the attack on his mother's reputation, Rose cannot allow her mother's "gift" to go unthanked; but more, even here, in the love that is so powerful that it makes her see herself "a clog," in the "withered" hopes that she recollects, and even more in the fever that threatens to kill her, we can see the tension between unfulfilled desire and some "pride" she carries with her – a struggle, of course, much like Nancy's.

In the scene at the hotel, Rose begs Nancy to abandon her life of "wickedness and misery," to leave this "terrible infatuation." Nancy's reply reverberates through the novel:

When ladies as young, and good, and beautiful as you are . . . give away your hearts, love will carry you all lengths – even such as you, who have home, friends, other admirers, everything, to fill them. When such as I, who have no certain roof but the coffin-lid, and no friend in sickness or death but the hospital nurse, set our rotten hearts on any man, and let him fill the place that has been a blank through all our wretched lives, who can hope to cure us? (366)

Rose cannot argue with that, for her love for Harry Maylie is precisely that absolute: furthermore, her identity, like Nancy's, is constructed around a "blank," the lost mother, the disgraced identity, the silent loneliness; she, like Nancy, cannot be "cured." The surprise of the contact between these two worlds, of Nancy's introduction to Rose, is that the whore does not disappear into the virtuous woman's story. Rather, the text constructs a "Banquo's sons" chain of seduced, innocent, loving women: Oliver's mother Agnes, Nancy, Rose herself, women who, in Nancy's phrase, "give away their hearts," only to be "carried all lengths." And it is that masochistic, overly generous love that the novel values: that love of the "blank" that saves Oliver; the love of Bill that redeems and destroys Nancy; that love of her own that leaves Rose, after her meeting with Nancy, so "overpowered that she sank into a chair, and endeavoured to collect her wandering thoughts" (366). Rose, after that "extraordinary interview" has become, at least in her own imagination, a story-telling streetwalker.

Nancy, of course, tells her story only to die: while she longs for a quiet death in the river, a tranquil, sexless exile with Bill, what she gets is a horrific murder, and a fame (a history) that generates the rest of the novel. Fagin is hanged for Nancy's murder, not his life of crime; it is the knowledge that Sikes is about to be apprehended that prompts Monks to talk – that, and the report of Nancy's eavesdropping success. Nancy, however, has left the novel: there is no place for her in the last chapter; she is even more anonymous than the unnamed "chief remaining members of Fagin's gang" who die abroad (276). (Bet, Nancy's friend, is last heard of going mad after seeing Nancy's corpse; she leaves the novel in a straight-jacket.) Nancy seems to be lost, forever, in the hero's story, in Oliver's "progress." But the novel does end with a lost, silent woman:

with Oliver's mother, Agnes, whose name is "as yet" the only one on a tomb in a silent church; whose name, like the name inside her ring, is unfinished by marriage – and by death. The narrator concludes,

I believe that the shade of Agnes sometimes hovers round that solemn nook. I believe it none the less because that nook is in a Church, and she was weak and erring. (480)

This seems to conjure up a forgiving narrator, one extending his generosity to the fallen. But it doesn't seem necessary here: Oliver's mother was told that her lover couldn't marry her; she is in every essential way presented as unsinning. Indeed, if her "sin" were to persist in the novel, her sister Rose's virtue might continue to be questionable, which is the last thing the novel wants. But portraying Agnes as "weak and erring," and more, portraying her as a "shade," allows back in the shadow-haunting Nancy, otherwise excluded from the novel's conclusion. In the original version of the novel, and in the 1841 edition, the final sentence left even more space for Nancy: the sentence read not "the shade of Agnes" but "the shade of that poor girl," and the fixing of the sign (deciding that "girl" must mean "Agnes") suggests that some of the ambiguity of the reference may have occurred to Dickens. His "erring" (wandering) woman seems to wander back into the book, listening and babbling when we least expect her.

The spectacle of Nancy's return is staged repeatedly throughout the novel and Dickens's career, much as the novel obsessively returns to the moment of Oliver's birth – a scene that we get early, and are told repeatedly we didn't get all of. More and more information needs to be packed into that scene; more and more needs to have happened there, just as more and more information seems to be encoded in the female body. "Carry your memory back" (331), Monks commands Bumble, and in that play on a maternal "carrying" we hear some connection of memory and conception – specifically, of the mother who "carried" Oliver, only to die. The novel seems often to forget the question of Oliver's inheritance ("What [is the] object?" asks Dr Losborne; "Simply, the discovery of Oliver's parentage, and regaining for him [his] inheritance," he is told, to which he replies, "Ah! . . . I almost forgot that!" [373]) but Oliver never forgets his mother. Nor does Rose, whose mother's obsessive concern with Oliver's existence is what generated all this mad plotting (his "beginning and finishing") in the first place. Dead women (particularly dead mothers) hold all the stories in this novel: from old Sally's confession of Agnes's dying words (the originary act elided from the first scene) to Oliver and Rose standing under the tomb, with the one name "Agnes" staring back at them, women do get the last word. The narrative seems only marginally to belong to Oliver, or even to male storytellers; at times, in its tensions, it suggests that Dickens himself is fighting to keep control of his narrative.

This lack of authorial control is reflected everywhere in the novel, as a confusion and slipperiness of point of view and – more – of narrative voice. Steven Marcus has suggested the ways in which the narrator of the opening chapters, in parodying Utilitarian prose style, takes on the limitations of that voice, and depends on an almost Malthusian habit of abstraction.[7] The narrator is habitually ironic – but one of his tricks of irony is that of identifying with the character he is mocking, of taking on that voice just long enough to make it ridiculous. So, when Oliver first sees the prostitutes and the narrator seconds his assertion that they are "nice girls" with his own "there is no doubt they were" (111), he tells us that there is every doubt they were. The narrator pretends to assume Oliver's innocence to get us to agree to his own knowledge – that is, he pretends an identification with the object of his satire, to insure our identification with his narrative authority.

But this process of narratorial identification, and our reading of this voice, becomes more difficult as the plot (and problems of identification in general) becomes more complex. In the scene where Nancy goes to recapture Oliver, assuming the dress of a respectable woman, the narrator assumes a new style of address:

"She's a honour to her sex," said Mr Sikes, filling his glass, and smiting the table with his enormous fist. "Here's her health, and wishing they was all like her!"

While these, and many other encomiums, were being passed on the accomplished Miss Nancy, that young lady made the best of her way to the police-office; whither, *not withstanding a little natural timidity consequent upon walking through the streets alone and unprotected,* she arrived in perfect safety shortly afterwards. (p. 140, emphasis added)

The narrator becomes "missish" here, stressing both his and his subject's gentility – both possess "natural timidity," and the heroine (who is, after all, a streetwalker) becomes equally genteel with the importation of this new language. And the language persists until she leaves the jail:

In a dreadful state of doubt and uncertainty, the agonized young woman staggered to the gate, and then, exchanging her faltering walk for a swift run, returned by the most devious and complicated route she could think of, to the domicile of the Jew. (p. 141)

Nancy's whole journey into this "state of doubt," this state of sisterly affection, is shared by the narrator – who only breaks out when she does, "exchanging" her walk for a run, moving into the old "devious and complicated" routes.

At no point does the narrator signal any separation from Nancy – but for whose benefit is this irony being exercised? It is the same ironic portrayal ("acting beautifully") that Nancy has put on to deceive the good characters, but why should it be used for us? It allows readers to enter into Nancy's fiction (the description may be an account of the way she is narrating her journey to herself, so she can better play her part) but since we are already in on the con, it also allows us to laugh at those who are taken in by it, increasing our identification with the thieves. Some of this irony, of course, is directed at Nancy, at her coarseness and *lack* of a need for protection (Rose Maylie would not be able to take this walk alone) and as such, it is one with the early illustrations of the overweight, blowsy Nancy – illustrations Dickens needed to separate from the rest of the novel, wishing later they had not been drawn. But reading this passage after the novel's conclusion, one can see in it some preparation for Nancy's later genuinely ladylike behavior: Nancy's "natural timidity" is her innate goodness, the quality Oliver's suffering will bring out in her. The "accomplished Miss Nancy" *will* die "alone and unprotected," and her last, dangerous, devious routes through the streets to the "domicile of the Jew" will be taken with exactly this doubt, this uncertainty, this agony. The uncertainty of the narrative voice, directed at no one, anticipating no reader's needs, pointlessly ironic, in fact allows the space for the rewriting of Nancy, for her complication of the narrative route. Nonetheless, it suggests a continuing uncertainty about how best to tell Nancy's story and give it meaning.

And yet, Dickens retold it repeatedly, told it publicly, and was most proud of his effect on audiences of women. "If one woman cries out when you murder the girl," the "ladies' Doctor" Priestley told him, "you may rely on it that . . . there will be a contagion of hysteria all over the place."[8] A contagion of hysteria is in part the state of the novel, with its sliding female sexuality and masochism; but it is also, of course, Dickens's own response to the reading. When he first came to, "try, alone by myself, the Oliver Twist murder," he told a friend he had "got something so horrible out of it that I am afraid to try it in public," but, like Nancy "trying it on," he "tried it" over and over, killing himself with the effort. When he performed the reading, his pulse-rate rose from 72 to 124; after reading it, he would collapse on a sofa, unable to speak; Wilkie

Collins, among others, believed that this reading "did more to kill him than all his work put together"; his physician forbade him to continue it – and yet, a friend reports that a day or two before his death, he was discovered in the grounds of Gad's Hill performing the death of Nancy.

One could see in Dickens only the vengeful, mad, driven Sikes, bludgeoning the vulnerable, loving girl, again and again, endlessly destroying women, unable to stop trying to close her eyes. But Dickens made a remarkable comment the last night he performed the reading publicly. "I shall tear myself to pieces," he whispered to a friend, echoing the division of self we saw primarily not among male, but among female characters in the novel. Just as Nancy, feigning repudiation of Oliver, claims, "sight of him turns me against myself," so in creating and murdering the woman, then destroying her murderer in turn, Dickens can "turn" against himself, and the novel can complicate its own generic moves – though it, like Thackeray's cathartic novel *Catherine*, also imagined as a critique of the Newgate sensationalism, may wind up emulating and exacerbating exactly what it set out to critique.

But the problems go deeper than this. The traces of the Newgate novel, and the intricate battle it stages between romance, realism, and violence, return throughout Dickens's career: the battered woman who forgives her merciless lover haunts not only the early fiction (in "The Hospital Patient" and "A Visit to Newgate" in *Sketches*; the stroller's tale, the madman's manuscript, and "The Convict's Return" in *The Pickwick Papers*) but the later, more generically coherent novels. Lucie Manette, standing outside the prison signalling Charles Darnay, and Amy Dorrit, standing inside the Marshalsea with her loving, devoted heart, carry echoes of Nancy, walking with Bill Sikes beside the walls of Newgate, saying that she would be true to him even if he were condemned to death – even if it were, as it is in this novel, her murder for which he were imprisoned. Masochism, written first on the body of the woman and then on the imagination of the violent man, is the power Dickens imagines women to have – the power to soften, to make disappear the stone walls of the prison. This is, as the career progresses, a power at once personal and political, individual and social, a power Dickens needed to believe in.[9] Dickens's faith in that power suggests something more about the roots of *Twist*'s progress (from the parish boy's progress into the harlot's; from Newgate to new realism), and the roots of the violence the narrative directs towards Nancy – a violence connected to its own narrative wanderings and anxieties; a violence that, not properly contained and narrated, would tear the author to pieces.

As the assemblage of images (babbling drabs, walking shadows, angelic heroines, and their specular doubles) suggests, there is more to the uncanny heroine than the spectacle of violence directed towards her, and it remains to ask, what do her various embodiments, her narratorial wanderings and "twistings," accomplish for the fiction and for the new author; in what ways does she serve as an opening for Dickens's literary career?

We might best answer that question by counterpoising Nancy's wanderings to Dickens's other spectacular heroine, little Nell, who similarly stages her own wandering mortality, and around whom Dickens stages his challenge to the novel. The central activity of any reader of *The Old Curiosity Shop* is watching Little Nell walk herself to death; as passionately as we are expected to follow the hunt for Nancy's murderer ("the eyes! the eyes!" cries Bill Sikes, as Nancy haunts him to his accidental but just hanging) so do we follow Nell's virtuous, painful, and lonely path to the grave. But as Dickens's Preface suggests, while on one hand we are caught up in Nell's wanderings, which become the peregrinations of the novel itself, on the other, we are to hold fixed in our mind the still, sad icon of goodness, the small girl in her bed, surrounded by misshapen and eccentric figures, among whom she is both a perfect object, and an object of perfect goodness.

The language of the Preface, as it contrasted her "innocent face and pure intentions" with "associates as strange and uncongenial as the grim objects that are about her bed" (42) suggests the power of Dickens's "fancy" about her, and the narrator's language goes on to recapitulate this theme:

the child . . . alone, unwatched, uncared for (save by angels), yet sleeping peacefully. So very young, so spiritual, so slight and fairy-like a creature passing the long dull nights in such an uncongenial place – I could not dismiss it from my thoughts. (55)

Master Humphrey takes repeated "turns" about the room as he "speculates" on Nell's "curious" wanderings, and his inability to move forward in his thoughts takes us in the same circular directions as does the novel, for the sections of description I have quoted were, like the Preface, written *after* the novel was finished – hence their uncanny prescience, which suggests not only the book's difficulty in proceeding but Dickens's own obsession with the uncared-for child, who manages to recapitulate not only Oliver's passive goodness, but Nancy's uncomfortable display of sexuality and self-sacrifice.

Master Humphrey cannot "dismiss her from my recollection, do what I would" (56). Or perhaps he means he cannot dismiss her from his *collection*, for he goes on to turn her into a different kind of curiosity, "imagin[ing] her in her future life, holding her solitary way among a crowd of wild grotesque companions; the only pure, fresh, youthful object in the throng. It would be curious to find – " and the breaking off of his thoughts suggests the dangers of following the girl, as he goes on to reflect, into "a region on which I was little disposed to enter" (56). But just as Nancy's wandering into the shadows of *Oliver Twist* seems to suggest some incipient unrest in the narratorial voice of that novel, so here the thematic and formal tensions of *The Old Curiosity Shop*, and its anxiety about Nell's place, suggest some of Dickens's own thematic and formal anxieties, and the wanderings of the novel some of the young Dickens's experiments in realism and its variations.

These experiments seem centered on the multiple speculations that characters (and readers) are encouraged to indulge in about Nell and her melodrama. Master Humphrey's "tender reflections," it unfolds, are only his fantasy: the "fairy-like" creature he perceives does not have the "light and sunny dreams" he imagines, and her tale progresses through a series of nightmare visions of flight, pursuit, and pain. Most of Nell's problems arise from the speculations of others about her, those who single her out as a "pure fresh youthful object" (56), selected by the idler Dick Swiveller for her fortune ("a young and lovely girl . . . saving up for me" [118]) and for her "pretty face, [her] very pretty face" (103); by the dwarf Quilp, to be my "number two," my "cherry-cheeked, red-lipped wife" (93); by her grandfather, as a guarantor of his luck in his gambling speculations. From the first, she is a particular kind of commodity: a "Fine girl of her age, but small" (103), or, as her brother says, "Nell will be a woman soon . . . [and will have] money" (64–5), or, as Quilp says, "such a chubby, rosy, cosy, little Nell!" (125). Her journey is similarly punctuated by evaluation: she is noticed by many people along the road who "praised Nell's beauty and were at once prepossessed in her behalf" (184), but also by equally many who, seeing "this fair young child a falling into bad hands, and getting among people that she's no more fit for, than they are to get among angels as their ordinary chums" (to quote the unsavory Short), "take measures for detaining . . . and restoring [her]" – that is, for kidnapping her, and profiting from her "fall" (199). In that way, everyone is interested in gazing at Nell – if not in making her among "their ordinary chums" – and it is the vulnerability of that object that moves them to desire it.[10]

The spectacle of *The Old Curiosity Shop* is organized around the alternate veiling and discovering of Nell's sexual vulnerability. Nell is a kind of pornographic object, and it would seem that the novel invites us to share in her fate as a pleasure victim, a tiny Justine, ready to be initiated into a Sadeian world of violence and perversion. But it is important to note the ways Nell does not participate in such a plot, and also to note our own discomfort with the ways she is imagined in the novel: the plot of the novel is largely Nell's attempts to escape Quilp (who spends a fair bit of time staring at Nell as well as playing in her bed) and the rape he has planned for her.[11] Quilp's fascinated viewing of Nell being kissed by her grandfather ("just upon the rosy part" [125]) seems to force us to participate in the structures of his desire. But the novel repeatedly forces our view away from his watching of Nell into Nell's anxiety about being watched; early in the novel, she stares into the darkening streets "wondering whether those rooms [opposite] were as lonesome as that in which she sat, and whether those people felt it company to see her sitting there, as she did only to see them look out and draw in their heads again" (120). Nell sees her own objectification as like (if more terrifying than) that of everyone else in London; she is both drawn to being looked at and terrified of the perceptions of others. But merely to read her as a "blank" to our projections (the customary role of the object in pornography) would be to evade both her pain at being the site of so much looking, and her willingness to look back, to participate in the visual world in which she seems to be only a "lonely figure."

Nell, like Nancy, is more than a passive object, and her progress takes her farther than her slight frame might suggest. She plans and executes her escape with her delusional grandfather; she travels across the wilds of industrial England, singing ditties to wild men on a barge; she enters into small towns and barters for goods; she sleeps one night on a factory floor, beside a begrimed and mysterious worker. At times, she anticipates the later work Dickens's investigative daughters will perform, interrogating the condition of England. But only rarely is she allowed to pause to examine what she sees: what she cannot escape on her journey is not (as most critics would have it) her own death, which certainly seems to be following her, but her own status as exhibition. The only times Nell seems to be happy is those few times when she can embrace her own "curiosity," and join in the show: these scenes, unlike the scenes in her

grandfather's shop or within the uneasy family circle, seem to offer Nell
some release, and the possibility of a looking-on not fractured by the
anxieties of voyeurism. When Nell joins Mrs Jarley's waxworks, she
enters into a wider world of curiosities:

> Rumbling along with most unwonted noise, the caravan stopped at last at the
> place of exhibition, where Nell dismounted amidst an admiring group of chil-
> dren, who evidently supposed her to be an important item of the curiosities,
> and were fully impressed with the belief that her grandfather was a cunning
> device in wax. (280)

Nell proves so adept at *being* a commodity, that she soon begins to move
freely *among* the commodities, and to exhibit the "devices themselves":

> The beauty of the child, coupled with her gentle and timid bearing, produced
> quite a sensation in the little country place. The Brigand, heretofore a source of
> exclusive interest in the streets, became a mere secondary consideration, and to
> be important only as a part of the show of which she was the chief attraction.
> Grown-up folks began to be interested in the bright-eyed girl, and some score
> of little boys fell desperately in love, and constantly left inclosures of nuts and
> apples, directed in small text, at the wax-work door.
>   This desirable impression was not lost upon Mrs Jarley, who, lest Nell should
> become too cheap, soon sent the Brigand out alone again, and kept her in the
> exhibition room, where she described the figures every half-hour to the great
> satisfaction of admiring audiences. (286–8)

The brigand really is a "cunning device in wax," but Nell might as well
be one here – she is the "chief attraction . . . of the show," producing
"quite a sensation" everywhere she goes, until, in fact, she runs the risk
of making herself "cheap."[12] In these scenes, Nell is threatened, but only
comically: a schoolmistress vows to have Mrs Jarley put in the stocks and
Nell forced onto the treadmill, but Mrs Jarley admonishes Nell that she
is to laugh every time she thinks of Miss Monflathers, and the novel
moves on unperturbed.[13]

But the sight of Nell on the road, collecting "desirable impressions" is
not always so benevolent. More often she is exposed to harm, vulnerable
to the schemes of onlookers, and fearful, most often, of course, not of
the threat she might encounter, but of the danger she carries with her,
her deluded and desperate grandfather, who (in the novel's darkest
moment) enters her room and removes the coins she has hidden in the
folds of her dress. The sexual threat her grandfather seems to represent
for her is a hidden one, but it lines up almost too neatly with the threat
that faces her in her travels: precisely that of being a woman on the road.
In a powerful scene, Nell meets a woman (almost certainly a prostitute)

at the races, and the woman, after buying flowers from her, begs her to stay at home. And here the eeriness of the waxwork child comes together with the other threats against Nell: to be in danger of becoming "too cheap" is one with the danger of becoming one of the goods yourself; if Nell must be on the road to achieve her status as iconic heroine and to die her sanctified death, she is also at the mercy of everyone who sees her on that road — of everyone who has a penny with which to look at her.

Dickens's Preface invited this speculative gaze, in drawing the "pure, innocent child" surrounded by "grotesque and wild but not impossible companions" (42), the object that gathers together all the value of his work of representation. But the longer we gaze at her – and indeed, the longer we speculate about the novel as a whole – the more Nell and the book seem equally "impossible," if not "wild" then certainly grotesque. While Nell is carefully situated (as are Kit Nubble and his family, the Garlands, and the girlish Barbara) to be an icon of good, to oppose the great eccentric characters like Quilp, the Brasses, and Dick Swiveller, she increasingly departs from any realist or even tidily allegorical conception of femininity: as she is converted by the narrative into a figure of redemption, she becomes herself no less freakish than her companions, another version of "the little lady without legs and arms" who arrives at the Jolly Sandboys having "jogged forward in a van" (203) – and Dickens's "constructed" tale takes on more of the flavor of the showman's improvisation, itself more curiosity warehouse than allegorical fable. But the curio collection is centered curiously on Nell's own body: Dickens will be attracted in particular to female carnival figures throughout his career,[14] and I will return to them later in this book, but in his earliest depiction of the powerful daughter, the *redemptive* daughter Nell is meant to be, he moves his heroine herself close to the realm of the female freak.

Parodic versions of Nell surround her throughout the novel: Sally Brass, the angular and angry sister of the spineless attorney Solomon Brass, is the "sphynx of private life" (466), "the Virgin of Bevis" (325), "The beautiful virgin" (542), "that amiable virgin" (348); showing "maiden modesty and gentle womanhood" (320), she is "the female who has all the charms of her sex and none of their weaknesses" (325). Further, she generates the same fascinated gaze that Nell does; Swiveller stares "with all his might at the beauteous Sally, as if she had been some curious animal whose like had never lived" (327). But the curiosity she conjures is more monstrous: Swiveller calls her "that strange monster"

(328); he claims he is "clerk to a female dragon"; he stares transfixed at her "vampire cap," which he – Perseus like – attempts constantly to knock off.[15] Yet her monstrosity is particularized as female – and as sexual:

"It's of no use asking the dragon . . . I suspect if I asked any questions on that head, our alliance would be at an end. I wonder whether she *is* a dragon by-the-by, or something in the mermaid[16] way. She has rather a scaly appearance. But mermaids are fond of looking at themselves in the glass, which she can't be. And they have a habit of combing their hair, which she hasn't. No, she's a dragon." (349–50)

The threat of Sally Brass is of a woman who *is* half-monster – and the other half alluringly feminine.

If Sally is a horrible parody, the Marchioness is the comic – and romance – version of Nell, an altogether more amiable freak. She is referred to repeatedly as the "small servant," but (like Nell) she is an "old-fashioned child in her looks and manner," so lost in her clothes "She might as well have been dressed in a violin-case" (332). And like Nell, she prompts wonder wherever she goes: she is "a very extraordinary person – surrounded by mysteries, ignorant of the taste of beer, unacquainted with her own name (which is less remarkable), and taking a limited view of society through the keyholes of doors." "It is," as her admirer, Dick Swiveller, goes on to note, "a most inscrutable and unmitigated staggerer" (532). She literally staggers, racing across London in one shoe to rescue Dick from illness, proving again her relationship to the plucky and staggering Nell, but what she shares most profoundly with Nell is her use literally as an object – in the Marchioness's case, she is "objectified" as a battering ram, as a slavey, as a projectile to be thrown downstairs to rouse the sleeping Gentleman; as an object of the rage of others, as in the horrific scene when Sally Brass "dart[s] suddenly forward, and falling on the small servant give[s] her some hard blows with her clenched hand" (353); the Marchioness is remarkable not only for her size and her mobility, but for her endurance.

These other versions of Nell suggest the way that the modest daughter is transformed into something monstrous, something that (as Susan Stewart describes it[17]) suggests the etymological roots of monstrous, both of showing forth (*monstro*) and warning (*moneo*). Nell, in her persistent emblematizing of goodness, is a monitory figure, but she also reminds us of the showman-like quality of all of Dickens's early fiction, the "mountebank" figure that David Musselwhite and others have located in the early Dickens, "Boz," the narratorial flâneur whose sheer pleasure in spectacle resists the joys of a tidy narrative.[18] What Dickens is showing off here is, in the Marchioness's eloquent phraseology, the heroine who is "such a one-er," both "a wonder" (and a cause of wonder in others) and a unique (one of a kind) spectacle in herself. The pleasures of the "curiosity shop" in which Nell is a principal display conjures up the anthologies of wonders that Dickens loved and collected, books like G. H. Wilson's *The Eccentric Mirror and Wonderful Characters*, which contained "authentic biographical accounts of persons . . . [who] deviat[e] in a remarkable degree from the ordinary course of human existence."[19] These "MALE AND FEMALE CHARACTERS, ANCIENT AND MODERN, who have been particularly distinguished by extraordinary QUALIFICATIONS, TALENTS AND PROPENSITIES, Natural or Acquired, comprehending singular Instances of Longevity, Conformation, Bulk, Stature, Powers of Mind and body, wonderful exploits, adventures, habits, propensities, enterprising pursuits, etc., etc., etc.," included dwarves, giants, misers; Margaret Lambrun, who dressed up as a man to kill Queen Elizabeth; Hannah Snell, "the Widow in Masquerade, or the Female Warrior;" the Queen of the Gipsies, "Louisa, the Lady of the Hay-Stack," women frozen for a week, living in caves or dressing like men, even a man who lives as his own dead sister. Dickens's Nelly would be considerably less unusual in this catalogue than his Preface suggests.

Dickens loved the extraordinary, but yearned always for the ordinary, and the longer he surrounds Nell with eccentrics, the more of a "one-er" she becomes. But her centrality to his vision poses a problem essential to his fiction: the question, to return to Wilson's title, of what the "Eccentric Mirror" reflects. Is it that the mirror is eccentric, and distorts what it reflects, or is the mirror (the novel) merely a "reflection" of an eccentricity ("adventures, habits, propensities") already existing somewhere outside it? We are, unexpectedly, led back to the problem posed by *Oliver Twist*'s rejection of the Newgate novel's false realism: what *Twist* depicts "is a contradiction, an anomaly, an apparent impossibility; but it is a truth." In the same way, Little Nell, however improbable she might seem, represents "the truth," and yet her very uniqueness challenges the "truth" of what is around her.

The question would seem to be, what kind of truth does the eccentric female body possess – and what kind of object is it? This returns us to the problem of the showman Dickens and his affinity with other, extranovelistic forms of spectacle. In Dickens's collections of "miracles of conformation," to quote Wilson, we would find several miniaturized icons of daughterhood: contemporary accounts include a boneless woman observed at the Bartholemew Fair by Robert Hooke in 1677, "A girl, above sixteen years of Age, born in Cheshire, and not above Eighteen inches long, having shed the Teeth seven several Times, and not a perfect Bone in any part of her, only the Head; yet she hath all her senses to Admiration, and Discourses, Reads very well, Sings, Whistles, and all very pleasant to hear."[20] The "Sicilian Fairy," Mademoiselle Caroline Crachami, a ten year old girl exhibited in 1824, was nineteen-and-a-half inches tall, her feet hardly more than three inches long and her forefingers less than one inch, her waist eleven-and-a-quarter inches around. A contemporary observer recounts that she was:

lively and interesting, . . . [she] sat upon a small tea-caddy with infinite grace, and listened to music with evident pleasure, beating time with her tiny foot, and waving her head just as any boarding-school Miss in her upper teens, and conscious of the beauty of her movements, would do.[21]

But a Mrs. Mathews, a less sympathetic observer, notes that when her husband, a "tireless" pursuer of "sights,"

entered the room, he found her seated on a raised platform, in seeming mockery of regal state, to receive her visitors: she was described to be of foreign birth. The man who attended her, attired in a strange garb, had a tall athletic figure, and formed an admirable contrast to the tiny proportion of his *daughter*, as he called her . . . The lady was a most disgusting little withered creature (although young), very white, and what my husband disliked very much in a woman, had a *powdery* look upon her skin. Her voice was pitched in the highest key of childish treble, indeed so thin, and comb-like, that it hardly reached the ear of those to whom she spoke. Her "papa," however, considerately repeated all she said, for the satisfaction of her patrons, adding many particulars not mentionable to ears polite.

The childish dwarf, the "little withered creature" displayed by her athletic papa, reads like a Dickens child, but that daughterhood is also a fiction: her real parents appeared in London only after she died of "exposure" (both of bad air affecting her lungs, and of receiving too many visitors – over two hundred in one day) and they arrived in the city, having heard of her death in the newspapers, only to find her in the process of being dissected.[22] As Thomas Hood wrote of "The Sicilian Fairy" in his poem, "Ode to the Great Unknown," "When she felt herself a show, she tried/ To shrink from the world's eye, poor dwarf! and died!"

What links Nell to these other displays of daughterhood (the Sicilian Fairy, the boneless girl, "Louisa, the Lady of the Hay-Stack") is not so much her display as her "shrinking" quality, the way she at once stays in circulation and evades representation. The text, in its "kind of allegory," attempts to reconcile these impulses, to read her death (her shrinking) as redemptive, as something that allows her image to continue to circulate. In that reading, the nation can gather to mourn that "Nelly, Boz's little Nelly is dead," and the grandfather is allowed, Lear-like, to weep over his "dear, gentle, patient, noble Nell." But if we were to ask again, why is Little Nell so little, what makes her such a spectacle, we might be able to turn in a different direction: to a reading of the redemptive daughter that took seriously her status as a 'freak' within the realist novel. For if we weigh others of Dickens's little women, the angelic quality of their diminution is less clear. Consider in this light Nicholas Nickleby's first meeting with the Infant Phenomenon and her father, after her somewhat remarkable (and quite ghastly) performance:

> "May I ask how old she is?" . . .
> "You may, sir" replied Mr. Crummles, looking steadily in his questioner's face, as some men do when they have doubts about being implicitly believed in what they are going to say. "She is ten years of age, sir."
> "Not more?"
> "Not a day."
> "Dear me!" said Nicholas, "it's extraordinary."
> It was; for the infant phenomenon, though of short stature, had a comparatively aged countenance, and had moreover been precisely the same age – not perhaps to the full extent of the memory of the oldest inhabitant, but certainly for five good years. But she had been kept up late every night, and put upon an unlimited allowance of gin-and-water from infancy, to prevent her growing tall, and perhaps this system of training had produced in the infant phenomenon these additional phenomena.[23]

This "training," of course, is also Little Nell's: she is similarly kept awake through most of the novel; repeatedly, she is too exhausted to eat; she shares her portions with her grandfather ("Her grandfather ate greedily, which she was glad to see" [426]); she refrains from asking for more. She is far from the only Dickens heroine to do so: Amy ("Little") Dorrit turns out to be so small because she takes her meals home from Mrs. Clennam's and feeds them to her father. When Arthur finds her in the Marshalsea, he sees that "She had brought the meat home that she should have eaten herself, and was already warming it on a gridiron over the fire for her father, clad in an old grey gown and a black cap, awaiting his supper at the table"[24] – it is, obviously, *her* supper he is awaiting.

That recasting of the novel suggests that Nell's death is not an image of female sacrifice but a vision of an abused young woman, hounded by speculators and tortured by an unseeing grandfather; that novel, we might imagine, is pushing closer to the realism of *Oliver Twist* and farther away from the allegory of fairy-tales and magical dwarves. That "realist" novel might push us to notice all the ways in which Nell is *not* a waxwork child: she is an observant, plucky, surprisingly brave traveler; she watches those around her and protects herself from their wiles; she invents dream-visions to save her grandfather from himself; she can even imagine for herself a happier end for her novel.

That, as a Dickens narrator might put it, was not to be; instead, a suspicious Dickens reader might point out, following John Ruskin, "Nell . . . was killed for the market, as a butcher kills a lamb."[25] This is in keeping with the reading I have been suggesting, that Nell's death is a site of value for Dickens, part of the cannibalizing of young children so central to his early fiction – and indeed, given the sweeping-boy Jo and little John Harmon, it was a taste Dickens was as slow to renounce as his readers. But it seems that Dickens was also slow to decide on the death of little Nell, and the alternative realism I am suggesting (feed her and buy her decent shoes) is an unexpected diversion from that allegorical and remunerative path. Something else, though, seems to be at work in the death of Little Nell.

Susan Stewart's brilliant study of the miniature might suggest some of the duplicitous work Nell's death – like her wanderings – might be doing in the novel, and in Dickens's career. Nell seems to encapsulate something at once monstrous and miniature: the "little" wonder. As Dickens uses her to anchor the brilliant wanderings of the novel, she stands as what Stewart calls a "souvenir," an emblem that "may be seen as emblematic of the nostalgia that all narrative reveals – the longing for its place of origin. Particularly important here are the functions of the narrative of the self: that story's lost point of identity with the mother and its perpetual desire for reunion and incorporation, for the repetition that is not a repetition."[26] Nell's body almost literally encapsulates that function, for, like so many Dickens heroines to come, her birth marked her mother's death, and yet she is the picture of her mother and of her grandmother, the latest miniature in "a portrait gallery." In this daughter, as her uncle remarks, the mother lives again; as Alexander Welsh once wrote, "if one has faith in the return of the repressed, the mothers in Dickens are not hard to find,"[27] and Nell represents the perfect moment of narrative, when origin and end (mother and daughter) come together.

The female body is sexually charged; it is vulnerable; it is impregnable. And that, of course, is the secret of Nell's body – that she is, at the

age of fourteen, on the verge of menstruation, of which the blood that
falls from her feet at every step is a hint.[28] Nell's wasting sickness is close
to contemporary accounts of diseases that attack women when they
begin to menstruate; it also resembles movie-heroine disease, which is to
say that Nell dies not only of exhaustion and malnutrition, but of
becoming a woman – or of excess femininity On the verge of reproductive possibility, Nell must die precisely so she can stay a miniature;
she can both stay small, and leave behind no double of herself; she can
stay a "one-er." It is for this reason that Dickens needs a fourteen-year-
old-freak, and he needs her at the moment before she becomes pregnant.
She must be preserved at the moment before sexuality, before reproduction, so that she can stay a "trace," a "souvenir," a "memento." Nell, in
that way, is not only a monument, she is her own epitaph; more, she
stands in the place of the whole novel, and for that reason, the novel can
become "the death of Little Nell." The still-miniature Nell suggests the
freak show domesticated. Richard Altick recounts that in the eighteenth
century wealthy patrons paid to have freaks exhibited in their homes;[29]
for more money, customers would be given private showings. The smallest of freaks would be brought in tiny boxes, and step out into the
drawing room; a freak who arrives in a small container for a private
showing is, in a way, precisely what little Nell is. The novel needs an
emblem, a "legend"; it is the female body – Nell's body – that comes to
our homes, that stays with us, that becomes that emblem.

But the female body is a notoriously slippery emblem: it threatens
always – as Quilp's jealousy, Dick Swiveller's jealousy, Nell's grandfather's jealousy, all suggest – to become "inconstant," to use the word the
novel uses of its own narrative when trying to tie together its plot. This
anxiety about stability might suggest why the novel is so concerned with
travel, even at the expense of its historical accuracy. Even Mrs. Jarley's
joyous wanderings suggest this obsession with the road: Madame
Tussaud, her historical model, had settled down in London by the time
Dickens wrote his novel; *The Old Curiosity Shop* insists on taking the
waxworks back on the road. Similarly, like Wilson, who claims in *The
Eccentric Mirror*[30] that only stepping *out* of the track of the ordinary
excites us, that "it is curious to observe Nature step out of the common
road and enter the precincts of the marvelous," the novel seems to claim
that it is "by deviations," by mis-steps, that it will "raise astonishment."

The novel takes its narrative power from the variety of objects it can
parade before us, but it also needs to find a steady place: indeed, its

moment of greatest anxiety comes at the book's end, when Kit Nubbles returns to show his children the site of the curiosity shop, only to find he can no longer remember it. It has disappeared, the narrator says, "like a tale that was told" (672). It is true that the novel ends with a happy marriage, one of the most contented sexual matches in all of Dickens, the union of Dick Swiveller and the Marchioness, but even that marriage suggests traveling on as much as forming more perfect communities: the Marchioness, after all, has been renamed "Sophronia Sphynx," in tribute no doubt to Sophy Wackles (whose love Dick sacrificed to his pursuit of Nell) and Sally Brass, the Marchioness's mother and the Sphinx of private life. The novel might be offering us a new form of domesticity, but it is still "swiveling," still offering, sphinx-like, to return us to the source of all narrative, the crossroads.

To make Nell Trent into a monument (the site of her own epitaph) is to ask again what it means that the daughter is to be the site of all value. This is the other note struck in Ruskin's late commentary on *The Old Curiosity Shop*, and it goes some way in accounting for the power these female figures have in Dickens's early fiction:

I think the experience of most thoughtful persons will confirm me in saying that extremely good girls (good children, broadly, but especially girls), usually die young. The pathos of their deaths is constantly used in poetry and novels; but the power of the fiction rests, I suppose, on the fact that most persons of affectionate temper have lost their own May Queens or little Nells in their time. For my own part of grief, I have known a little Nell die, and a May Queen die, and a queen of May, and of December also, die; – all of them, in economists' language, as good as gold, and in Christian language, only a little lower than the angels, and crowned with glory and honour. And I count the like among my best-loved friends, with a rosary of tears. [31]

In Ruskin's account, little Nell's "realism" is lost in the language of "a little lower than the angels," and the power of the girls is not only their death but the affection that has surrounded them *in people's recollections*. It is the work of the daughter to gather memory, and to convey the past, at the same time that it is her job to stand on the bridge of culture, the moment of reproduction that insures the transmission of value. It is no accident that Nell here is not only the standard of Christian value ("crowned with glory and honour") but also her very own *gold* standard: "as good as gold" in "economists' language".

But how are we to move from the hysterical realism of *Oliver Twist* and the uncanny allegory of *The Old Curiosity Shop* to the domestic realism of the later novels, the novels (to follow Musselwhite) not of "Boz" but of "Dickens"? Perhaps we could follow the train of connection suggested by Ruskin's equation of women and "value" if we paused briefly at one final, early Dickens novel, *Nicholas Nickleby*, which takes up a female figure closer to the middle and late novels – a woman not noticeably "eccentric"; a woman, that is, presented in her familiar, Dickensian guise as daughter and sister. Kate Nickleby forms an interesting parallel to her brother Nicholas: she can travel the world, exploring a variety of female employments (governess, dressmaker) and undergoing a series of threats against person and pride (primarily from drunken noblemen and their foul henchmen) but Kate's true narrative employment is to embody herself – to be, as the text repeats in a series of guises, "pretty as a picture." When she works for a mantua-maker, she is soon promoted from sweatshop seamstress to model; employed as a governess, she is besieged by suitors and spends more time being courted than offering instruction – indeed, her chief labor seems to be reading society fiction out loud to her employer. But Kate's chief "value" (as character and as plot device) is her silent work in the marriage plot. She is the subject of her mother's and everyone else's fantasies in the novel: Nicholas imagines that she will marry a nobleman; her mother's similarly imagines "pleasant visions":

On Tuesday last, at St George's, Hanover Square, by the Right Reverend the Bishop of Llandaff, Sir Mulberry Hawk, of Mulberry Castle, North Wales, to Catherine, only daughter of the late Nicholas Nickleby, Esquire, of Devonshire. "Upon my word!" cried Mrs. Nicholas Nickleby, "it sounds very well." (419)

If *Nicholas Nickleby* made its effect on Dickens's career in its depiction of poor Smike and the boys at Dotheboys Hall, it marks Dickens's entrance into domestic realism through Kate's escapades, and through what Ralph Nickleby (Kate's uncle, and the usurous authorial surrogate of the novel) refers to quite accurately as a world of match-making mothers – although as his example (and that of his crony, Gride, attempting to marry the beautiful Madeline, beloved of Nicholas, by buying off her *father's* debts) suggests that the world of patriarchal exchange is every bit as deadly to women.

Nicholas Nickleby, with its range of literary pastiche and full-blown authorial anxiety[32] suggests that that world of male exchange and female value *is* the world of domestic fiction: the true threat to Kate comes from within the family, and while Nicholas is free to roam the world of boys' adventure books, she must sit still, representing a value she cannot wholly possess, and which she is not free to employ in any market. The economy of *Nickleby*, an economy primarily of exchange and usury, of surrogacy and doubles, will become the obscure economy of Dickens's major fiction, and the role of the good, quiet, daughter (like that of good, quiet, patient, Nell as well as that of the less patient Nancy) may well be to represent a patrimony she cannot, yet, possess for herself. The novels that follow, beginning with *Dombey and Son*, will play with exactly that opposition – and with the novel's deployment of female economic value, the separate property that women represent in the Dickens world.

But what an essentially pragmatic deployment of women cannot will away is that other essential element of the Dickensian femininity that this chapter has been tracing: the uncanniness of the daughter. One more scene from *Nicholas Nickleby* suggests what is at stake in the daughter's plot: in a pivotal moment in the novel, the usurous uncle and surrogate father, Ralph Nickleby, escorts his niece Kate to her carriage:

As the door of the vehicle was roughly closed, a comb fell from Kate's hair, close at her uncle's feet; and as he picked it up and returned it into her hand, the light from a neighbouring lamp shone upon her face. The lock of hair that had escaped and curled loosely over her brow, the traces of tears yet scarcely dry, the flushed cheek, the look of sorrow, all fired some dormant train of recollection in the old man's breast; and the face of his dead brother seemed present before him, with the very look it wore on some occasion of boyish grief, of which every minute circumstance flashed upon his mind, with the distinctness of a scene of yesterday.

Ralph Nickleby, who was proof against all appeals of blood and kindred – who was steeled against every tale of sorrow and distress – staggered while he looked, and reeled back into his house, as a man who had seen a spirit from some world beyond the grave. (316)

The daughter's ability to conjure spirits "from some world beyond," to fire "some dormant train of recollection," to re-present the dead, to embody the past – precisely to embody *resemblance*, is terrifying, to the point of being *physically* staggering to the man of "steel." Here, Kate's habitual passivity, her ability to sit still and be the "picture" of goodness, becomes the physical embodiment of memory, and the promise (the dangerous promise) of connection which precisely will undo the usurous bonds of exchange and surrogacy upon which Ralph (and the novel) depends. It is Dickens's work Kate is doing here, but it remains (in the scene, and in the novel, where it is never explained) uncanny and

spectacular: Kate herself, not unlike Nell and Nancy, is at once a
material girl and a presence from some world "beyond." That magical
property, at once reproductive and already dead, is the source of the
daughter's terrifying and promising uncanniness, and it is, somehow,
enough to send a strong man reeling.

PART TWO

On not committing adultery
in the novel

CHAPTER TWO

Dombey and Son: *the daughter's nothing*

Dombey and Son marked a new beginning for Dickens in many ways: it was the first of his novels for which he wrote number plans in advance; the first to use complicated and involved metaphors for itself; the first he spoke of as 'branching' off in the ways we think of his novels developing. For the argument of this book, *Dombey and Son* marks another beginning, for it was in this novel that Dickens began to isolate those characteristics of the daughter, in particular the writing daughter, which were the hallmark of his later career. But the breakthrough idea of the novel (which Dickens was never to carry out with quite the same level of poignancy) was the bringing together of the good and the dark heroine under one roof; the domestication of the story of the wanderings of *Oliver Twist* and *The Old Curiosity Shop*. In the meeting of Florence Dombey and her stepmother Edith, and in the toll it exacts for the daughter to separate herself from the dark heroine (whom she refers to as "my beautiful mama"), Dickens posed the problem of the daughter within the patriarchal house, both Dombey's house and the novel, which he was to work out in the rest of his career. In a series of scenes at the novel's end what he does is to make clear the contractual nature of the negotiations between the daughter, the angry mother, and the silent father, the final resolution a Lear-like bargain which he can work out only through the daughter's silence and renunciation, the renunciation that will culminate in Amy Dorrit's selflessness and in the almost complete dispossession of Estella in *Great Expectations*. In *Dombey* he traces out the path of the seemingly adulterous virtuous daughter, the problem of how the daughter is to remain true, through the painful severing of her bond with the other/mother whose adultery, although also illusory, can nonetheless never be forgiven.

Dombey and Son is, more fully, *Dealings with the Firm of Dombey and Son, Wholesale, Retail, and for Exportation*, but a reader might be drawn to ask, "what is that when it's at home?" for the novel, *Dombey and Son*, is more properly the story of (what the firm is usually called) "The House of Dombey."[1] The novel begins with father and (very young) son toasting before the fire like muffins; it celebrates and then destroys the reign of what it ironically calls "anno Dombei"; it traces the rise and weakening of the young "son and heir," only to kill him brutally in the fifth number part; and then, finally, celebrates the rise of the forgotten and over-loving daughter of the house, Florence, who proves that "Dombey and Son is a daughter after all."[2] But the portrait on which it focuses throughout suggests that it is as much the story of the house as of any external dealings, and that house a rather haunted one: ghosted by the dead mother; vexed by the daughter's rebellious and loving spirit; troubled by the image of a relentless paternal will and an ominous, self-invoked destructive fate. It is a house, to quote one of the book's many prophetic characters, in which there is "One child dead, and one child living: one wife dead and one wife coming"(460). That story of replication, replacement, and destruction suggests that the story of the family "firm" is a rather dark one, though the firm deals "often . . . in hides, but never in hearts" (50). What this book traffics in is domestic love, and in particular, in "daughter(s) after all."

The force of the novel's plot is to make of Florence Dombey's love a gift, offering her father another, more redemptive form of circulation. To read the novel as that form of exchange means taking domestic economy seriously in a way most critics cannot: for the novel's most penetrating critic, Julian Moynahan, the daughter's plot is most dangerous in its shying away from the novel's otherwise potent social critique, ignoring "the sphere of actual social existence which must be transformed if Dickens's project for the transformation of society by love is to work."[3] For Moynahan, the triumph of the novel's "wet" characters over the harsher, drier Mr Dombey is the danger of sentimentalism overtaking hard-headed political thinking; for him (as, interestingly, for many subsequent feminist critics), Florence is an image of human feeling viewed with quasi-religious fervor, and the reader's interest is unfairly forced to her. The book's complicated and (for Dickens) newly plotted tightness has led critics to want more: a deeper critique of the capitalism that seems to underwrite the novel's harsh view of human nature; the wider view of society its almost desperate invocation of visual acuity ("Oh, for a good spirit who would take the house-tops off. . . ."[738]) would offer; a true view of the "condition of England" and the problem of hides and hearts.[4]

What Moynahan and others have objected to, then, is what we

observed in the earlier novels: the specular or uncanny quality of Florence Dombey, the book's reverence towards her iconic status, and their own inability to account for her centrality both in the novel's and the author's explicit statements. "Oh, forgive me, for I need it very much," prays Dombey at the end (940), and the reader must be led to accept the father's rebirth at his daughter's gentle hands. Florence is made the agent of social and personal rehabilitation, while (seemingly) never leaving her father's house. But that reading ignores the other quality of the heroine's uncanniness that we have noticed elsewhere, one that is the most striking element of Florence's role as Dombey's daughter. The daughter here begins by being *alien* to the paternal order, outside of it. She must come to understand that order through her passage through the mother's plot (in this case, the far more interesting plot of her stepmother, Edith Granger) and then, having left the father's house in disgrace and anger, return to it as domestic angel. This journey is the heart of the transformative process of *Dombey*'s plot: the daughter begins, in Mr Dombey's phrase, as "base coin" and ends as the "golden link," the "glorious sunshine" of her father's life.

Alienation is the novel's keynote. The first chapter pans back from its opening shot of father and son, toasting by the fire, to the rest of the family: first, to Mrs. Dombey, on her deathbed after giving birth to her only child – or, as the novel is constantly correcting itself, her only son – and then to the lonely daughter. As the novel puts it, the marriage "had had no issue. – To speak of; none worth mentioning" (51). The abrupt break between clauses, marked in the text by a paragraph break, suggests Florence's initial position, which is "in a corner." As the narrator goes on, "There had been a girl some six years before . . . . But what was a girl to Dombey and Son!" (51). The absenting of Florence from the plot seems absolute: her attention to her mother is read instantly as indifference to her brother; her hysterical embrace of her mother is a "very ill-advised and feverish proceeding" (52). And yet the mother and daughter hold on, the mother "clinging fast to that slight spar within her arms [as she] drifted out upon the dark and unknown sea that rolls round all the world" (60). While "in the capital of the House's name and dignity" Florence is "merely a piece of base coin that couldn't be invested – a bad Boy – nothing more" (51), for her mother (and for all the romantic forces of life, death, and the unknown which the sea represents in the novel) she is the one piece of firm material: the spar to which the novel will cling.

Just what kind of "nothing" the daughter is, remains a puzzle for the novel.[5] For "the House's name and dignity" it is clear that Florence doesn't count since, as Susan Nipper says, "girls are thrown away in this house" (79), but it does not seem inevitable that, even in a world in which the sun rises and sets for Dombey and Son, a daughter is "base coin," not currency that can be spent or invested. The novel is curiously silent on why the "curious child" is so very alien to her father – or rather, it talks a great deal, but always in suppositions, none of which is confirmed until we are told much later that Dombey has now, as he (perhaps) always feared he would, come to hate Florence. While he lives in a world of terrifying proximity to his young son, in which he imagines a stunning unity of identity and purpose (after all, he himself was once the son of Dombey and Son; so, in effect, he still is, while his son is alive), the daughter stands as "the flesh and blood he could not disown" (142). Florence is not the only family member to stand in such relation to Dombey, of course; his own wife would be missed only "as he would miss a piece of the plate or the furniture" (54), and when Mr. Chick imagines, given the absence of a mother to provide mother's milk, that "something temporary [could] be done with a teapot" (63) he is unknowingly echoing his brother-in-law's view of female relations. The same economy of affection informs the introduction of Polly Toodles as nursemaid into the Dombey household: she is not to regard herself as having any relationship with the boy she nurses ("a mere matter of bargain and sale, hiring and letting" 68), and when she (the "treacherous attendant") is summarily dismissed, the "question of wages," as Dombey thought their agreement, is to be entirely at an end; she becomes to him, if not to his children, an "obscure stranger" (142).

But that phrase might apply to Dombey's daughter as well, for she remains a stranger to him and his household, in spite of her instant success in every other household she enters. Indeed, some of what is remarkable about Dombey's relation to Florence is that while every other parent in the novel is turning a daughter *into* gold (Mrs. Skewton selling Edith; Good Mrs. Brown selling Alice), Dombey cannot see in his already golden daughter any investment possibilities at all. For him, as for Clarissa Harlowe's brother, "daughters are chickens brought up for the tables of other men."[6] To marry Florence off (to treat her as dispensable property) is necessarily to alienate her from "Dombey and Son" – and to admit that the family is not enough in itself. The daughter holds for Dombey no promise of social alliance, and to the extent that she does, she seems to threaten his necessary economic independence, and all mentions of her beauty seem only to remind him of her alienability. But Dombey seems to have alienated his daughter in advance: whereas even Doctor Blimber can offer his daughter, Cornelia of the flashing spectacles, to the eager and ambitious Mr. Feeder, B.A., along with his freshly repainted house, Dombey cannot allow himself to see his daughter as even *of* his house; Florence (the "no issue – to speak of; none worth mentioning") seems worse even than a "bad boy." She is a drain on the family fortunes, less than the plate or furniture, not even (despite her spectacular showing elsewhere in the book) worth displaying.

But the pathology of Dombey's dislike of his daughter suggests a deeper anxiety about the mobility of property, something else at stake in the "base" coin. The metaphor reaches us first as "mere" metal, a lower form of coinage not worth investing in the firm's capital. But as Dianne Sadoff has pointed out, "the metaphor of 'base coin' signifies not only valueless currency but also illegitimate genealogical origin";[7] the coin is forged, adulterated, "bastard" issue. Since Florence's lack of resemblance to Dombey is the point held most against her, one might wonder if her allegiance to her mother doesn't suggest an adulterous prehistory to the novel, but the more damaging aspect of her character seems to consist in her willingness to render her father illegitimate: to exclude him, by the ferocity of her clinging first to her mother and then to her brother, from a differently formed family. It is in her willingness to be "in league" with these others against him that she seems most "base" – at the same time that the novel seems always to be pushing us towards another reading of "base," that of foundation or core element, the way Dombey will come to see Florence not as his "issue" but as his true child: the source of his real authority and firmness, the "spar" to which he should cling, the home that cannot be taken from him.

To be redeemed as the true home, Florence must pass (as must the novel) through the adultery plot; must seem to wander off and be restored, so she can do the work of restoration. Just as Florence's mother stands as an icon at the book's beginning (Mrs. Chick is described as "a common-place piece of folly enough, compared with whom her sister-in-law had been a very angel of womanly intelligence and gentleness" [106]), so Florence will spend the second half of the novel posed against her darker angel, the fierce and moody Edith Granger Dombey.

If a daughter's affection exists to be alienated, for Dombey a wife exists to be owned – to be an extension of the firm, of the house, of the name of Dombey. The genius of the plot of *Dombey and Son* is that with the entrance of Edith into the novel, the language of domestic economy is both fulfilled and eviscerated: Edith's self-conscious position as possession (as a possession that, having been bought, refuses to be owned) points up the daughter's possibility of self-possession, as powerfully as her stepdaughter's sympathetic vision points up Edith's own escape from the world of hides and hearts. In Dombey's view, Edith is "his wife, a part of himself"; as a separate entity she has, as Carker the manager expresses it, "no existence in his mind" (718). Dombey is, as he himself says, "accustomed to 'insist,' to my connexions and dependents," and his wife "should partake – or does partake, and cannot help herself – of both characters" (651). The closest thing to interest he shows in Florence in the novel (and it is a parody of parental instruction) comes when he insists she stay at the table while he rebukes Edith, saying he would have his daughter learn the kind of wifely obedience Edith needs to display; this sense of her (subliminal) inability to learn either "connexion" or dependence is fulfilled when he sends Florence out into the streets after her stepmother, where presumably the two of them, "in league," can offer their wares to other, unsuspecting men.

The great irony of the novel is, of course, that while Dombey imagines Edith (or his wife) as the only possession he can possess completely (unlike even his son, whose affection he regretfully had to share, to his constant mortification), and imagines his daughter as a possession already alienated (chickens for another man's table), these positions are entirely reversed in the novel: his daughter lives for his love alone, and his wife exists only to scorn him and rebuke his pride. In that sense, Edith's passionate love of his daughter is precisely the blow to his possessiveness he insists it is: to love his daughter is to love the possibility of alienation, and his logic seems to be that Edith has, rather, followed Florence into the streets, for the daughter's love is always ready to be dispersed, to be spent elsewhere. Florence spends a fair part of the novel already in the streets: lost, only to be retrieved by that hoarder of daughterly beauty, Mrs. Brown; scorned by her father, taking refuge in the home of Sol Gills, the home that will become hers when she marries Walter Gay. But where Florence's plot carries out the father's fantasy, that his home will be exchanged for the streets, Edith's carries out the father's nightmare, that his home is already no different from the streets, a place of exchange and barter, a place where his ownership (indeed, the mastery that to him is self-ownership) is already incomplete.

For Dombey, the home is primarily a site of display. After he and Edith are married, and after they have revealed the marriage to be a miserable and painful farce, they begin entertaining: "If none of the new family were particularly at home in private, it was resolved that Mrs. Dombey at least should be at home in public" (593). Mrs. Dombey, who has the most compelling private life of any character in the novel, already sees herself as entirely a creature of publicity, a slave made for the purchasing vision of the marketplace: "*She* is regularly bought, and you may take your oath *he* is as regularly sold" (598), in Cousin Feenix's accidentally accurate diagnosis. For Edith, every item of her married life reminds her of her enslavement: everywhere she looks in her home, "she [sees] some hateful atom of her purchase money" (503); she tells Dombey she will not be shown off, saying "I will be exhibited to no one, as the refractory slave you purchased" (748). Her metaphors for herself range from slavery to prostitution, and the novel participates in this discourse: "He sees me at the auction, and he thinks it well to buy me" (473); her courtship is "a matter of traffic in which she is a reluctant party" (464); she "made and delivered [the sketch Dombey asks for] as if it had been bargained for and bought . . . her haughty face . . . had been that of a proud woman, engaged in a sordid and miserable transaction" (470); "she had beauty, blood and talent, and Dombey had fortune" (453); and (in her harshest self-examination) she claims she has asked herself what she is "more than once" when she sat by the window "and something in the faded likeness of my sex has wandered past outside; and God knows I have met with my reply" (514).

It is proof of Florence's unworldliness (and how little her life has shown her of real love) that she imagines she can learn from Edith how to please her father – that her "beautiful mama" can give her the key to winning the affection she has spent her life trying to gain. The Dombeys (who can never be at home in private) have only one character intent on mastering domestic life, and that is Dombey's obsessive daughter. Here again, the logic of Florence's life is not that far from her father's: it is to enter the world, only to bring all metropolitan goodness back into the house. The movement Florence makes into the city belies the passivity critics have noted in her: she is far from an unworldly or extra-worldly creature. To teach her brother, she purchases all his school books and learns his homework before he does; she negotiates the streets of London to return to him; in weaving the web of connection which will bring about the novel's happy ending (and the redemption of the family firm) she moves from the highest realms of English society to the casual working-class poverty of the Toodles and the decaying gentility of the Toxes and the Gills. But the world for Florence remains domestic: it *is* her father's world. When she is lost in London, she announces to young Walter Gay, "my name is Florence Dombey, my little brother's only sister" (134), and her only way of asking directions is to ask for "Dombey and Son"; when she becomes a mother, it becomes for her only a way of understanding how she *should* have loved her own father. For much of the novel, Florence's love of her father isolates her from the rest of the world. when she reads books, she listens only for descriptions of unloving fathers; in society, she is aware of her orphaned state only in that it seems to suggest (unfairly, to her view) some reproach upon her father.

But just as Edith's slavery seems to draw our attention to a world of marketplace relations (Mrs. Pipchin's middle-aged niece is "her good-natured and devoted slave" [161]; Joey Bagstock's native servant "had no particular name, but answered to any vituperative epithet" [346]), so Florence's daughterly abjection draws our attention out into a world of social connections, one that rather than, as Moynahan would suggest,[8] narrowing into the world of female masochism and sickly sentimental saintliness offers a near-anatomical understanding of the layering of English society. This becomes clearest in the "study" Florence Dombey makes of other daughters, in her poignant quest for the behavior, the magical difference that will make her father love her. The chapter title ("The Study of a Loving Heart") works doubly, suggesting both Florence's patient examination of daughters, and the narrator's examination of her – Florence is at once *doing* the work of criticism, and *in* it. As she studies it, her patient heart becomes less a freak of nature and more clearly a social phenomenon: she is only one in a world of daughters with fathers. Further, her "study," even if inadvertently, takes her widely abroad, through class as well as familial relations. She examines an orphan adopted by a wealthy aunt; four "little sisters" (presumably middle-class) waiting for their father's return from work; one father, seemingly direct from the pages of Henry Mayhew, wandering the banks of the river looking for "bits and scraps in the mud" (424), while caring for his unloving, misshapen, ugly daughter, whistling at her for a sign of affection because, "the day'll come, and has been coming a long while . . . when to get half as much from that unfort'nate child of mine – to get the trembling of a finger, or the waving of a hair – would be to raise the dead" (426). Florence, like so many Dickens heroines, herself a budding sociologist, seems to have cross-sectioned her society, running the knife of daughterly affection and curiosity through the sample, surveying almost surgically, almost geologically, the layering of patriarchal relations.

Florence's obsessive observation of her father, and the habit of watch-fulness it instills in her, makes her not only a domestic voyeuse but an affectional stalker: indeed, the mutual watchfulness of the Dombey family renders the home more of a battlefield than any place of haven. As the novel progresses, spying takes the place of any more powerful affective bond, and the family firm is rendered increasingly shaky on its legs. In fact, domestic surveillance is linked to the novel's own way of knowing, as it is when the novelist, in one of his more famous narratorial intrusions, asks for "a good spirit who would take the house-tops off, with a more potent and benignant hand than the lame demon in the tale, and show a Christian people what dark shapes issue from amidst their homes, to swell the retinue of the Destroying Angel as he moves forth among them!" (738). Such a spirit would bring forth a day, Dickens says, that would rouse "some who never have looked out upon the world of human life, to a knowledge of their own relation to it," that would make them "acquainted with a perversion of nature in their own contracted sympathies and estimates" (739). But "no such day had ever dawned on Mr. Dombey, or his wife," and so the novel progresses (739). The spirit that would "show" is that of the narrator, the Dickensian imagined benignant author, like the editor of *Household Words*, who could move like "a shadow" through English homes and hearts. But while this language in Dickens usually suggests the ravaging force of vice in the wider social world (think of Ignorance and Want, huddling in the skirts of Christmas Present), here the vice, the "perversion of nature" lies in "contracted" sympathies – not only those reduced to a smaller space, but those here contracted by marriage into the unhappy house of Dombey. The spirit of Asmodeus will reveal not the disruptions of mercantilism or industrialization or even the demon railways, but the perversions of the marital bed.

The chapter which invokes the "potent and benignant hand" is "The Thunderbolt," and it sketches the final marital battles of Edith and Dombey, Edith's supposed flight with Dombey's evil manager, Carker, and Florence's attempt to comfort her father in her beautiful mama's absence – that is, it traces the domestic unraveling of the fabric of English society. In particular, it traces the violence the father turns on the loving daughter:

[I]n his frenzy, he lifted up his cruel arm, and struck her, crosswise, with that heaviness, that she tottered on the marble floor; and as he dealt the blow, he told her what Edith was, and bade her follow her, since they had always been in league. (757)

For the first time, we gather just what kind of threat the daughter might be, and what power she holds over her father. The power he invokes, that of her "league" with the mother, haunts the novel in several guises: in its own way, the love between Edith and Florence is the secret of the House, the anxiety that women can do quite well without the firmness of Mr. Dombey. Edith's real betrayal of Dombey and her "contract" comes not with Carker (the "man with white teeth") but with his own daughter – who in turn, once she receives Edith's love, can finally pull away from her father, beginning to treat Dombey as if he were already dead, or someone she had loved long ago.

But the danger of the alliance between women goes beyond the distance it imposes on Dombey, through another form of plotting the women join forces to bring about. The link between mother and daughter, in particular, surfaces repeatedly in the novel, not only in Florence and her dead mother or Florence and her "beautiful mama," but between Good Mrs. Brown and her daughter Alice, Edith and her mother, and (eventually) between Alice and Edith, both of whom are seduced by Carker, and who indirectly conspire to destroy him. After "the thunderbolt," Dombey comes to Mrs. Brown to discover Carker's whereabouts, so he can pursue and kill him. When he meets Alice, who has been following Carker all this while, he asks her why she chooses to betray him. Or rather, he doesn't ask, for he knows: "Money," he says, "will bring about unlikely things, I know" (819). This is not the first time he has been wrong about money: even little Paul, who (asking his father what money can do) on being told it can do anything, asks "Why didn't money save me my Mama?" (153). Dombey, ever slow to learn, is here catechized again, this time by Alice Marwood:

"Do you know nothing more powerful than money?" asked the younger woman, without rising, or altering her attitude.

"Not here, I should imagine," said Mr. Dombey.

"You should know of something that is more powerful elsewhere, as I judge," she returned. "Do you know nothing of a woman's anger? . . . A woman's anger is pretty much the same here, as in your fine house." (819)

Female anger here, more powerful than money but nonetheless imagined as a currency, is a universal force – and is, indeed, what has just destroyed his "fine house." And more, it is something Dombey cannot possess: as Alice says, her connection to his house "is my story, and I keep my story to myself" (820).

Edith, too, keeps her story to herself, and the unraveling and rewinding of the plot in the novel's last third is the tracing of her adulterous wanderings – more specifically, the revelation that she has *not* betrayed Dombey with "the deceased person with white teeth" (966), but has used man against master to her own triumphant end, staging an escape from what was already a rather stagy script. Edith's great secret – that she is not, despite all narratorial conspiring to the contrary, an adulterous or a fallen woman – works most powerfully as a revelation of her own narratorial skill; she has gone from being an instrument of male plots (and an object of property and the proprietary gaze) to being herself the master plotter. This is one of Dickens's favorite devices, and will resurface in other novels of the 1850s, including *David Copperfield* and *Hard Times*. But in a novel whose first great climax sends both wife and daughter into the streets, and plays with the image of female (sexual) wandering throughout, it raises more questions than it answers.

Edith's seeming transgression has a contaminant force in the novel, radiating outward into both plot and thematics. What her adultery does most explicitly is not separate her from Dombey (for she was already as distant from him as could be) but separate both herself and Dombey from Florence: it is Florence who walks the streets after this chapter, finding herself back in Sol Gill's house, still mourning the loss of Walter Gay, the boy who found her in her first street-wanderings, and who carries about his neck the little purse filled with money she gave him on his ill-fated voyage on the "Son and Heir." At first, it seems that Florence walks herself into safety, for she walks directly into a marriage plot. Walter returns almost immediately (as if recalled to life by her presence in his house) and she, almost as immediately, proposes to him in a great renunciatory burst. In her domestic purposefulness, she seems to still the waters Edith has disturbed – but her own rhetoric is hardly calm:

"If you will take me for your wife, Walter, I will love you dearly. If you will let me go with you, Walter, I will go to the world's end without fear. I can give up nothing for you – I have nothing to resign, and no one to forsake; but all my love and life shall be devoted to you, and with my last breath I will breathe your name to God if I have sense and memory left." (806)

This speech provides a category of the virtues that Florence is here to represent, and that separate her from Edith: she is patient, she is good, she loves "dearly." Being "nothing" pays off at this moment, for Florence (unlike Edith) has "nothing to resign." Nonetheless, in Florence, as in her magical change-purse, nothing will ever be lost, and the world's end will bring no fear. The more Florence gives away, the logic goes, the more she has; the more she loves, the more she deserves love; the more she is

forgotten, she more she will remember. She reverses the scarcity
economics her father modeled, making her pain a principle of narratorial organization: "Pray . . . do not wish me to forget anything in our
acquaintance. I never can, believe me" (799).

But that power of memory and the power of self-renunciation (which
here, as elsewhere in Dickens, is the power of true self-possession) has its
own links to Alice Marwood's anger, the "something more powerful than
money" that is the same in her mother's hovel "as in your fine house." It
was Alice, too, who has remembered and tracked down Carker; Alice,
like Edith, who remains a scoreboard of past injuries and pain, particularly the pain her mother has written on her bartered body. As elsewhere
in Dickens, it is the daughter's job both to embody and to recompose the
past – and indeed, when Alice watched Dombey leave Mrs. Brown's
house, it was "The daughter's dark gaze [that] followed him to the door,
and noted [him]" (832). Florence, no less than Alice and Edith, writes
the book of memory.

Edith and Alice would seem to be distinguished from Florence by
being daughters not of neglectful fathers, but of mothers – and in particular, of plotting mothers. But for much of the novel, Florence
identifies herself as Edith's daughter, and it will take much of the labor
of the novel not only to make Florence the repository of all redemption,
but to make her back into her father's daughter. That it does take so
much work to effect this change suggests the power of the link between
Florence and the darker women of the text – and the attraction of the
novel itself to female scheming. As I suggested earlier, the novel's
strength is in depicting not only the painful bond between the father and
the daughter, but the cost it extracts from the daughter's "patient heart"
to bring that bond to life. But just as Florence must make her way
through the adultery plot to prove her own "truth," to remind him (as
Dombey says before her return) that "he always knew she would have
been true to him, if he had suffered her" (936), so she must make her
way through the intricacies of female plotting before she achieves closural redemption.

Critics like Moynahan, praising the quasi-religious fervor surrounding
Florence and the other "wet" characters, write as if it were easy for
Florence to achieve the redemptive force at the end – as if she need only
release the feeling she has already so powerfully contained throughout
the novel, weep over Dombey, and work her transformative magic.[9] But
the work of the text goes beyond the sacred rituals Moynahan is some-

what ironically invoking – indeed, the process it depicts is labor-intensive and filled with authorial analogues. If Florence's generation of sentiment seems in some way alchemical, as the "base coin" is turned into gold almost as romantically as the fairy-tale Dick Whittington story that follows her romance with Walter, it seems equally composed of a series of contractual negotiations between the principal parties to her ascendancy: Florence, her father, her "beautiful mama," and the "person with white teeth," Carker. These negotiations seem in part quite practical, for they determine who exactly is to "manage" Dombey in the future – who, to borrow a legal term, is to serve as Dombey's agent. But they also sketch out a process of magical writing, a series of half-promises and queries that are labyrinthine, suggesting again the complicated path the daughter follows to any kind of agency, even the partial and perilously complicit role we think of as an "agent of patriarchy."

As Audrey Jaffe has noted, Florence's victory is "essentially a victory of emotion over convention, of the natural over the artificial, and of private life over public life," but it is achieved in a series of scenes that can only be labeled "melodramatic," "scenes in which behavior seems to transgress conventional boundaries."[10] Jaffe links this effectively to the novel's interest in "managing" secrets, in effacing the work of the emotional labor Florence in particular stage-manages as private, natural acts; but the scenes also offer us contractual exchanges between the characters, in which a small series of objects are magically transported between a very few players, and the play of bodies and words signifies a heightened register, almost a theatricality of property and persons.[11] The exchanges begin when Edith leaves Dombey, flinging the rich jewels he has given her on the ground and pulling down her rich bright hair, leaving him "without a word, without a shadow on the fire of her bright eye." She leaves behind her the "deed of settlement he had executed on their marriage, and a letter" telling him she has left with Carker; he races out of the room and out of the house, "with a frantic idea of finding her yet . . . and beating all trace of beauty out of the triumphant face with his bare hand" (756). When he returns to the house he is greeted by an overwrought Florence, whom he strikes down with one blow, forcing her into the streets, where she finds herself "insensible to everything but the deep wound in her breast" (758).

The melodramatic language of flowing hair, wounded bosoms, and fiery eyes is curiously mixed in with the technical details of deeds of settlements and admissions of criminal conversation, as it will be in the scenes of confrontation that follow. The first of these, the scene between

Carker and Edith, is in some ways the stagiest, but it marks the moment when Edith goes from being the object of domestic spectacle to the staging of her own revenge against her husband and Carker. In turn, the language shifts from that of spectacle to those of account books. When she asks him "how many times" he has mocked her, assailed her with outrage and insults, "laid bare my wound of love for that sweet, injured girl, and lacerated it!", "fanned the fire on which . . . I have writhed?", all examples of the most tortured melodramatic language imaginable, Carker answers quite simply: "I have no doubt, Ma'am, that you have kept a good account, and that it's pretty accurate" (856). When she lists the process through which she has been "shamed and steeled," "put up and appraised," "paraded and vended"; explains that "every tie" between herself and her friends "has been deadened in my breast"; concludes that "you know that my fame with [the world] is worthless to me," he replies, "Yes; I imagined that" – and she strikes back immediately, "And calculated on it" (856–7).

Her scene of triumph is a reverse calculation, one based on predicting where his plotting will take him:

"In every vaunt you make," she said, "I have my triumph. I single out in you the meanest man I know, the parasite and tool of the proud tyrant, that his wound may go the deeper, and may rankle more. Boast, and revenge me on him! You know how you came here tonight; you know how you stand cowering there; you see yourself in colours quite as despicable, if not as odious, as those in which I see you. Boast then, and revenge me on yourself." (859)

Edith has effected a perfect economy of revenge here, turning Dombey and Carker evenly on each other, and herself on them, escaping precisely their nets. Much to Carker's – and the reader's – surprise, she has no interest in the adultery plot, nor even any interest in him *per se.* Indeed, the indifference that has been her salvation all along turns out to be her chief weapon here:

"I have thrown my fame and good name to the winds! . . . I'll die, and make no sign. For this, I am here alone with you, at the dead of night. For this, I have met you here, in a false name, as your wife. For this, I have been seen here by these men, and left here. Nothing can save you now." (860)

As she confronts him, it is her willingness to die – as well as her willingness to kill him – that saves her; the willingness to be misunderstood, to "make no sign."[12] All the infamy that has attached itself to her becomes her weapon, much as her heaving bosom, in which she now clutches a knife she carefully positioned near herself, becomes an arsenal instead of a seductive trap. As Carker watched her,

He saw that she was desperate, and that her unquenchable hatred of him would stop at nothing. His eyes followed the hand that was put with such rugged uncongenial purpose into her white bosom, and he thought that if it struck at him, and failed, it would strike there, just as soon. (860)

In this final meeting between them, as she flees, as he is confused by "the frustration of his schemes," Edith turns on Carker everything that had seemed to trap her, slamming the door in his face, trapping only her "veil" as she seems, as well, to escape the novel, having squared her "accounts," and left the master and the manager to fight it out for themselves. But the text is equally clear on the cost to her of this escape: "the taint of his kiss upon my cheek," the "meeting with [Florence] while that taint was hot upon me," the "shame and degradation [I brought] on her name through mine" (858) – all that makes Edith not only, in her own speech, "divorce" her husband, but, seemingly, divorce her from herself, self-denial being the only power left to her after her defeat of the men who have pursued her, and pursued each other through her, and whom she has used against each other – at considerable cost to herself. Her last warning to Carker ("You have been betrayed, as all betrayers are" [860]) and her last gesture ("He turned white, as she held her hand up like an enchantress, at whose invocation the sound had come" [860]) suggest her power, but also disembody her, turning her into a ghost of herself, into the "veil" that is all she leaves behind. Her scene seems to promise no exit except revenge, and no power except anger and a series of betrayers and betrayals; its logical conclusion is Carker's desperate last leap that lands him, of course, in the path of the oncoming train, coming, like his own desires, to betray him in turn, abandoning him to the force of the new economy he seemed to unleash, and attempted to master. For Edith, the scene between them seems to promise only a dark room, and a dark path into a foreign city, in which the novel (at least temporarily) loses her, while it turns back to Dombey and daughter.

While Edith's language, here as elsewhere, seems to embrace the terms of her enslavement, turning the language of the market against the merchants, Dombey's resurrection seems designed to undo the economy of affection that has obtained so far, in favor of a language of what Susan Horton has called "human love, compassion and forgiveness."[13] After all, Dombey's great cry, when his daughter re-enters his house and his arms, is, "Forgive me, for I need it very much." But the scene, coming after the fall of Dombey's house and the great auction that follows, all that has emptied out his "credit," seems unfortunately but hardly accidentally like forgiving a debt, an action (and a concept) that has underwritten much of this novel. The great reconciliation scene seems like nothing so much as turning the "base coin" of the daughter into a credit card that will erase Dombey's financial and spiritual debt with one gesture, through the daughter's redemptive agency.

The scene itself is largely, like Carker's inadvertent suicide, a dialogue for one, the division of Dombey himself into master and man. Its end is, logically, a moment when he sees himself (as he once saw Edith) reflected in a mirror, with a penknife in his hand, about to kill himself. The self-reflexivity of the scene extends to the novelist, who must quote himself to make his point, as he re-intones "Let him remember it in that room . . ." (934), repeating the phrase twice more, as if to prove himself even more right. But the scene nicely captures the total interiority of an already interior thought, as if the emptying of the furniture of the Dombey house (the escapades of the advertised "Capital Modern Household Furniture," going from "on view" to "on sale" to "in the course of removal" in these chapters) had emptied out what little interior life Dombey had, as well. One is reminded, almost inadvertently, of young Paul at school, "with an aching void in his young heart, and all outside so cold, and bare, and strange, . . . as if he had taken life unfurnished, and the upholsterer were never coming" (215). His father, conversely, seems intent on disposing of what emotional furniture is "furnished him," and emptying the house of all life – animate and inanimate. But the novel must refurbish or flesh out Dombey's world: here, Dombey's fantasy that he might "give up what his creditors had spared him" (his life) promises, in Dickensian fashion, that he is now ready to live, which really means that he is ready to allow himself to be loved by his daughter. It only remains for her to break the silence of his monomania, break through the walls of the house, displace the knife from his hand, and claim, as he stops, "arrested by a cry – a wild, loud, piercing, loving, rapturous cry," that it was all her fault all along (939). In their reunion, the key elements of Edith's flight and dismissal of Carker are magically reordered: the knife, the heaving bosom, mysterious documents and even the veil return:

Upon the breast that he had bruised, against the heart that he had almost broken, she laid his face, now covered with his hands, and said, sobbing:

"Papa, love, I am a mother. I have a child who will soon call Walter by the name by which I call you. When it was born, and when I knew how much I loved it, I knew what I had done in leaving you. Forgive me, dear Papa! oh say God bless me, and my little child!" (939–40)

All of the melodramatic apparatus (the veil of her hair, the bruise on her bosom, the power of speech, the invocation of the name and the blessing) are converted to the process of conversion – and yet, it is only her own conversion Florence can recount. Somehow, her realization of how much she loves *her* child has demonstrated anew to Florence how much she should have loved her father, and not how much *he* should have loved her; her earlier fantasy that she could die and her father would miss her has been translated into how much she would grieve if her child left her. Dombey plays a small part in the scene, seeming as empty as the family house, which now, "dumb as to all that had been suffered in it, and the change it had witnessed, stood frowning like a dark mute on the street; baulking any nearer inquiries with the staring announcement that the lease of this desirable Family Mansion was to be disposed of" (942). Dombey, too, stands frowning like a dark mute, baulking inquiries, staring at his own reflection, "so proud . . . in his ruin . . . that if he could have heard her voice in an adjoining room, he would not have gone to her" (936). But of course, he does not have to "go to her," for she (his redemption, his stay of execution) comes to *him*, speaking volumes, stopping him from praying to her, "clinging," "clasping," "keeping close to him" lest he should look around and be reminded of their "last parting." And does she remember? – or is the memory of that last parting lost altogether in her plea that "Never let us be parted any more, Papa. Never let us be parted any more!" (940).

To answer this question, I need to turn to the final staged encounter of the novel, the last meeting between Florence and Edith. This scene, too, works with a few basic elements: reflection, bosoms, tears, promises, negotiations. Florence is tricked by cousin Feenix into meeting with the disgraced Edith, Edith into revealing her innocence to the still loving Florence; the two then part forever. Where Dombey's crisis was punctuated by images of blood and execution, Edith's redemption comes through images of shadows and dreams, of the veiled life that has been hers through so much of the novel. And where Dombey's redemption seemed to remind us of the differences between him and his daughter, this scene draws Florence and Edith, once again, closer together:

> They stood looking at each other. Passion and pride had worn it, but it was the face of Edith, and beautiful and stately yet. It was the face of Florence, and through all the terrified avoidance it expressed, there was pity in it, sorrow, a grateful tender memory. On each face, wonder and fear were painted vividly; each so still and silent, looking at the other over the black gulf of the irrevocable past. (964)

The keynote of the scene is this reciprocity, that is also the site of a "gulf." Florence, the "first to change," cries out "Oh, Mama, Mama! why do we meet like this? why were you ever so kind to me when there was no one else, that we should meet like this?" And continuing, as "Edith stood before her, dumb and motionless,"

"I dare not think of that. . . .I am come from Papa's sick bed. We are never asunder now; we never shall be, any more. If you would have me ask his pardon, I will do it, Mama." (964)

There seems to be no immediate reason to insist that Edith ask for *Dombey*'s pardon. Florence offers her own, Walter's, their children's; her insistence seems to be on getting Edith to *ask* for forgiveness from Dombey, as if that might parallel either her own asking forgiveness from him, or Dombey's asking for it from Florence – though of course, he asked it not directly of her (he would not cross the room at the sound of her voice), but of God.

Edith, as always, cares only for Florence. She refuses to repent of her "blind and passionate resentment" (965), but as before, her love for Florence wrings from her the denial that "nothing else in all the world . . . would have" – "No love, no hatred, no hope, no threat. I said that I would die, and make no sign. I could have done so, and I would, if we had never met, Florence" (965). As Cousin Feenix reveals his dissemblance in bringing Florence to startle Edith into confession, Edith ignores him, taking Florence to a sofa where they sit side by side, "in the deepening darkness" (967). Instead of confession, Edith offers a sealed paper she has in her bosom, something she wrote "in case of dying suddenly or by accident" (967), something that presumably clears her of the false adultery charge and describes to Florence (and anyone she chooses to give it to) what we witnessed in the scene with Carker. But Florence continues to press her for a message to Dombey, and Edith continues to resist, until she concedes:

"Tell him that if, in his own present, he can find any reason to compassionate my past, I sent word that I asked him to do so. Tell him that if, in his own present, he can find a reason to think less bitterly of me, I asked him to do so . . . When he loves his Florence most, he will hate me least. When he is most proud and happy in her and her children, he will be most repentant of his own part in the dark vision of our married life. At that time, I will be repentant too – let him know it then – and think that when I thought so much of all the causes that had made me what I was, I needed to have allowed more for the causes that had made him what he was. I will try, then, to forgive him his share of the blame. Let him try to forgive me mine!" (968)

This is far from Dombey's monosyllabic, and almost anti-narrative, repentance: Edith's is contingent, careful, dependent on *his* having reformed as well; her forgiveness is a secret to be revealed only when he has earned it, and one that continues to bind her to Florence, and bind Florence to her. But her adieu, which follows "the last words I send him!" is more fierce than anything in the earlier scenes of confrontation: "Now, goodbye, my life!" (969). And when Florence leaves her, "never" to meet again, she returns, "When you leave me in this dark room, think that you have left me in the grave. Remember only that I was once, and that I loved you!" – and Florence leaves, "seeing her face no more, but accompanied by her embraces and caresses to the last." The scene bears out one's sense that Edith is both the most powerful agent of narrative in the novel, with her proleptic forgiveness and retrospective resentment, and the one the novel (and Florence's view of the world) can least easily accommodate.

But the scene has a power beyond these negotiations and half-promises. It can be read in two diametrically opposed ways: either as a "wrapping up," a scene that brings Edith back long enough to clear her name and absolve Florence of the neglect of her beautiful mama (the one person who was good to her, as Florence points out), or as the climactic scene to which the novel was heading, providing the resolution still lacking after Florence's forgiveness of her father. It certainly has more drama than the earlier scene; it has more suspense, and more action, as the two women take turns falling on each other and crying; it goes fairly far in reconciling more of the deeper tensions (of debt and forgiveness, love and obligation) than does Florence's forgiveness of her father, most of which took place off-stage, and is barely narrated to us. Where Florence has entered with an already changed heart on her father's pain and illness, here, what we witness is much more like a complicated negotiation between two fellow sufferers – indeed, almost fellow travelers – and a complicated agreement to part, a negotiation by definition closer to the mood of readers (of authors?), about to part from the characters they have been living with so closely for so many months of the original part publication.

To read this scene, rather than Florence's reunion with her father and redemption of the family firm, as the novel's climax, is to see the novel as truly being the story of "a daughter after all," and this scene as the end of the story of "the day I met my beautiful mama." While it repeatedly stages the daughter's quest for the father's authority, her desire to act as his one true agent, it takes up the far more complicated problem of mothers and daughters, one that *Bleak House* avoids by Honoria's refusal to have anything to do with Esther. It is the dilemma of the woman who wants to have, as well as be, a mother; the dilemma of the woman who has both a father and a mother; the dilemma of the woman who (moving between father and husband) can never sign her own name to any agreement. There is something profoundly troubling in Florence's assumption that she must choose, finally, between her father and her mother, and that she must choose her father. Certainly, it is her father who needs her – but it has been her mother who has loved her all along. Her mother has, it is true, wronged "her name," but careful readers remember that the bait in the trap Carker laid for Edith was her passionate love for Florence, and his knowledge of Florence's "disgraceful" friends, the Cuttle/Gills ménage. Edith has sacrificed all along for Florence, and does so, again, at the end, when she "gives up" her silence, handing Florence the sealed text.

Florence, ever the negotiator, is slow to give up the fantasy of reconciliation, convinced, still, that she can bring her parents together as she could not when she was a child. The energy she exerts in this effort suggests, somewhat painfully, the power these old scenes still exert over *her* – and her inability (even though married, happy, a mother) to outgrow that darker childhood.[14] But Florence's insistence that Edith play this game, too, that she relive the dream, the "dark vision of our married life" she has left behind, and forgive and forget as Florence did, makes final the gulf between the two women, and, we feel, between Florence and the darker part of herself, the "cruel mark" that still stains her bosom.

What Edith does offer Florence is that final, unnarrated letter, the final production of Edith's magically signifying bosom that now produces not the knife it waved at Carker (which went on nearly to kill Dombey), but an alternative female text. This unread letter conjures up an earlier letter from a "beautiful mama," one that also went unread by the novel's readers. Fanny Dombey, who died "clasping her little daughter to her breast" (59), left behind, upon her death, a letter in a cabinet in her chamber, which her husband found. The letter might be to Dombey; it might be to the man she loved, whose death leaves her heart so frozen that it can tolerate marriage to the frigid Dombey. When Dombey found the letter, he

read it slowly and attentively, with a nice particularity to every syllable . . . When he had read it through, he folded and refolded it slowly several times, and tore it carefully into fragments. Checking his hand in the act of throwing these away, he put them in his pocket, as if unwilling to trust them even to the chances of being re-united and deciphered . . . (104)

It is almost as if in Edith's letter that fragmented text were made whole, passed on to the daughter, brought back to the father, still (in some essential ways) sealed, as was so much of Edith's plot, as is so much of the mother's plot, to all readers.

For now, this text closes on a world of repetitive parenting, one in which, to echo Toots's praise of the Nipper's daughters, "the oftener we can repeat that most extraordinary woman, my opinion is, the better!" (972). The Nipper has a Susan and a Florence; Florence Dombey Gay has a Florence as well, leaving us with two Susans and three Florences at book's end, as if for security against the premature deaths of children. It leaves us with only one little Paul, though one stronger than the original (presumably nurtured by mother's milk) and with a series of stronger houses: the new firm that has grown through Walter's exertions, and even, at the Blimber's school, a repainted version of the original house, occupied by the beamish Mr. Feeder, and his bride, Cornelia Feeder, née Blimber. All the daughters have brought home husbands to redeem their fathers' infirmity, and yet everywhere the old houses thrive. Dombey plays, at last, in the sea with children; Edith has fled back into the foreign shadows from which she arose; Florence seeks no further for her beautiful mama.

But if, in their final scene together, the dagger Edith turned on Carker and was willing to use on herself, the dagger that became the penknife Dombey considered committing suicide with, turned (penknife into pen, perhaps) into a female text, *Dombey and Son* retains its sense of that text's power – and of its roots in female anger – and female pain, as if "the cruel mark" that was "on [Florence's] bosom yet" had begun to speak, but only barely. "What shall Cordelia do?" Florence might earlier have asked, "Love, and be silent?"[15] Like the story of Dombey's love for Florence's daughter, the love he quite properly "hoards" in his heart, "That story never goes about" (975). The daughter's text doesn't quite emerge here; Florence's habitual self-abnegation echoes what we observed earlier of Alice Marwood: "the daughter was dumb" (576). And yet, the novel seems to point forward, to those daughterly narratives crafted by Esther Summerson and by Amy Dorrit; the texts that might represent more fully both the power and the pathos of being in an economy that traffics in women, and that does not (yet) let them out of the shadows of representation. Those texts, in a world of false agency, painful accounts, and bitter contracts, might reflect somewhat more crazily the difficulties of being "a daughter – after all."

CHAPTER THREE

Hard Times *and* A Tale of Two Cities
The social inheritance of adultery

The early Dickens novel depends upon stories of identity: *Oliver Twist*, *Nicholas Nickleby*, and *Martin Chuzzlewit* all concentrate on the young hero's assumption of his patrimony and his personality – a process that comes to the fore in the autobiographical "favourite child," *David Copperfield*. In that light, "a daughter after all" seems a mere distraction – the literary equivalent of the "base coin" Florence Dombey's father thought her. How much more ephemeral seems the plot of the daughter's adulterous mother, or the daughter's own progress through the meanderings of the adultery plot. And yet, as Dickens moved from these novels of identity toward the wider screen of the social novel, it was the adultery plot that served him in better stead – that allowed him to move from stories of identity to those of social position; to question the connections between individuals and the forces of historical transformation.

One example from *David Copperfield* might suggest why this is so. Mid-novel, David meets Annie Strong, the young and beautiful wife of his teacher, Doctor Strong. While Doctor Strong adores Annie, calling her "the dear lady" and his "contract-bargain,"[1] Annie is flighty and nervous, and seemingly infatuated with her cousin, the bounder Jack Maldon. The young David is incapable of recognizing her wandering ways; the older, narrator David seems more cognizant:

she was looking up at [her husband]. But with such a face as I never saw. It was so beautiful in its form, it was so ashy pale, it was so fixed in its abstraction, it was so full of a wild, sleep-walking, dreamy horror of I don't know what. The eyes were wide open, and her brown hair fell in two rich clusters on her shoulders, and on her white dress, disordered by the want of the lost ribbon. Distinctly as I recollect her look, I cannot say of what it was expressive, I cannot even say of what it is expressive to me now, rising again before my older judgement. Penitence, humiliation, shame, pride, love and trustfulness – I see them all; and in them all, I see that horror of I don't know what. (304)

The retrospective narrator David is here playing with the reader's sense of the ignorance of the *character* David, for what we are meant to "see" (what the young David cannot see – or more accurately, can see but cannot "know") is the guilt of adultery.

But the narrator is being disingenuous here: the older David, narrating, knows that Annie was never an adulteress, and in fact, her shame comes from something quite different. By keeping that shame a vague horror, he can manipulate the reader's desire to read for the adulterous plot, a desire to *see* her fall, and still hold on to the didactic efficacy of her alleged misprision – while never exactly telling the distinct untruth, never saying directly that she was untrue to her husband. Annie's secret is in fact not sexual but financial: what she fears is that her husband will think she married him for his money, dreading "the mean suspicion that my tenderness was bought – and sold to you, of all men, on earth" (729). What Annie wants made clear is not that she is not an adulteress, but that she is not a "contract-bargain". Annie's misery comes from her husband's generosity and the financial demands of her family (in particular her mother), for she is "unhappy in the mercenary shape I was made to wear" (730). "Mercenary," in that sentence, takes the place of "adulterous," and in similar fashion, David's ignorance must be transformed from sexual blindness to economic mystery: what he (and the Doctor) cannot know is the guilt of someone assumed to be nothing but a commodity. What seems more important, at this moment, than David's initiation into sexual wisdom, is the revelation of exchange relations: what Annie Strong reflects on is her own status as property, and the narratives spun around female ownership and material worth – in essence, her legal status as property and as conveyor of property. Though the other characters, David and Aunt Betsey in particular, think that Annie has been using her husband's money to pay off her lover, this is a sign only of their blindness: Annie *seems* to have been playing both a sexual and a property game, but in fact, she has been faithful and honest, a "contract-bargain" indeed.[2]

David, led in part by Annie's example, and by her words of warning, makes his way through the path of the false heart to perfect happiness and narratorial authority; Dickens, in the undoing of his marriage that took him through the 1850s, not only named his daughter Dora Annie, after the two wandering heroines of the novel, but found himself at the end explaining that his long-lived and many child-producing marriage was itself the mistake of an "undisciplined heart."[3] The Dickens novel, as it makes its way through the historical and social minefields of the same decade, has a less easy time of it. At the heart of the social novels, in particular *Hard Times* and *A Tale of Two Cities*, is a now familiar anxiety over the daughter's ability to signify truth – to stay true to their husbands, their fathers, the past. Repeatedly, as with Annie Strong, it is the male anxiety over female erotic wandering that is mistaken, a wandering off from the truth. But the plot of mistaken adultery provides not only a period of suspense for the reader, but a kind of suspension of meaning and of social coherence. In these two novels, anxieties over social coherence and the transmission of history – anxieties, in short, about authority and authorship – are tested through the plot of female disruption, and the daughter's adulterous plot turns out to be the key to the better ordering of society, and the proper uses of fiction.

Dickens returns in *Hard Times* to the central question of *Dombey and Son*: what use is the daughter? As in the earlier novel, he finds a variety of ways to test the daughter's true worth; and as in *Dombey and Son*, he allies the daughter's plot to the economic critique at the novel's core.[4] In *Hard Times*, Louisa Bounderby's plot is the one that most clearly parallels that of the workers, and her destiny seems to be worked out through theirs; she is also the character who comes closest to understanding and expressing the sense of impending revolt that the dangerous masses represent in the novel – however mild Dickens chooses to make their chief representative, Stephen Blackpool. But where Louisa and Stephen meet most fully is in their shared participation in the divorce plot, and it is in Louisa's sexual frustration, the anger she seems to inherit from Edith Dombey, that she most illustrates the forces the novel needs to contain. In this novel, the daughter is passionate, angry, and gains the most power by straying from the paths of narrative virtue.

Louisa herself makes the connection between her plight and that of the workers when she is told by her father, the Utilitarian Thomas Gradgrind, that she is sought by his friend, the blustery Josiah Bounderby, for his wife. Staring out at the "works," Louisa comments on how quiet they look in the evening; and yet, she says, "when the night comes, Fire bursts out."[5] The threat of her own fire, the passionate nature she suppresses, jostles the novel along far more compellingly than does the somewhat inadequate plot of workers' revolution, but even more striking is the connection Dickens makes between her sexual wandering and the "wonder" that is to suffuse the workers' blighted lives. In a sleight-of-hand metaphorical twist, Dickens aligns the workers, Louisa's bad marriage, and the faulty education of the Gradgrind children, all as a form of repression, an unnatural growth, ready to bear stunted and (were such a thing possible) violent fruit.[6]

The central evildoer in this fairy-tale would seem to be the children's father, Thomas Gradgrind, who gets his own fairy-tale introduction. When Louisa goes to meet her father in his study, we are told that "although Mr. Gradgrind did not take after Blue Beard, his room was quite a blue chamber in its abundance of blue books" (75).[7] The odd conjunction between fathers, daughters, and the Arabian Nights continues in an anecdote Sissy Jupe tells of her father and the days when she would read to him from "wrong books." She tells Louisa, whose capacity for "wonder" has been locked up by the domestic Blue Beard, that these books

"kept him, many times from what did him real harm. And often and often of a night, he used to forget all his troubles in wondering whether the Sultan would let the lady go on with the story, or would have her head cut off before it was finished." (49)

Sissy's story does more than remind Louisa of what a truly affectionate father and daughter share: it suggests the power of fiction in a world of harsh (and harmful) reality. The intrusion of Scheherezade into the text suggests further the ways Dickens's sexual plot – and the readerly desire generated in particular by the adulterous plot – will immunize the reader against what might do "real harm." If Stephen Blackpool had read fairy-tales, he might not be tempted to threaten revolt; if Louisa Gradgrind had learned the narrative striptease Scheherezade practiced, she would neither have married the wrong man nor have been isolated from the lives of those who surround her.

The reader who follows Louisa's plight is drawn on through another fantasy altogether, that crafted by Mrs. Sparsit, Bounderby's house-keeper. Mrs. Sparsit's *ressentiment* (she is a down-on-her-luck gentle-woman, freed from the tyrannies of her mysteriously bed-ridden cousin Lady Scadgers only by the genteel employment granted her by Mr. Bounderby) turns to sexual resentment when the beautiful young Louisa comes into the house. When Harthouse, one of the fact-party's minions, comes to town and is entranced by the young Louisa, Mrs. Sparsit makes it the "business" of her life to imagine Louisa's sexual fall, in an elaborate conceit that the narrator follows wholeheartedly:

Now, Mrs. Sparsit was not a poetical woman; but she took an idea in the nature of an allegorical fancy, into her head. Much watching of Louisa, and much consequent observation of her impenetrable demeanour, which keenly whetted and sharpened Mrs. Sparsit's edge, must have given her as it were a lift, in the way of inspiration. She erected in her mind a mighty Staircase, with a dark pit of shame and ruin at the bottom; and down those stairs, from day to day and hour to hour, she saw Louisa coming. (150–151)

The passage is a curious mixture of authorial and characterological insight: Mrs. Sparsit's "observation" of Louisa's "impenetrable demeanour" echoes Harthouse, who, pondering Louisa, remarked that she "baffled all penetration"; at the same time, the capitalization of "Staircase" suggests that the narrator, at least briefly, looks with Mrs. Sparsit's eyes. She is granted a vision beyond her own, and we are asked to share it – and for all that her "allegory" eventually fails, it is our path through the novel.

Mrs. Sparsit's plot is compelling largely because it has generic coherence: it has a melodramatic sequence of events, and Louisa is patently a melodramatic heroine, heaving bosom, flashing eyes, and all. From the scene where her father proposed Bounderby, when she addressed the "Fire [that] bursts out" (78) at night, Louisa has seemed a sleeping-beauty heroine, waiting for erotic awakening. The progress that started when Sissy Jupe entered her home and introduced those dangerous Arabian Nights narratives to the fiction-starved children cries out for physical embodiment – which it will find, eventually, not in Louisa's successful sexual escape with James Harthouse, but in her collapse into the loving Sissy's arms. More than mere embodiment, it seems to cry out for physical violence: the first sign of Louisa's sexual nature came early, when Bounderby demands a kiss from her, and she submits in stony silence – only to rub the area red after he leaves, and tell her brother he could cut it out with a knife, and she wouldn't cry out. The violence of Mrs. Sparsit's imaginings of the fall satisfies the reader's sense of Louisa's masochism, and of the vivid (repressed) desires that underwrite it – here, as elsewhere, the novel carries out the narrator's initial pronouncement, that fantasy, repressed in one space, will grow in cramped and warped form in another.

But it is Dickens who needs Louisa's fall – or more accurately, her near-fall. Mrs. Sparsit, in her quest for Louisa's ruin and her own return to power in the Bounderby household, has used a metaphor near to Dickens's heart: "Eager to see [the descent] accomplished, and yet patient, she waited for the last fall, as for the ripeness and fulness of the harvest of her hopes" (153). So, too, does Louisa's descent seem to Dickens the *proper* harvest of her own hopes: when she collapses on Sissy's breast, Louisa cries out, "Forgive me, pity me, help me! Have compassion on my great need" (168). The words are almost exactly Dombey's, when he cries out to God and Florence, "Forgive me, for I need it very much." Only those who know they have nothing stand any chance of gaining anything in a Dickens world, and the adultery plot seems to work (unlike the workers' plot, which gives to those who have nothing even more of nothing) by this image of stores replenished by a heavenly (loving) reward. But Louisa's progress through the bad marriage plot, past the dangers of the adultery plot, and into the plot of daughterly redemption (the plot in which she is saved by her return to the father; and he by her return) has actually had to make its way as well through a plot of property, of dispossession, and of repossession. This, in turn, reflects back on the connection between the fiercely angry, hard-hearted woman and the gentle, muddle-headed worker: the worker and the woman, it turns out, have in common that they are bodies that cannot possess themselves; they are subjects who can only uneasily become bodies of their own.

Images of violent disembodiment haunt the novel: the battered body of the woman worker; the fall of Stephen Blackpool down the Old Hell shaft; Louisa's collapse at her father's feet after she flees her husband and her would-be lover. Where these images coalesce is in the connections (of plot and of imagery) between Louisa's and Stephen's stories. Despite his representative status as "hand" in the novel, Stephen, far from being the most radical of the workers, has (nobly) refused to join his fellows in their strike, thereby allowing Dickens to avoid the direct representation of radical action and staying closer to the hearts (and hearths) of the workers. But this commitment to the domestic yields two important sub-plots, the first, Stephen's legal and moral bondage to his drunken, filthy wife; the second, the introduction of Rachael, the woman worker who offers a different version of the worker's miseries. Stephen's wife is the reason he visits Bounderby and meets Louisa in the first place; eventually, his inability to be freed from her will offer another point of connection for Louisa, chained to her marriage to Bounderby. While Bounderby's explanation of Stephen's obligation offers Dickens a brief moment of Chancery-like irony (Stephen is reminded, essentially, that divorce is cumbersome and marriage a moral obligation – except for wealthy people), Stephen's encounter with his wife offers the description of urban slime that is missing from Dickens's description of the workers. Dickens's Coketown is rather clean: there is virtually no ooze of the sort Engels, and novelists like Elizabeth Gaskell, depict – a primeval slime more familiar to us from *Bleak House* and *Our Mutual Friend*. Though

Coketown seems to resonate with filth, the city is more often seen as a vague blotch on the horizon than as specific trails of grime: only James Harthouse seems to notice that it is an "extraordinarily black town," where the workers appear "to have been taking a shower-bath of something fluffy" (92).

All the dirt that does not exist in Coketown seems, conveniently enough, to have found its way onto Stephen's alcoholic wife, who represents in her person all the ills of industrial decay – even though there is no evidence she has been near a factory in recent years.

Such a woman! A disabled, drunken creature, barely able to preserve her sitting posture by steadying herself with one begrimed hand on the floor, while the other was so purposeless in trying to push away her tangled hair from her face, that it only blinded her the more with the dirt upon it. A creature so foul to look at, in her tatters, stains and splashes, but so much fouler than that in her moral infamy, that it was a shameful thing even to see her. (55)

The foulness not only shames everyone who sees her, it contaminates even Stephen's apartment, "a room . . . as neat, at present, as such a room could be . . ." in which "the furniture was decent and sufficient, and, though the atmosphere was tainted, the room was clean" (54–5). This description precedes Stephen's discovery of his wife in the corner, and seems initially a description of the foulness of the Coketown air – but in fact, the atmosphere turns out to be more susceptible to her drunken foulness than to any of the ills of industrial pollution; the foulness is both encapsulated in her body, and miasmically fluid: when she scrambles up, it is "dangling in one hand by the string, a dunghill-fragment of a bonnet," and when she falls asleep, Stephen, cowering with his eyes covered, gets up but once, "to throw a covering over her, as if his hands were not enough to hide her, even in the darkness" (55). This is a dirt stronger than hands, stronger than fabric, stronger than darkness itself.

Stephen is incapable of cleaning up his room, or his wife, just as he is incapable of taking on the ills of industrialization ("a' a muddle," as he describes the chaos of social change).[8] Only Rachael's gentle hands can restore the realm of female sanctity, replacing his wife's "disgraceful garments [which] were removed, and some of Rachael's were in the room" (66). Indeed the whole room is restored to order: "everything was in its place and order as he had always kept it, the little fire was newly trimmed, and the hearth was freshly swept" (66). What Rachael cannot reorder is society, and she remains a voice of hopeless (and somewhat irresponsible) harmony: her requirement that Stephen pledge he will not join the striking workers leads to his social isolation ("You are the Hand they have sent to Coventry," says Bitzer, singling him out [110]) and, eventually, to his death in the tricky plot of Tom Gradgrind.

The vow he takes for Rachael suggests a further connection with Louisa Bounderby's plot, and offers another icon for the daughter's representative plight in the machinery of industrialization. Rachael has requested Stephen's oath that he abstain from political action (and here the illogic is Dickens's, and not my own) as a result of the tragic fate of her little sister. In a passage Dickens cut at a late stage in the publication of the novel, Stephen recalls Rachael's sister's dismemberment at the hands of the machinery:

"Thou'st spokken o' thy little sisther. There agen! Wi' her child arm tore off afore thy face!" She turned her head aside, and put her hand up to her eyes. "Where dost thou ever hear or read o' us – the like o' us – as being otherwise than onreasonable and cause o' trouble? Yet think o' that. . . ." (247)[9]

The violence directed against the sister here seems to indict, fatally, the system of factory labor that otherwise needs only to be "moderated" so that workers and masters can both continue to prosper – Stephen goes on to echo one of *Household Words*' own editorials on "rend[ing] and tear[ing] human creeturs to bits in a Chris'en country!" (247). But Dickens's excision of the violence against her not only (for socially minded readers) limits the "realism" of this venture into the arena of social fiction, it wreaks havoc with Dickens's conventional fictional skills: this scene explained Stephen's vow to Rachael that he would not enter into the strike against the masters, and without it, his obstinacy seems mere muddle-headedness. With the departure of the maimed sister from the text, Stephen is an even less effective speaker for the workers than he might be, and his refusal to join the strike seems more novelistic, and less credible, than ever.

Dickens wants to keep Stephen and Rachael clean, unsullied by the rebellious sludge (the "fluffy men") of Coketown, but he needs – without provoking revolution – to suggest the powers of those banked fires that Louisa imaginatively conjures. Stephen is protected from active rebellion; Louisa is kept from committing adultery; and yet, both suggest – perhaps in the very nobility of their nearing and then refusing an action that would embody their discontent – a revolutionary force that the novel cannot quite contain.[10] The connection between female rage and workers' resistance accomplishes some of this – and indeed, Bounderby himself makes such a connection when Louisa's father returns to ask her husband for patience in her unhappy state of mind:

"I know the works of this town, and I know the chimneys of this town, and I know the smoke of this town, and I know the Hands of this town. I know 'em all pretty well. They're real. When a man tells me anything about imaginative qualities, I always tell that man, whoever he is, that I know what he means. He means turtle soup and venison, with a gold spoon, and that he wants to be set up with a coach and six. That's what your daughter wants." (179)

Bounderby is not entirely wrong. Louisa, like the workers, wants something she can't name – it is the same "wild escape into something visionary" (162) which betrays her in her marriage; that something which is "not an Ology at all" (149) which she missed in her education at home. She has been transformed into someone who feels the unspoken connection with others always at the heart of Dickens's social program – and, as is often the case in a Dickens novel, a changed heart seems to be the substitute for social transformation.

That is not, however, entirely true in Louisa Bounderby's case, nor does Dickens's critique stop with her transformation. He went to considerable trouble to set up the connections between Louisa and Stephen: not only the parallel miseries of their bad marriages, but the scenes in which they meet and talk, in which he explains the workers' disenfranchisement. The plot drags Stephen into the web of deceit practiced by Tom Gradgrind, but Stephen (we believe) instructs Louisa in the web of social connection that restores her to herself, beginning the work Sissy Jupe will finish when Louisa returns home. All this works to quiet social outrage and to promote the ideological work of social connection – like the introduction of Honoria Dedlock to Jo the crossing sweep, or Arthur Clennam to poor Little Dorrit, these cross-class meetings prove the deeper connections between us in the great weavings of time, and Dickens thought of them (as in the meeting of Nancy and Rose Maylie in *Oliver Twist*) as his best ideas.

Hard Times goes farther, for it suggests not only that Louisa must meet and understand the abused victims of society, but that she herself is one. In some sense, this is the work of the adultery plot, for Louisa becomes an element of social disruption, another strand in the unweaving of society. Once the slime of industrial despair has been moved to Louisa, once she is an element of adulteration, she can be cleaned up and society reordered simply by removing from her the stain of adultery and restoring her to sanctimony and moral cleanliness. As Mary Douglas famously wrote of dirt, "if uncleanness is matter out of place, we must approach it through order. Uncleanness or dirt is that which must not be included if a pattern is to be maintained."[11] Culture needs dirt – in its own special place – in order to exist, and in this novel, Louisa provides both the dirt and the spot of cleaning up. This is accomplished through Mrs. Sparsit's hunting down Louisa on what she thinks is the great night of adulterous passion. Mrs. Sparsit follows Louisa into the garden, then into a train, and then back to Coketown, expecting to catch her in the act of degradation, only to wind up herself an ungodly mess:

> Wet through and through: with her feet squelching and squashing in her shoes whenever she moved; with a rash of rain upon her classical visage; with a bonnet like an over-ripe fig; with all her clothes spoiled; with damp impressions of every button, string, and hook-and-eye she wore, printed off upon her highly connected back; with a stagnant verdure on her general exterior, such as accumulates on an old park fence in a mouldy lane; Mrs. Sparsit had no resource but to burst into tears of bitterness and say, "I have lost her!" (160)

Louisa escapes both Mrs. Sparsit and the act of adultery – she has, to echo that earlier phrase of James Harthouse's, baffled both the reader's penetration and that of the characters nearest to her. But with all her moral ambiguity "printed off upon [Mrs. Sparsit's] highly connected back," Louisa is freed for the higher work of the plot, the industrial slime has been cleaned up and modern society reframed through the body of the tragic daughter, and the adultery novel seems to have contained all of the collective rage (workers; torn bodies; angry daughters) of the novel.

Louisa's abrupt rescue from the adultery plot returns us to the model Annie Strong offered David Copperfield: that being an adulteress is no more shameful than being called a mercenary. *Hard Times* encourages us to read Louisa's plot not as sexual desire but as the discontent of a woman *owned* by her husband. Louisa's flight is as much from the "contract-bargain" of marriage as from the disgusting sexual advances of her husband, the "bully of humility."

Bounderby may not "buy" Louisa as directly as Dombey purchased Edith Granger, but he certainly views her as an acquisition, another sign that he has risen from poverty and can acquire trophies. He is fond of introducing her as "Tom Gradgrind's eldest daughter Loo," crammed with lots of "expensive knowledge" (98); their betrothal took on a "manufacturing aspect," in which "Love was made on these occasions in the form of bracelets . . . Dresses were made, jewellery was made, cakes and gloves were made, settlements were made, and an extensive assortment of Facts did appropriate honour to the contract" (83). The wedding feast is an array of "imported and exported" objects, with "no nonsense" about any of it – in short, the marriage is a parody of the "party of Fact" 's pure materialism (83).

But so, also, is Louisa's affair, both in that she is the victim of Harthouse's tired seduction routine because she has no grounds but material grounds on which to make romantic choices, and in that the secret of her marriage, which Harthouse learns and uses to seduce her, is that she has sold herself into marriage not for her own improvement but for her brother's. Her father's system has left her viewing herself only as a commodity best exchanged for the good of others, in another dreadful parody of the maxim of the Utilitarians, the greatest good for the greatest number, and it is as a property plot that the adultery plot unfolds.

Louisa first reveals her sexual volatility to Harthouse through her devotion to her brother, "the whelp." Harthouse watches her brighten in response to her brother, and thinks, "it would be a new sensation, if the face which changed so beautifully for the whelp, would change for him" (126). In the overall coldness of Louisa's presence, her devotion to Tom is the only sign that she is at all penetrable. But the scenes in which Harthouse wins Louisa's sympathy, and begins to win her erotic attention through his own attention to her brother, center on her brother's siphoning off of her money, and her own dubious relationship to her property. Harthouse, insinuating his knowledge of the lack of affection between her brother and her husband, asks, "may there be a better confidence between yourself and me?" (129), asking not for sexual favors, but financial information:

"Tom has borrowed a considerable sum of you?". . . .

"When I married, I found that my brother was even at that time heavily in debt. Heavily for him, I mean. Heavily enough to oblige me to sell some trinkets. They were no sacrifice. I sold them very willingly. I attached no value to them. They were quite worthless to me."

Either she saw in his face that he knew, or she only feared in her conscience that he knew, that she spoke of some of her husband's gifts. She stopped, and reddened again. If he had not known it before, he would have known it then, though he had been a much duller man than he was.

"Since then, I have given my brother, at various times, *what money I could spare: in short, what money I have had.*" (129–30; emphasis added)

What money Louisa could spare, which turns out to be all her money, must be the money she is given by her husband, for she can have, we know, no money of her own: similarly, she can sell her jewelry for him, for it is the only part of her property that belongs expressly to her – and to sell it says clearly to Harthouse that its "giver" is of no value to her.

Harthouse's "penetration" into Louisa's economic relationship with her brother automatically gives him entrance into her economic relationship with her husband. As the whelp complains, Bounderby will give him no money; his father "draw[s] what he calls a line," and "here's my mother who never has anything of her own, except her complaints. What *is* a fellow to do for money, and where *am* I to look for it, if not to my sister?" (132). Looking to his sister involves describing the sustained prostitution which is his sister's marriage to Bounderby:

"She could get it. It's of no use pretending to make a secret of matters now, after what I have told you already; you know she didn't marry old Bounderby for her own sake, or for his sake, but for my sake. Then why doesn't she get what I want, out of him, for my sake? She is not obliged to say what she is going to do with it; she is sharp enough; she could manage to coax it out of him, if she chose. Then why doesn't she choose, when I tell her of what consequence it is? But no. There she sits in his company like a stone, instead of making herself agreeable and getting it easily. I don't know what you may call this, but *I* call it unnatural conduct." (133)

This perverted sense of what is unnatural follows a description of the interweaving of erotic energy and familial debt that is chilling; no less so is the "confidence with her" that Harthouse has established "that absolutely turned upon her indifference towards her husband, and the absence, now and at all times, of any congeniality between them" (134). This financial knowledge (and secret intimacy) seems as damning as sexual intimacy – but it is through her "indifference" that the largely indifferent Harthouse intends to trap Louisa.

That she escapes him suggests the way "mere" materialism will not save her: Louisa must find another answer to her questions of "what matters" than material goods. However, material goods – in the form of marital property – continue to follow her moral progress as her father and Bounderby negotiate over what turns out to be the return of Louisa – and her property – to her father's house. In some ways, she has never left it: Mrs. Sparsit, ever the reader's friend, helps us towards that reading by her inability to remember Louisa Bounderby's married name, calling her, variously, "Miss Gradgrind," "Mrs. Gradgrind," and – most tellingly – "Miss Bounderby" (145).[12] Gradgrind's attempts to impress Bounderby with Louisa's new self-knowledge ("I see reason to doubt whether we have ever quite understood Louisa" [178]) impress Bounderby only with Gradgrind's having been "brought low." In his version, there is "what people call some incompatibility between Loo Bounderby and myself," and he translates that immediately to mean "that your daughter don't properly know her husband's merits, and is not impressed with such a sense as would become her, by George! of the honour of his alliance" (179). Rejecting her father's plea that he "aid in trying to set her right," *he* responds by transforming the conversation immediately into one about property:

> "As to your daughter, whom I made Loo Bounderby, and might have done better by leaving Loo Gradgrind, if she don't come home to-morrow, by twelve o'clock at noon, I shall understand that she prefers to stay away, and I shall send her wearing apparel and so forth over here, and you'll take charge of her for the future. . . ."
>
> So Mr. Bounderby went home to his town house to bed. At five minutes past twelve o'clock next day, he directed Mrs. Bounderby's property to be carefully packed up and sent to Tom Gradgrind's; advertised his country retreat for sale by private contract; and resumed a bachelor life. (180–1)

The dissolution of the marriage, which ends the chapter, is marked not by romantic discussion, or even the erotic exchange suggested by Louisa's flight from her father's friend to her father's party-mate, but by the removal of her property (or that of her fictional legal self, "Mrs. Bounderby") and the sale of Bounderby's estate – his "private contract" here not marriage, but resale, and marital status not, as Gradgrind wished, an arrangement in "a friendly manner" (180) but merely a question of land ownership and rentals.

The novel's efforts focus on the attempt to avoid the accounting book model of marriage – indeed, of all human relationships – and Louisa's abrupt departure from her marriage is no exception. Bounderby remains committed to counting: his will calls for the founding of a house for orphans and the creation of twenty-five identical copies of himself; after Bounderby dies of a fit in the street, the will lingers in a Dickensian maze of "little service and much law," never yielding a result (218). Louisa returns to her father's house, leading a life of "not fantastic" duty, with "happy Sissy's happy children loving her," and with herself holding her course "simply as a duty to be done" (219). Louisa Bounderby, like Edith Dombey before her and Honoria Dedlock after, does not return to the happy ending, but is allowed a filial attachment. Her much-changed father, who clutched his favorite child to his bosom, only to hear her cry out "I shall die if you hold me! Let me fall upon the ground!" and see the "triumph of his system" lie an insensible heap at his feet (163), is now himself returned to sensibility, his system redeemed by her fall and her resurrection into a "gentler and a humbler" Louisa (218).

What Louisa Bounderby wanted from the world, her equivalent of "turtle soup and venison, with a gold spoon," is something more, what

Bounderby calls with equal contempt, "imaginative qualities." From the book's beginning those qualities are summed up in the word "wonder," but from the time of Louisa's fall, we might rename them "wandering." What the novel wants is for people to learn to adulterate: to mix fact and fancy, to allow for the release of natural forces, to be "amuthed." "There ith a love in the world, not all Thelf-interetht after all, but thomething very different" that "hath a way of ith own of calculating or not calculating" which is "hard to give a name to" (215). In *Dombey and Son*, of course, the only thing greater than money was the joy in another's destruction. In *Hard Times*, Dickens moves through a woman's joy in her own destruction to posit something like a moral awareness – only slightly undercutting it in the circus master Sleary's voice by aligning it to what dogs know. But in this novel, Dickens also imagines that the most imaginative and sensitive character in the industrial world, the woman who tries to imagine a destiny for herself beyond material interest, might fall short of her own imaginings; while her father is transformed, and her brother learns her value, and happy Sissy's happy children love her, Louisa Bounderby sits silent and alone by the cold hearth fire, an emblem for readerly rebirth, but unable herself to wander, to adulterate, to rejoin the plots of marriage and childbirth. She is left with no "fantastic vow, or bond, or brotherhood, or sisterhood, or pledge, or covenant, or fancy dress, or fancy fair; but simply . . . a duty to be done" (219), and she does it, but despite her powers of prestidigitation by the fire, she sees no "blessing and happiness" for herself. The wandering daughter may be the road to social salvation, but for herself, at least in this novel, her only inheritance is the general good.

Readers of *A Tale of Two Cities* can only be amused by the extent to which it remains a "Dickens novel": it features a quiet, gentle daughter; an angry, passionate, dark woman; a father baffled by imprisonment and history; a husband, somewhat tamed and listless in the face of duty; and a dark, willful, charming, and dissolute lover, who must be forced (by love and destiny) to own up to his own inheritance and *act*. The novel, in effect, domesticates the French Revolution, and returns it to the key motifs we have been tracing: the daughter and her uncanny double, the heroine's perilous trek through the adultery plot, the maternal text from beyond the grave.[13] Indeed, revolution in *A Tale of Two Cities* is a plot carried out by fathers and daughters: Dickens self-consciously quotes the key-note of Thomas Carlyle, who, in characteristic fashion, referred to the guillotine as "Doctor Guillotin's daughter"; we can only note, in

keeping with the pattern of doubling and daughters we have been stressing throughout, that this novel is patently "A Tale of Two Daughters" –
and of the daughter's duplicitous progress through history.[14]

The novel begins with the release from prison of Dr. Manette, the
"good doctor of Beauvais," who has been in the Bastille for eighteen
years, buried alive. He is reunited with the daughter he did not know he
had, but whose image kept him alive all these years: she is 17, small,
earnest, loving, with a head of golden hair, hair that will become, the
narrator tells us, the "golden thread" that will lead Manette from prison,
connect his present with his past, and serve as the narrative thread connecting the sections of the book.[15] In this way, Lucie (whose very name
suggests the light of reason and memory she represents) will fulfill a
familiar plot: the daughter's duty is to be the memory of her family, her
father, her culture, the novel itself. And in a book obsessed with memory,
restoration, connections – a book in which a character, Sydney Carton,
is nicknamed "Memory Carton" – this is the central role, the melodramatic fulcrum of the novel.

But as the daughter's memory becomes the crisis-point of the novel,
so she enters both the adultery plot and the plot of historical change.
When the Manettes return to England, where Lucie has lived for many
years, they become friends with a young French emigré, known to them
as Charles Darnay. He is tried for treason in England, and acquitted, in
part because he is shown to have an uncanny double, Sydney Carton,
who works for Darnay's lawyer. Carton, like Darnay, is soon in love with
Lucie, whom he nonetheless describes with devastating accuracy as a
"golden-haired doll."[16] Unlike Darnay, Carton is a wastrel, a drunkard,
a ne'er-do-well and probably a rake; still, his love for Lucie is the one
golden moment of his life, and (conveniently for the plot) he promises
one day to do something to redeem his wasted life and "embrace any
sacrifice for you and for those dear to you" (183). This seems a safe
promise, but no sooner has Lucie married Darnay (despite some
mysterious shrinking on the part of her father, Dr. Manette) than the
French Revolution appears on the scene, drawing all the characters back
to France and into their destiny. Darnay is arrested as an aristocrat and
an emigré (a capital offence under the new regime); he is saved in a melodramatic trial scene by his father-in-law, whose status as a survivor of the
Bastille carries considerable power in revolutionary France. The book
could end here – except that Darnay is re-arrested, and charged with the
past crimes of his family, crimes documented in a buried letter written
by none other than Dr. Manette, and hidden by him in the Bastille.

The manuscript was recovered (and Darnay hunted down) by the book's most memorable character, Madame Defarge, wife of Manette's old servant, and (in the book's metaphorical scheme) the chief planner of the revolution, a tiger woman, who (pleasantly occupied in knitting throughout the whole novel) has been keeping within her needlework a secret register of those to be killed. "What do you knit?" a stranger has asked her; "many things," she replied; "For instance?" "For instance, shrouds" (203). Indeed, the narrative suggests, Madame Defarge has knit nothing less than the entire French Revolution, and as the book moves to its conclusion, the guillotine, under her watchful eye, carries out the deaths inscribed in her handiwork.

So far the novel's symbology seems carefully set up along conventional lines: Lucie Manette, the golden-haired doll, keeps a quiet home, filled with tactful French touches, though she has never lived in France. She has a worried little forehead, capable of a myriad expressions, and always at work – but *her* only work is to make a home for her father, choose the proper suitor to marry, and then reconcile her father to her marriage. Hers is an aggressively private life, calm and stable, the daughter's perfection of her domestic duty. Her opposite, in every way, is Madame Defarge, walking barefoot through the streets of France, a "tigress . . . without pity" (391). It is Madame Defarge who keeps the spirit of the revolution: when her husband fears it will never come, that "we shall not see the triumph,"

"We shall have helped it," returned madame, with her extended hand in strong action. "Nothing that we do, is done in vain. I believe, with all my soul, that we shall see the triumph. But even if not, even if I knew certainly not, show me the neck of an aristocrat and tyrant, and still I would – "

Then madame, with her teeth set, tied a very terrible knot indeed. (208)

The "terrible knot" she is tying is the revolution, and specifically the executions that will follow; she "enforces" the conclusion of her advice to her husband by "striking her little counter with her chain of money as if she knocked its brains out" (208–209).

Madame Defarge is associated here, as elsewhere, with the violence of the guillotine and the spectacle of revolution: it is she who takes the humble "mender of roads" to see the royal family:

"As to you," said she, "you would shout and shed tears for anything, if it made a show and a noise. Say! Would you not?"

"Truly Madam, I think so. For the moment."

"If you were shown a great heap of dolls, and were set upon them to pluck them to pieces and despoil them for your own advantage, you would pick out the richest and gayest. Say! Would you not?"

"Truly, yes, Madam."

"Yes. And if you were shown a flock of birds, unable to fly, and were set upon them to strip them of their feathers for your own advantage, you would set upon the birds of the finest feathers; would you not?"

"It is true, Madam."

"You have seen both dolls and birds today." (204)

It is the sheer unexpectedness of this passage – not only the violence, but the placidity of Madame Defarge's diction and its eerie resemblance to instruction, the deceptive gentleness of dolls and birds – that accentuates its viciousness: it is also the undoing of Madame Defarge's "womanly" character, and the uncanny invocation of Lucie Manette, called a "golden haired doll" by Sydney Carton and "Ladybird" by her servant, Miss Pross, in the specter of the "heaps of dolls" and "flock of birds" that are to be set upon, stripped, and despoiled. Madame Defarge's violence is an undoing of domesticity; the same violation of womanhood represented by the crowds of women on the streets, who break down the laws of public and private when they dance the Caramagnole; a "fallen sport – a something, once innocent, delivered over to all devilry – a healthy pastime changed into a means of angering the blood, bewildering the senses, and steeling the heart" (307). For Dickens, the terror of the dance was that it "perverted all things good by nature" – by which he means femininity: "The maidenly bosom bared to this, the pretty almost-child's head thus distracted, the delicate foot mincing in this slough of blood and dirt were types of the disjointed time" (307–308).

What Madame Defarge wants is precisely to disjoint that scene: to her and her henchman, Lucie, with her "pretty almost-child's head," is only a threat, the wife of the traitor Evrémonde and the mother of his daughter. In their view, all this only adds to the spectacle she will make before the guillotine:

"She has a fine head for it," croaked Jacques Three. "I have seen blue eyes and golden hair there, and they looked charming when Samson held them up."

Ogre that he was, he spoke like an epicure.

Madame Defarge cast down her eyes, and reflected a little.

"The child also," observed Jacques Three, with a meditative enjoyment of his words, "has golden hair and blue eyes. And we seldom have a child there. It is a pretty sight." (388)

This could stand not only as a representative conservative denunciation of revolution ("Look, they don't spare even women and children," as we might paraphrase it – or as Jerry Cruncher summarizes the revolution, "a goin' on dreadful round him, in the way of Subjects without heads" [337]), but as a representative icon for Dickens's art. Women, children, golden hair, and blue eyes: "a pretty sight" in the "way of Subjects" indeed.

But this is not all that links pretty, blonde, blue-eyed Lucie Manette to the spectacle of the French revolution, and Dickens begins to complicate the daughter's relationship to history. Lucie has also become part of the spectacle around her: while her husband has been imprisoned, she has been seen daily outside his prison, waving and kissing her hand to him, holding up their daughter to his eyes. In the revolution's breakdown of public and private spheres, Lucie's movements mark her as a spy, and the woodcutter whose hut she stands near is prepared to testify against her, for she has been "making signs and signals to Prisoners." Her devotion, Carton reports, will be read as "a prison plot, and . . . it will involve her life – and perhaps her child's – and perhaps her father's . . ." (373). Here Dickens's view of the interpenetration of domestic and political space anticipates Lynn Hunt's: "the other side of the rhetorical refusal of politics was the impulse to invest politics everywhere. Because politics did not take place in a defined sphere, it tended to invade everyday life instead." In what Hunt calls the "compulsive publicity" of the revolution, and what Dickens calls the "universal watchfulness," there is no private life left.[17]

Lucie is linked even more powerfully than through paranoia with the book's spectacle of political life, however: the central image of the novel (and the revolution) is apostrophized in terms uncannily like those that summon up our heroine. There was no more potent symbol of the revolution's power (and the terror it conjured) than the guillotine; and yet the guillotine, as imagined by Carlyle's *French Revolution*, is "the product of Guillotin's endeavors, gained not without meditation and reading; which product popular gratitude or levity christens by a feminine derivative name, as if it were his daughter: *La Guillotine!*"[18]. Dickens, as well, refers to the "sharp female newly-born" (283), the "sharp female called La Guillotine" (302), but in bringing together these two images (the sharp female, the dutiful daughter) he seems to be bringing together his own two opposite poles of femininity, Lucie Manette (whose father is called, by one character, "a doctor with a daughter" [156]) and Thérèse Defarge, whose sharpness is the terror of the novel.

The guillotine, that public spectacle, is at the center of daily life in the revolution – indeed, it is relentlessly domesticated by the novel. It was, the novel says,

the popular theme for jests; it was the best cure for headache, it infallibly pre-
vented the hair from turning grey, it imparted a particular delicacy to the com-
plexion, it was the National Razor which shaved close: who kissed La Guillotine,
looked through the little window and sneezed into the sack. (302)

A recent scholar has commented that Dickens, typically, has recorded
virtually all the contemporary humour surrounding that "sharp female
newly-born"[19]: in his account the blood is merely "red wine" for La
Guillotine, "to slake her devouring thirst." The wood-sawyer who
watches Lucie at the prison calls his saw "my Little Guillotine" or "Little
Sainte Guillotine," for "the great sharp female was by that time popu-
larly canonised" (305, 307). But that "canonization" is also Dickens's way
of treating small, soft women, and the description invokes both heroines.
The guillotine is a not an uncommon sign for male anxiety, but the
anxiety reaches further into the culture: as Jacques Barzun wrote of
Berlioz's generation, they were "as much haunted by the guillotine as we
are by the death camps".[20] The images of the guillotine are poised
between the gothic animation of the "sharp female," and the mecha-
nization of death the guillotine represented: quick, impersonal death,
meant to mimic the impersonality and equality of justice, emphasizing
that government by the people is exclusive of all expressions of individual will; that, as Robespierre wrote, the virtue with which the people are
imbued consists precisely in the "sublime sentiment [that] prefers the
public to all private interest."[21] As Daniel Arasse summarizes it, the guillotine from this standpoint exemplified "the very principle of revolutionary democracy: it emphasized the individuality of each of its victims the
better to annihilate it – more exactly, to deny this individuality by the
mechanical process with which the victim was destroyed."[22]

It is not in the nature of novels to prefer the public to the private –
indeed, the work of the novel seems the opposite of the very trans-
parency of the private sphere the revolution called for, the rendering of
each event public, political, momentous. The world of spies called forth
by the Terror, one subtly invoked by Dickens, is one in which the most
random gesture signifies a political stand – and it is a world in which citizens could be charged with not supporting the Revolution with enough
enthusiasm; a world in which, Marat said, citizens could not be blamed
for making false accusations against others, for their vehemence suggested their passion for the revolution; a world in which "twenty-one
Girondins were dispatched in twenty-six minutes;" in which the skin of
aristocrats was tanned, for its softness, and the hair of victims was turned

into wigs; a world which, indeed, suggests a horror of impersonality we fear we live with; a world of spectacle gone awry, in which prisoners would practice their own guillotining, so as to make a noble show for themselves.[23]

But it is also a world of chummy violence, horror rendered (to return to our central terms) domestic: as one recent account has it, the guillotine "became a tourist attraction, inspired songs, was reproduced in fashion items (earrings, gowns *en guillotine*), and even appeared as a household appliance, in the form of a bread slicer."[24] This suggests the reverse of the process I have been charting, in which the revolution reveals the horror in the domestic; in this account, we might say, the revolution comes home.

Or perhaps, as Dickens's novel suggests, it *begins* at home. If gentle Lucie Manette, receptacle of cultural and paternal memory, is allied in unexpected ways to the guillotine, the force that cuts through the novel, she is thus allied to Thérèse Defarge, who seemed merely her evil double. The novel's doubleness is so powerful that it can be read in the opposite direction as well, for with the revelation of Thérèse's family history, with her movement back into the private sphere, the public revolution becomes more sympathetic, and her anger at "birds of the finest feather" moves closer to Lucie's fierce defense of home. Thérèse's sister was raped by Charles Darnay's uncle, and her father and brother were killed to conceal the crime – a crime revealed in Dr. Manette's prison narrative.[25] The real crime in the novel, the omission that the revolution must fill in, is Charles Darnay's inability to complete his mother's last request, for his mother had come to the doctor to see the girl, who is, alas, already dead: "Her hope had been, she said in great distress, to show her, in secret, a woman's sympathy" (360). Further, "she had reasons for believing that there was a young sister living, and her greatest desire was, to help that sister." In the doctor's presence she makes Charles, her "pretty boy," swear to "bestow, with the compassion and lamenting of his dead mother, [money little beyond the worth of a few jewels], on this injured family, if the sister can be discovered" (360). Charles has not pursued this search zealously enough: Madame Defarge has been under his (and our) gaze for the whole of the novel, and her "vengeance" (the Revolution) is her response:

"I tell him, 'Defarge, I was brought up among the fisherman of the sea-shore, and that peasant family so injured by the two Evrémonde brothers, as that Bastille paper describes, is my family. Defarge, that sister of the mortally wounded boy upon the ground was my sister, that husband was my sister's husband, that unborn child was their child, that brother was my brother, that father was my father, those dead are my dead, and that summons to answer for those things descends to me!'" (370)

At that moment, with Thérèse Defarge's "answer," the Revolution and its terror become the daughter's revenge, the act of memory this novel seems to have been calling for: Lucie's story and Thérèse's have come together, and the Revolution has become a female narrative, born in a story of rape, violation, and filial memory.

In some compelling ways, adultery is the only outcome of this text, primarily because of the text's relentless doubling: not only are there two daughters, but (at various times) the novel becomes a tale of two cuisines (Miss Pross learns to cook dinners "half English and half French" [129]); two decorating styles (Lucie's London lodging "appeared to have innately derived from [the country of her birth] that ability to make much of little means" [124]); two banks (Tellson's London and Paris offices, which exchange the documents that generate the plot); and of course two languages (little Lucie speaks in "the tongues of the Two Cities" [240]). The novel worries constantly about the relationship between these doubles: are they truly separate; can they be merged in a happy marriage; can the two be reconciled in one historical narrative? But with the same force that Lucie Manette is haunted by Thérèse Defarge, twin daughters of history-swept fathers, so is her husband, Charles Darnay, mirrored by Sydney Carton, his physical double, and the tale of the two husbands proves more complicated, however much they are drawn together. After Carton saves Darnay's life the first time, he mockingly asks him, "Do you think I particularly like you?" (115). But the scene ended with Carton's muttering to himself in the mirror, "why should you particularly like a man who resembles you? There is nothing in you to like; you know that" (116). Different versions of "like" seem constantly at risk in this text, and it is worth noting only the central characterological resemblance between Darnay and Carton: both are sons of devout mothers, haunted by the image of a mother who wants them to reform, and both imagine carrying out that reformation through Lucie. Charles's mother, from whom he has taken his English name, represents the force of historical restoration, the wrong never righted that must somehow be avenged; Sydney Carton, whose body will take the place of Charles's in that great historical righting of the wrong, hopes in that action to appease his mother and fulfill the promise of what he would have been had he followed her guidance. That promise is repeated in the novel – specifically, and adulterously, to Lucie Manette, who proves (like all good daughters) the stand-in for all mothers (historical, memorialized, and in any way fetishized) in the novel.

Carton's fantasy of maternal remembrance and fraternal resemblance becomes explicitly sexualized as the novel goes on, and takes the specific form of imagining himself as adulterous father to Lucie's children. The scene in which he first does this is the climax of the book's middle, nominally courtship, section: Lucie Manette has been pursued by three suitors, Darnay, Carton, and Stryver, the self-impressed lawyer. These men may be courting Lucie, but we never actually see any of them propose to her: Darnay speaks to her father prior to an offstage proposal; Stryver discusses the matter with Jarvis Lorry, who (also offstage) raises the question with the Manettes, and returns to repeat his advice that Stryver not attempt a proposal; and Carton begins his odd pursuit of Lucie by remarking that it is fortunate after all that Lucie does *not* love him. This absence of propositional scenes serves to throw attention not on Lucie and Darnay's dance of attraction (which is of minimal interest at best) but rather on the relationship between Darnay and Lucie's father: the tension of the middle of the book leads up to the scene in which Darnay (again, offstage) reveals to Dr. Manette that he is the son of the Marquis St Evrémonde; that his father and uncle raped the sister of Thérèse Defarge and murdered her father, brother, and husband – and that Dr. Manette is the only witness to their deed. This secret remains a secret from the reader until the great trial scene of the third volume, but readers are poised to be more curious about the secret meeting between bridegroom and father than about anything that happens between Darnay and Lucie.

Into this erotic void sidles Sydney Carton. Although his dissipation is merely hinted at ("the life I lead," he says, "is not conducive to health" [180]) his very posture singles him out as the erotic other in the novel: rather than striding or standing erect, he "leans" (112, 132), he "lounges" (133), he "wander[s]" (342), he walks aimlessly – he is, for the heroine, the guide to the erotic wanderings that mark (off) the adulterous path. The scene in which he approaches Lucie comes after her engagement, at a moment when he is "thankful" that she cannot feel tenderness for, or return the love of "the man you see before you – self-flung away, wasted, drunken, poor creature of misuse as you know him to be" (180). The work of the novel is to remake that self-flinging into the heroic self-sacrifice Carton effects at the end, when he takes Darnay's place first in the prison, and then at the guillotine; its origins are in this scene of secret meeting, when he tells her "you have been the last dream of my soul"; that in her presence he has "heard whispers from old voices impelling me upward, that I thought were silent for ever"; that "with . . . a sudden mastery you kindled me, heap of ashes that I am, into fire" (181). The scene, with its heightened, eroticized mixture of self-loathing and adoration, ends with two gestures on Carton's part: his request that "my name, and faults, and miseries [be] gently carried in your heart" (182); the second, his promise that

"when the little picture of a happy father's face looks up in yours, when you see your own bright beauty springing up anew at your feet, think now and then that there is a man who would give his life, to keep a life you love beside you!" (183)

The burden of Carton's meeting is that the "last confidence" of his life be carried by her, and by her alone. That shared secret creates the twin progeny of the scene: his relationship to her children, and his mastery over her husband's life.

Carton's presence in the perfect domesticity of the Darnays is, as he wants it to be, that of a "useless . . . piece of furniture" (237), or would be were it not for Lucie's imploring her husband to be gentle with the wanderer who carries "wounds" in his heart – and if not for her child's sympathy with him, for, the narrator assures the reader, "No man ever really loved a woman, lost her, and knew her with a blameless though an unchanged mind, when she was a wife and mother, but her children had a strange sympathy with him" (241). Carton is the "first stranger" to whom little Lucie holds out her chubby arms; he is the last ("almost at the last") person to whom the "little boy" speaks before death: "Poor Carton! Kiss him for me!" The adultery plot works itself out not only through Carton's sacrifice, and his continued presence – however furniture-like – in the Darnay menage, but in this displaced paternity: his ability, at his death, to invent still more children to remember and name him.

This fantasy matters so profoundly because questions of memory and proper naming (questions of inheritance and descent) are essential not only to the familial but to the historical plot of the novel. Indeed, the adultery plots register not only as part of a more general anxiety about male paternity and female fidelity, but an anxiety about the transmission of value: as the anthropologist Carol Delaney has argued, adultery disrupts the motions of transmission upon which orderly society depends, not only of paternity, but of honor and masculine identity. As Delaney summarizes it,

Contrary to the evidence of the senses, paternity has meant the creative, life-giving role. Paternity is over-determined, and in proportion so too are the social measures constructed to ensure the legitimacy of paternity . . .[26]

These measures are harsh to the degree that women are perceived as vulnerable – indeed, in an unexpected echoing of Lucie and Carton's secret meeting, Delaney reports that in Turkish village society, women are held to be so incapable of containing their own boundaries that if men and women are alone together for more than twenty minutes it is assumed they have had intercourse, and this constitutes grounds for divorce. "It is because women are thought to be so vulnerable, so open to persuasion, that they must be socially closed or covered";[27] it follows, then, that a man has access to social authority – to the legitimacy of paternity – only through a female property defined by its vulnerability.

In *A Tale of Two Cities*, that legitimacy takes the form of historical authority – the ability to inscribe not only views of the future, but visions of the past. Madame Defarge's memory, enhanced by her knitting (which includes names, dates, and faces) contends with the (loving) memory of the Darnay/Manette party, who bind people to themselves with affection and recollection. The most horrifying moment of the novel, and the one bit of suspense it maintains, is that it is Dr. Manette's own *written* text, one written to preserve the memory he feared was fading in the darkness of the Bastille, which will condemn Charles Darnay to death – just as, with similar irony, it is Darnay's attempt to honor his mother's memory, to enact her dying wish that he make amends to the Defarge family, that leads him to the Manettes in the first place; his loyalty to Gabelle, the estate's manager, that draws him back to the ruins of France, and his own probable death. The letter Gabelle sends to "Monsieur heretofore the Marquis" (270) is only one of many documents within the text inscribed to persons who are already ghosts.

To write to ghosts – or to expect ghosts to fulfill promises; or in any way to expect the future to "right" the past – is to impose an uneasy burden through inheritance and through memory. While the novel is in many ways on the side of history, the persistence of memory is synonymous with the Terror itself: the "Ghosts" of La Force prison ("the ghost of beauty, the ghost of stateliness, the ghost of elegance, the ghost of pride . . . all waiting their dismissal from the desolate shore" [285]) may be harmless "apparations" (286), but Madame Defarge's determination to extinguish the entire "race" (370) of Evrémondes suggests that one's family will write one's story forever, and one's individual deeds count as nothing. Not only individuals but the society will be unable to forget; all existence will become a haunting. *A Tale of Two Cities* shares its ambivalence about this inheritance with much of Dickens's later fiction, and registers a departure from some of the earlier work of good daughters like Florence Dombey, who claims she can never be made to forget. As the selfish but honest Fanny Dorrit cries out, to her obsessively memorial sister Amy, "are we never to be permitted to forget?" Amy Dorrit's insistence that it would be cruel to forget places where people have been kind to one takes on a nightmare twist in Thérèse Defarge's "Dickensian" repetition of the past: "that sister . . . was my sister, that husband was my sister's husband, that unborn child was their child, that brother was my brother, that father was my father, those dead are my dead, and that summons to answer for those things descends to me!" (370). In the power of the "me" who answers is a "me" who is *never* permitted to forget, and out of whom will be born nothing of promise.

The problem of memory becomes not only one of proper transmission, but of when time is to have an end, of what thread is to bind the past to the present and the future, and whether that thread should run uncut. As in *The Old Curiosity Shop*, *Dombey and Son*, and *David Copperfield*, the key to memory is the daughter who, in her resemblance to her mother, *is* the thread that binds the generation – in that daughter, the mother lives again. Without the assurance of that connection, Dr. Manette would wander forever in the darkness of the Bastille; Darnay would leave no progeny; the book would end, one assumes, without hope. Nonetheless, when Lucie first appears to Dr. Manette, he is terrified, and Lucie is terrorized by her own guilt at somehow not having known that her father was alive all along. The terror is not that memory will fade but that it will perilously persist – it will be "buried alive."

If the daughter's memory in this novel holds real terror, much as Madame Defarge's memory provokes the Terror of the Revolution, one alternative form of memory is away from maternal or daughterly transmission, and through the illicit progress of the adultery plot. As in *Hard Times*, adultery suggests a possible reordering of narrative and the social order: here, it further suggests a profound ambivalence about historical descent. The way this novel ensures a future is not through Darnay, but through his wandering, dissolute, and seemingly sterile double, Carton, whose evocation of future generations generates the end of the novel, and suggests the power of history to continue.

When Carton is finally on his way to save Darnay, he walks the city streets, and the narrator claims "It was the settled manner of a tired man, who had wandered and struggled and got lost, but who at length struck into his road and saw its end" (342). That passage suggests the end of the adultery plot, the end of wandering and the substitution of a firm goal (the road's end) for the dilatory travails he has indulged in so far. The road's end is still clouded in secrecy for the reader: Carton arrives secretly ("who could that be . . . who must not be seen" [309]), plots secretly (he has "business . . . in his secret mind" [327]), and, whatever is in his mind, he "never mentioned Lucie's name" (373). He progresses in silence through the complicated plot of substituting himself for Darnay and dying his death, but he nonetheless transmits one message: he kisses the unconscious Lucie, and "The child, who was nearest him, told them afterwards, and told her grandchildren when she was a handsome old lady, that she heard him say, 'A life you love.'" (366). She repeats, unknowingly, the promise he had made in his earlier scene with Lucie, and it is the daughter who becomes the fulfillment of their secret memory-pact.

But Carton is not satisfied with one child or one inheritance: his final vision is of Lucie "with a child upon her bosom, who bears my name"; of himself "hold[ing] a sanctuary in their hearts, and in the hearts of their descendants, generations hence"; of "that child who lay upon her bosom and who bore my name, a man winning his way up in that path of life which once was mine" (404). And finally, Carton sees *that* child become a man ("foremost of just judges and honoured men") bringing "a boy of my name, with a forehead that I know and golden hair, to this place – then fair to look upon, with not a trace of this day's disfigurement." The figure he summons, a child with his name and Lucie's face, the child of a child she doesn't have yet, will repair the disfigurement: the child who is somehow theirs will not only redeem the legal profession (no small feat in a Dickens novel) but restore the beauty of history, making the hideous fair to look upon, as well as justly judged. If Carton's final historical vision is to "see the evil of this time and of the previous time of which this is the natural birth, gradually making expiation for itself and wearing out," he must conjure up a rather unnatural birth to carry out that redemption of France, the family, history itself.

This fantasy of male birth through adulterous passion is, however, far from all-conclusive. Carton seems to capture all narrative authority to himself through his heroic self-sacrifice and his posthumous narration, even dictating his suicide note to the hapless and impotent Darnay, but the text presents several important counter-arguments to his version of history. Carton's final prophecies, his (the text's) closing words are variously imagined as passing through not masculine but feminine ventriloquism, and invoke again a literary authority slightly at odds with Dickens's intense overidentification with the adulterous, wasted, heroic ne'er do well and his theatrical end.[28] The conclusion of *A Tale of Two Cities* makes its way through a series of spectacular women, and invokes a literary inheritance far different from that of the lone hero facing his death and his possible erasure from history.

Carton's valedictory message is introduced by the narrator's invocation of the most famous scribbling woman who faced the guillotine, Madame Roland:

One of the most remarkable sufferers by the same axe – a woman – had asked at the foot of the same scaffold, not long before, to be allowed to write down the thoughts that were inspiring her. If [Carton] had given an utterance to his, and they were prophetic, they would have been these. . . . (404)

What follows is a series of visions: "I see . . . long ranks of the new oppressors who have risen on the destruction of the old perishing by this retributive instrument"; "I see the lives for which I lay down my life, peaceful, useful, prosperous and happy," "I see Her with a child upon her bosom, who bears my name . . ." and so on (404). It is odd enough that these meditations are invoked in such a dreamy way, with the narrator's series of conditional clauses: there is no guarantee either that Carton had a vision or that it had the truth of prophecy.[29] What is more remarkable is that they are invoked through Madame Roland, whose prison memoir was one of the central documents of the revolution circulating in England. When Carton goes to "give utterance," he follows in the path of an unfinished manuscript by a woman writer – one whose last letter, interestingly enough, was to her daughter, and whose last note, in her memoir, was of her pleasure that her property would, upon her death, pass to that daughter. Not only the novelist's vision, but the vision of "a beautiful city" rising from the ashes is handed over, by extension, to a prophetic, propertied, "remarkable" woman.

The text dilutes still further Carton's closural authority – or rather, dilates it through the gaze of another prophetic woman. In the tumbril on his way to the guillotine, Carton meets a young seamstress who was in prison with Darnay, the one fellow-sufferer to recognize that Carton is someone else. She asks if he dies "for him" – "Yes," answers Carton, "and his wife and child," repeating again his earlier promise to Lucie (384). The seamstress's fate is more interesting: when he asks her what she is in prison for, she answers "Plots." "But," she goes on, "who would think of plotting with a poor little weak creature like me?" (384). The question opens up the novel once more: like the guillotine's specular display of the heads of small women and their beautiful children, the seamstress's plaintive cry comments on Dickens's own narrative as the spectacle of the suffering of "poor little weak creatures." But yet once more, it also suggests the ways that the revolution (with its blurring of public and private, familial and historical) *is* a plot by poor little weak creatures: in a world where Madame Defarge's knitting sends many to their deaths, what is so innocent about being a seamstress?

Most interesting of all, at the end of this rather reactionary novel of political change and upheaval, the seamstress unexpectedly gets one of the most radical statements the novel allows itself. As they ride to their deaths, she asks Carton a question:

"I have a cousin, an only relative and an orphan like myself whom I love very dearly. . . . Poverty parted us, and she knows nothing of my fate – for I cannot write – and if I could, how should I tell her! It is better as it is. . . . If the Republic really does good to the poor, and they come to be less hungry, and in all ways to suffer less, she may live a long time: she may even live to be old. . . . Do you think . . . that it will seem long to me, while I wait for her in the better land where I trust both you and I will be mercifully sheltered?" (403)

For the first time in many pages in the novel, someone reminds readers of why the revolution was necessary: the Republic could do good to the poor, and they could come to be less hungry. There was a brief, similar moment when Darnay is walked to La Force prison, and is suddenly invisible, for at this moment, that an aristocrat, "a man in good clothes should be going to prison, was no more remarkable than that a labourer in working clothes should be going to work" (283). When the seamstress turns to history she connects her own imminent death with the labor of Dr. Manette at his shoe-making and Jerry Cruncher at his "resurrection": for Dickens, the Revolution is in part the terror, and in part, the problem of social order and labor, much more in the vein of *Hard Times* (and of Thomas Carlyle's social writings) than of romantic historical fiction. Carton, characteristically, ignores that part of the seamstress's question, and assures her they are going to a place where "there is no Time . . . and no trouble there." Like his final invocation of the "better rest" he goes to, his response gestures at a space outside narrative, history, memory, where all revolutions, including the normal revolutions of plot, will cease to matter – although, of course, his prophecy depends on the transmission of his historical message through Lucie's as-yet unborn children.

The *seamstress's* final invocation of vatic authorship, however, suggests something else: "for I cannot write – and if I could, how should I tell her!" Neither Lucie nor Madame Defarge, the text's twin "daughters of time," is allowed such a prophetic moment, and the novel ends by suggesting that the events of these dark days remain unreportable – in contrast to Sydney, the daughter is more hesitant to claim the authority over history, and as I have suggested, her inheritance is troubled by its affiliation with the other terrors of the novel. "That story," in the words of *Dombey and Son*'s narrator, "never goes about": like the good daughter, it must here remain domesticated. But *A Tale of Two Cities* hints at something more: that not male prophecy but female property will go on to tell a different story, and that the daughter's hand will write another revolution. If she could write, this novel suggests, the daughter would have *much* to tell, and in a letter to another (even if unknown) woman, would open a different account book of history.

If the role of the adultery plot in all these novels has been to adjust the balances of social order, and return everyone to a rightful (righted, written) place within plot and history, the daughter's story has been the fulcrum of that balancing act, whether in the circus of *Hard Times* or the carnival of the French Revolution. In *Bleak House*, however, when the daughter claims a different "portion," and the mother bestows a different inheritance, female writing will offer another story, one that as yet cannot be told ("How should I tell?"), but will come to have its own revolutionary matrix.

PART THREE

The daughter's portion

CHAPTER FOUR

Bleak House *and the dead mother's property*

The specter of female inheritance walks a revolutionary path in *Bleak House*. The novel brings together the strands we have been tracing – adultery, history, and writing; more explicitly, it takes up the plot of the portionless daughter, playing these larger questions through the bastard daughter's quest for her legacy. But *Bleak House* imagines a different form of inheritance. Here, inheritance is not the father's name, the father's word, or even the father's house; instead, it is the mother's, it is dispossessed and homeless, and it is the daughter's revenge. The questions of history and adultery that circulated throughout *Hard Times* and *A Tale of Two Cities* come home in this novel to what is truly a bleak house, emptying out the inheritance plot and the lines of property, to ask what is property; what is the role of the will; and what can the dispossesed, illegitimate daughter inherit? In *Bleak House*, the daughter stages her own revolution: her recapture of weapons of writing, which in this novel are the weapons of property. *Bleak House* is the novel the orphan daughter writes to reclaim her property; more than that, it is the autobiographical fiction the bastard daughter writes to ask, "who killed my mother?"

In *Bleak House*'s split narration, however, Esther Summerson, the novel's bastard daughter, seems initially to stand apart from the work of the law plot – which in *Bleak House* seems to be the work of critique, for the novel constitutes English literature's most extended attack on the legal system that determines the inheritance of property. The novel is about, to the extent that any novel this long and this divided is about any one thing, a suit that is caught in Chancery, in the only equity court in the land.[1] The suit is about a will – or, to quote John Jarndyce, who refuses to be an active suitor to it, it was about a will when it was about anything at all. In the present the will, as John Jarndyce puts it, is "a dead letter": "through years and years, and lives and lives, everything goes on, constantly beginning over and over again, and nothing ever ends. And we can't get out of the suit on any terms, for we are made parties to it, and *must be* parties to it, whether we like it or not" (88–89). This ungainly suit is everywhere as the novel begins. The famous first sentences, "London. Michaelmas term lately over, and the Lord Chancellor sitting in Lincoln's Inn Hall" place us before the law; the passage that follows ("Fog everywhere. Fog up the river, where it flows . . . fog down the river, where it rolls . . .") ends "at the very heart of the fog, sits the Lord High Chancellor in his High Court of Chancery . . ." (5–6).

The first chapter closes with the story (proper) beginning, as two suitors, a boy and a girl, stand before the Lord Chancellor waiting to be awarded to a guardian, John Jarndyce; the next chapter takes us into the world of fashion, and another petitioner in the case, the lofty and lovely Lady Dedlock; only the third chapter seems to take us out of it, with the introduction of the novel's heroine, and other (first-person) narrator, Esther Summerson, a modest young woman whose opening, "I have a great deal of difficulty in beginning to write my portion of these pages, for I know I am not clever" (17) is as far removed as anything could be from the magisterial slowness of Chancery – but whose first chapter ends, as did the first of the novel, with the boy and girl, Richard Carstone and Ada Clare, before the lord chancellor, at the very heart of the fog.[2]

This is the uncanny doubleness readers have noticed throughout the novel, but it puts into question Esther's relationship to the legal (public) world of the novel. The novel, that is, seems to pose, and then collapse, some essential differences. The third-person narrator tells us of the law, of London, of wills and inheritance and procedure, of slowness; Esther, whose "I" shatters the complacency of those initial chapters, tells that other story of inheritance of maternal disgrace; a story of origins, unlike the will, in which the quest for knowledge of maternity and paternity is personal, individual, affective rather than functional. The question of what Esther's inheritance is to be (one, in the novel's terms, of fear and disgrace, or of love and connection) seems light-years (as the crow flies) from the elaborations of the "maces, bags, and purses" of Chancery (9) – a question, to quote the name of her first chapter, of "A Progress," rather than the circular motions of a Chancery suit. As Esther herself tells us, early on, she is "no party in the suit" (52).

But Esther's disingenuousness (her position outside the law) is the novel's central trick. As the plot proceeds, we learn that Esther *is*, indirectly, a party in the suit. The seemingly random second chapter, which finds the beautiful and icy Lady Dedlock reading the papers from the Jarndyce suit, and unintentionally starting on recognizing a familiar handwriting, places Lady Dedlock in both the will plot and an adultery plot; the handwriting is that of Esther's absent father, Captain Hawdon, now living, secretly, as "Nemo," the law-writer.[3] Lady Dedlock's insistence on staying in the suit is not her husband's reason, which is that it is a "slow, expensive, British, constitutional kind of thing" but her own: it was the only property that she brought into the marriage. And among the names in the suit, we learn early, are Carstone, Clare, Dedlock, and Barbary – the name of Esther's supposed godmother, in fact, her aunt, Lady Dedlock's sister.[4] *Both* parts of the narration, however circuitously, are "In Chancery," and it is female curiosity about property that brings the connection to light.

The text goes to considerable trouble to mask this double plot of property; Esther, in her narrative, never makes it explicit, though much of the evidence – including that last piece, about the names – appears in her narrative, in ways I will return to later. Rather, she clings to the division with which the novel begins: that unlike the "Chancery" narration, her narration is personal, is familial, is about powerlessness.[5] Her stylistic quirks, as a narrator, encourage this reading. Esther is modest, she is coy, she is indirect, she has a strong tendency to veer into the parenthetical. Throughout, she expresses only anger that she is "obliged to write all this about myself!" but assures us (and herself) that "my little body will soon fall into the background now" (27). She seems to incorporate the worst of female self-presentation in her discourse, and in her relations (of all sorts) to others – the only person to whom she speaks firmly is herself, when admonishing herself to "collect herself," "remember herself," to repress emotion or suppress anger. If, as D. A. Miller has noted, Esther keeps her place only by her constant striving to earn it, so she also keeps her social place (as ward, as the "person in authority" at Bleak House) by struggling to earn that, and by never questioning it – including the strategic silence she maintains about her family: her origins, her relations, her place within the suit.[6] The "place" she accepts is one that the split narration seems to need as well: it thrives on the contrast between that magisterial (a.k.a. Dickensian) third-person narrator, who dares to address the "lords and gentlemen" of England (572), to speak with Carlylean tenderness to Jo as "thou," to call on the forces of night and apocalypse, that voice of complete authority and Esther's still, small voice – the voice of the least powerful person in the novel who is still capable (as the crossing-sweeper Jo and the diminutive servant Charley are not) of penning a narrative. Esther's allotted portion of these pages, in this model, might be answered by the Pardiggle children, each of them condemned to an enforced charity; Dickens describes how the youngest, Alfred, is forced to contribute his mite to the anti-tobacco (and by extension, since his mite is his whole allowance, anti-pastry) league the "Bonds of Joy." As the eldest child demands the shilling he has been "boned" out of, he cries out in frustration, "Why do you call it *my* allowance, and never let me spend it?" (97) Esther Summerson might make a similar cry.

But we might question Esther's relational and legal powerlessness when we turn back not just to her modes of narration, but to the fact that it is Esther's "relations" that connect the two narratives – both her familial relations and the stories she relates to us. It is her little body, with its annoying refusal to "fall" out of the novel, that connects Chancery and family, and the two models of inheritance the book proposes, the one of property, the other of affection. While "Jarndyce and Jarndyce" represents a material property (or a relatively material one: its only representative in the novel is "Tom All Alone's," itself an uneasy syn-ecdoche for Tom Jarndyce, who blew his brains out waiting for the law's resolution), Esther's seems to be a moral one. As her religious aunt warned her, the sins of the fathers will be visited on the children, and "[she herself] is [her] mother's disgrace, and [her] mother [hers]" (19). The fulfillment of this promise is that the daughter will come to under-stand, and live again, her mother's sin; that she will come into the prop-erty of her own disgrace. It would seem, that is, that that plot could be resolved only through the mother's moral redemption, and through her bequest to her daughter.

But both these plots are unexpectedly linked by the mother's desire to own property and to transmit it to her daughter. In the first plot, Lady Dedlock's presence in the Chancery suit is what brings her supposedly dead lover's handwriting (his distinctive legal hand) to her attention; it is her start of surprise that brings her guilty secret to the lawyer Tulkinghorn's attention, and starts off the plot.[7] In the other, more obvi-ously, it is the daughter's need to find her mother and reread her own (sexually charged) inheritance that will motivate the plot, and lead to Dickens's customary genealogical response: that "I was as innocent of my birth as a queen of hers" (454). Esther is somehow in the suit, and out of it; she inherits and does not inherit her mother's sin. For Esther's story, too, is "about a will," when it is "about anything at all" (88). The story of story-telling which is *Bleak House* is not the ridiculousness of property, but Esther's *lack* of relationship to it. This is presented in the novel literally in a whisper: when Esther goes before the Lord

Chancellor, he asks if "Miss Summerson is not related to any party in the cause," and Mr Kenge "leant over before it was quite said, and whispered," and the Lord Chancellor "listened, nodded twice or thrice, turned over more leaves, and did not look towards me again, until we were going away" (32). The whisper re-enters the text in a conversation Esther does not hear, when Mrs. Rachael, now Mrs. Chadband, asked about "Miss Summerson" says, "*I* call her Esther Summerson . . . There was no Missing of the girl in my time" (242). Her real name (Hawdon) goes unspoken, but her illegitimacy is implicit in every snub enacted by Mrs. Woodcourt, whose invocation of the aristocracy of Wales (Morgan ap Kerrig and the poetry of "the Mewlinwillinwodd" [365]) is a constant source of pain to Esther, and underwrites her refusal to speak aloud her love for Allan Woodcourt. Indeed, Esther's proud assertion that "I was as innocent of my birth as a queen of hers . . ." (with its invocation of the illicit Queen Esther, Jewish interloper, also implicit) seems as much a spirit-booster as a deeply held tenet (454).

But Esther's lawlessness suggests several important things for any discussion of the daughter's inheritance. The first is that, in the eyes of the law, she did have specific rights: in particular, a right to support from the mother and "reputed father." If the "putative father" or "lewd mother" run away from the parish, their "rents, goods, and chattels" may be seized to bring up the "said bastard child."[8] (Since the obligation to maintain illegitimate children passed on to a woman's husband, this raises the interesting question of whether or not Sir Leicester has unknowingly been shirking a legal responsibility for Esther for all the years of his marriage.) But the other element of importance is that Esther has no right to inherit anything – in fact, she has no right to any *name*: she is, as the law says, "nobody's child" – as indeed, in this novel, being the daughter of Nemo, she is "nobody's daughter."

If Esther's story is legally a "bastard" narration (another version of "nobody's story," told by "nobody's daughter") then it raises the question not only of what property Esther can inherit (legally, none) but of what property her narrative can possess. The novel is everywhere obsessed with the alienability of property and of identity, which it insists on aligning at every moment. At its most haunting, the body itself turns into portable property, and parts of the body can no longer speak the story of the "whole" body. The eeriest of these moments comes when Allan Woodcourt asks Krook, the rag-and-bone dealer in used, broken, and scrap items, about the identity of his boarder, the now-dead Nemo. Woodcourt asks who Nemo might have been when he was "somebody," for he had the look of someone distinguished about him, someone who had had a "fall." Says Krook, "You might as well ask me to describe the ladies whose heads of hair I have got in sacks downstairs" (127). This connection between the body, less real than the women's hair, and the past, less real than Nemo's body, and both as somehow uncapturable, suggests the dangers of a disembodied identity that reign in this novel – dangers suggested no less when bits of Krook's body, in the various forms of oil, ash, and dust, begin to float back into his neighborhood after his combustion, leaving only a suggestion of "chops." But Krook's analogy, in this novel, seems even more ominous for women, who can be more easily separated from that "identity." When Krook first meets Esther and Ada, he picks up one tress of the latter's hair and says "Here's lovely hair! I have got three sacks of ladies' hair below, but none so beautiful and fine as this" (50). In the manuscript, curiously, appeared the line "I buy hair," a line that marks the hair as a form of female property, but that direct cash-nexus disappears; nonetheless, hair continues to suggest something at once individual and alienable about female identity. Esther customarily identifies Ada as behind her "halo" of golden hair – indeed, the "rich golden hair" opened Esther's first description of her "darling girl" (30), and when Ada confesses her love for Richard, her "bright hair" is all Esther can see. At the height of Esther's fever, her hair becomes alienable as well, for "it had been in danger" of being cut off (444); we learn this only when Esther lifts the hair, which has become a "veil," in order to see her altered face. The hair, which is still "long and thick," is at once the thing that is *not* altered, and something that has become alien, a "veil of my own hair," suggesting the veils Esther raises and lowers throughout the novel, as she tries to read the way the world reads her "new face." But as the hair is alienated, made a veil, made a reminder of Esther's alteration, so it also becomes a reminder both of Ada's permanent "halo," and the alienability of female property, like the bags of hair Krook can dispose of, sell, buy, but not "read," something that can no longer describe or denote identity or history.

However alienable her identity may become, Esther never thinks of selling her hair – but during the scene in which Krook imagines acquiring Ada's for his collection, Esther learns something of even more usefulness to her propertyless self, something that suggests she might have a different relationship to the property wars that frame her text. As he is introduced to "the wards in Jarndyce," Krook shows off his knowledge of the case: there was a Carstone, a Clare, a Barbary, and a Dedlock, he lists, running through what is of course also a list of characters for the novel (51). Ada and Richard can be forgiven their complacency upon hearing this story; they know themselves wards in Jarndyce and "in Chancery." It is the relation of this to Esther, whom one character calls Fitz-Jarndyce, that remains a puzzle: why does Esther not ask, since she knows by now that her aunt's name was Barbary, "what is my relationship to this suit?" Does it never occur to her that she, too, might be a ward in Jarndyce – and, hence, that she might be spared the burden of jingling her keys, repeating her duty to herself, and being the novel's "Dame Durden"?

This portion of her pages, however, suggests that her interest even in her own secrets falls victim to her terrible discretion – or it would, if her narration were any reliable guide to her real interests or desires. The fact that Esther doesn't say something means very little: her narrative is made up almost entirely of delays, gaps, absent disclosures, coy ellipses. After all, she never refers directly to her love for Allan Woodcourt; she never criticizes directly any of those who are cruel to her; she depicts her narrative not as one of moving towards prosperity, but moving towards emotional security: her quest, as she movingly reports, is to "win some love to myself" (20). The narrative's ambition throughout is the hoarding of affection, not acquiring worldly goods. And Esther's emotional bank balance seems to depend on her not asking certain questions: every time her guardian asks if she has anything she wants to ask, she replies, immediately, no; and certainly, she would be a very bad Dame Durden, and not advance too far in her struggles to win love, if she were to ask John Jarndyce if she stands to win any property from the suit.

But *Bleak House* suggests a range of female responses to property, often less modest than Esther's obligatory evasions. Lady Dedlock has no such scruples, and indeed has a very different relationship to property in general. In this, her closest ally would seem to be an earlier Lady Dedlock, whose act of marital and political defiance haunts the novel. This Lady Dedlock is a rebel, aiding the forces of Cromwell in the English Civil War against the propertied interests of her husband, Sir Morbury Dedlock. She is motivated in part by family feeling (her favorite brother was killed by the Royalists, by a relative of Sir Morbury), but she is also in revolt against her own situation, and she has taken political power into her own hands: she has stolen into her husband's stables, the pride of Chesney Wold, to wound the horse that will carry money to the royalist supporters. When her husband discovers her and tries to stop her she is injured, and lamed for life. For the rest of her days she walks along the terrace of Chesney Wold, "up and down, up and down, up and down, in sun and shadow," until she drops to the ground, and says, "fixedly and coldly," to her husband: "I will die here where I have walked. And I will walk here, though I am in my grave. I will walk here, until the pride of this house is humbled. And when calamity, or when disgrace is coming to it, let the Dedlocks listen for my step!" (84). These steps do echo, and are listened to, throughout the novel. When the reader first hears the story (by a "fast-darkening" window [83]) we are told that where the sound is clearest is from "my lady's pillow" (85), from the room of the woman whose pride, coldness and fixedness link her most clearly with the first Lady Dedlock – the present Lady Dedlock, Honoria, Esther's mother.

For Honoria, the novel's living ghost, the earlier Lady Dedlock provides what Derrida might term a "hauntology," a specter both dogging and designing her path.[9] The first Lady Dedlock's story is important for its ability to foretell, both shadowing and foreshadowing Honoria's own "story for twilight" (149). For the latter, as well, sexual transgression and property transgression come together, both in her (pre-narrative) adultery, and in her desire to pursue her "own" property. Even her names are linked to both sexual sin and political realities: Honoria, her "honor," we learn very soon is a sham, for she has already born a child out of wedlock; the second, her husband's name, is no less a joke, for the Dedlocks are already dead, both a dead issue (no child will come from this marriage) and dead to the history-of-the-present, for they are irrelevant to the country they presume to lead. (Indeed, the scenes that surround Sir Leicester are marks of that morbidity, the alphabetic parody surrounding those upper-class flunkies Boodle, Coodle, and Doodle who supposedly rule the country itself arriving fairly dead on the page.) Even more, her name suggests that she will not survive the novel's lethal maternal melodrama. As we follow the twists of plot (the threat of the revelation of her secret; her encounter with Esther; her involvement in the murder of Tulkinghorn) it becomes clearer and clearer that the novel needs her to fulfill her name and die; like the earlier Lady Dedlock, she can only walk in the same steps over and over, till the plot has done with her. For that reason, her death ends the book, and we are reading for that death, but her death walks a complicated path.

The heroine who walks through history is never far from Dickens's imagination, from Nancy's wandering shadows in *Oliver Twist* to Madame Defarge's confident tread through the streets of revolutionary France in *A Tale of Two Cities*. But since at least *Dombey and Son*, those wanderings have been linked to female adultery, and the daughter's dangerous alliance to the mother's illicit trek. The fear has been that the daughter, too, would take to the streets, leaving the path of domestic virtue. *Bleak House* raises some of the same anxieties, as Esther Summerson becomes more and more like her wandering mother: in the novel's most uncanny moment, she treads the Ghost Walk at Chesney Wold, realizing, at that moment, that she herself is the doom of Dedlocks, come to foreshadow her mother's death and her own deprivation. But the daughter (here, at once virtuous and adulterous; the daughter, and her own mother) never walks alone: the story of the earlier Lady Dedlock walked a similarly uncanny path, from Mrs Rouncewell, the housekeeper, to the maid, Rosa.

Soon after Mrs Rouncewell announces that Lady Dedlock would have been better for having a daughter, Rosa is taken up by Lady Dedlock, becoming the specular double of the absent daughter, Esther. But Rosa is also the double of Hortense, the beautiful and fierce French lady's maid, who in turn is the double of (and occasional stand-in for) Honoria; when Hortense leaves Lady Dedlock's service, she offers herself instead to Esther, who refuses her ("I keep no maid –") only to accept, at the end of the same chapter, the services of yet another double-daughter, the girl Charley, who is given to Esther as a "gift" by John Jarndyce. Charley, with her round eyes and sweet manner, seems again to double both Esther herself, the round-eyed orphan, and this chain of maidservants and mistresses the novel has served up – along with Caddy Jellyby, the novel's angriest daughter, and even Ada Clare, the novel's most gentle. This chain of female resemblance (caught up somehow in the indistinguishability of mistress and maid, of mother and daughter) is unleashed in the original scene between Mrs. Rouncewell and Rosa, not by any of the principals, but by the *portrait* of Lady Dedlock, and by the curiosity of the young man Guppy, who is drawn on equally by his fascination with the beautiful Lady Dedlock and his love for her (illegitimate, secret, unknowing) daughter, Esther, whose inheritance he wants to uncover and in whose service he weaves some of the webs of suspicion surrounding her mother. In Guppy's mind, resemblance equals inheritance and inheritance leads to property, but in this novel, it also leads back to history. When Hortense makes her offer of service to Esther, Esther says she "seemed to bring visibly before me some woman from the streets of Paris in the reign of terror" (286); earlier, as she walked away from Esther, walking barefooted through the grass to remind herself of the vow of vengeance she has taken against Esther's mother, the keeper's wife, watching her walk, claims she is walking through the water as if "she fancies it's blood" (231).

In the figure of Esther and her lost mother, as in all of the doublings and mirrorings I have cited ("there's three of them, then"), the versions of femininity Dickens has elsewhere tried to polarize come radically back together, but what they repeatedly suggest is the loss of that first dyad, the severing of the mother and daughter. As Honoria is lied to, told her daughter is dead, so is Esther deceived, told her mother died giving birth to her. All the doubles the novel (and the novel-writing daughter) acquires are an attempt to fill that empty space at the narrative's heart. The real pursuit in this novel is of that other inheritance: the mother's love, the daughter's embrace, the absent (now icy) kiss they never shared. That scene can only be replayed as a Gothic scene of return in *Bleak House*, but it comes back in its most powerful form as the fantasy of female inscription.[10] In this novel, as in *Dombey and Son*, the mother's property is that torn, fragmented letter Dombey destroys and Florence never sees: it is the mother's legacy that will restore the daughter to her lost property (her lost self), and that property is writing.

It is never clear in *Bleak House* what kind of property the daughter could hope to inherit. In this Chancery-infected world, as critics have noted since the book's initial publication, property is figured as a graphic chaos, documents that multiply as meaning slips further and further away.[11] Relationship is figured by the repetitions of names (Jarndyce *and* Jarndyce) and the disintegration of homes: to be "in Chancery" is to be in decay. To be "in Chancery" is also to be entirely in the place of writing: what distinguishes Chancery from other courts is that there is no oral testimony within it; all testimony is in the form of endlessly duplicated pieces of paper, and no suitor is ever without his or her documents, behind which (we must imagine) stand real properties – however decayed, lost, misplaced, misused. And yet, it is in the nature of these documents never to come to anything: much as the suit itself "melts away," dissolving itself in its own costs, so the documents shred and multiply in the "ecologically terrifying" world of Chancery.[12] Within the other world of female inheritance, relationship seems to be figured in what I have identified as a more Gothic (and more Byzantine) fashion: wandering women, fractured resemblance (Esther seeing her face in her mother's as "in a broken glass" [225]), the series of portraits and portrait-like doubles invoked here. But the particular form male property takes in this novel (documents, wills, testimonies) has its parallel in the forms of separate female property: narrative secrets, contagion, resemblance, a bastard line of property.

One final, uncanny return of Esther's mother suggests the relationship of tattered documents and female inheritance. Miss Flite, the
Chancery petitioner who carries in her reticule her "documents" (in her
case, mere scraps of paper) comes to see Esther after Esther's illness.
Miss Flite tells Esther the story of a "lady with a veil inquiring at a
cottage" after Esther, and taking with her a handkerchief because it was
Esther's (438). The lady (whom we recognize by her disguise, one worn
earlier when she visits Hawdon's grave, and worn later by Hortense to
frame Honoria for Tulkinghorn's murder) is Lady Dedlock, following
the trail of her missing daughter; the handkerchief had covered the dead
baby of the brickmaker's wife, a dead baby whose presence recreates the
presence of the baby Lady Dedlock took for dead (Esther herself) all
those years ago. But Miss Flite offers another explanation:

"in *my* opinion . . . she's the Lord Chancellor's wife. He's married, you know.
And I understand she leads him a terrible life. Throws his lordship's papers into
the fire, my dear, if he won't pay the jeweller!" (439)

Miss Flite's anecdote accomplishes something the rest of the novel can
only hint at: the destruction of all the documents of Chancery in a blaze
of fire, fed by the hands of an angry woman.[13] But the motive she
imputes to the Lord Chancellor's wife returns us to the world of female
property, reminding us that under the laws that govern marriage, women
were incapable of making a binding contract, and a husband bore the
responsibility of paying all his wife's debts – including the jeweller's bill.
The connection this narrative makes between female allurement, female
property, and female anger has its darker relationship to Chancery as
well: it is at this moment in the novel that Miss Flite tells her own story
of being "drawn into" Chancery, and the story of father, her brother,
and finally her sister, "drawn. Hush! Never ask to what!" (440). The
sister's destruction, presumably through prostitution, carries us back to
that realm of sexual transgression outside the law – and to the transgression that caused Esther's birth, the adultery the novel never narrates, but
that Miss Flite alludes to, subtly, in her way of naming Esther: it is she
who calls her "my dear Fitz-Jarndyce," invoking the age-old name of
bastards in English law.

The tale of the writing of female property (fragmented, charred,
impassioned) is one best told, as *Bleak House* is, by a female bastard: it is
the story I have been telling here, of Honoria's surprise at seeing her
dead lover's handwriting on a legal document; of her interest in pro-
tecting "the only property" (15) she brings into her marriage (the "piece"

that binds her, and binds Esther, into "Jarndyce and Jarndyce"); the story of Esther's different version of the monstrous suit. Within the story Esther is telling, the story figured psychically as the story of the dead mother and the dead child, there is a different story of inheritance: one we can follow only through the fragments, torn documents, the story of resemblance written on the wandering "face" of the female plot. Where it leads is not only a different version of *Bleak House*, but a different version of property altogether: the daughter's quest for her maternal legacy.

It is not clear, from the beginning of Esther's quest, what form that bequest could take. On one hand, *Bleak House* presents all property as abstraction, tied up in a mystical suit that hasn't been about anything for so long that no one ever formulates the property it (as it were) entails. On the other, property is of the basest and most material kind: hair, bone, old clothes, old paper, broken hearts. There is a kind of technicolor horror to property in *Bleak House*, as if a cliche of criticism (that identity is property) were being materialized before our eyes: the self is no more than the propertied collection of its body parts, and the novel's job is to accumulate these parts, to remorph the hair, bones, and clothes of Krook's shop, the memory fragments of Esther's past, and remake a person; narratives of redemption becoming like pawn tickets, as the coherent social identity is reassembled. In the novel's economy of identity, Esther's fragmented aggrieved self seems to be redressed through the dissolution (into hair and dress) of her mother, a salvaged, perhaps thrift-shop identity.

In such a world, what kind of property is the self? As in the pun that runs throughout Margaret Atwood's *The Handmaid's Tale*, "I compose myself," the self in *Bleak House*, no less than elsewhere in Dickens, is a made thing, composed, patchwork, patched together. When it falls apart, it falls (back) into pieces, like the shattered brains of Tom Jarndyce, or the house in Tom-all-Alone's; it fails, one organ at a time, first movement, then breath, then sight, then speech, then the heart, which breaks last and hardest.

Esther's narration proposes that the self similarly dissolves, decomposes, recomposes, into its many names, like Esther, Dame Durden, Cobweb, Mrs. Shipton, the Little Old Woman . . . so many nicknames, Esther says, "my own name soon became quite lost among them" (90). So, too, when left to itself, the self can only talk to itself, saying "Esther, Esther, Esther, Duty, my dear!" (76), shaking the keys like so many bells ringing itself on. No wonder, we might speculate, Esther talks so much to herself – by midway through the novel, she is the only person remaining who calls her (self) by her own name. The only question still to be asked, in this version of the novel, is, by what name does her mother call her? And to which "name" does Lady Dedlock leave the property she has, in the course of the novel that courts her death, collected?

The silence at the heart of their story makes it difficult to imagine any real inheritance for Esther. The mother–daughter plot of *Bleak House* is one that, in many ways, dare not speak its name: if the illegitimate daughter can gain a name, Blackstone's *Commentaries* says, only by "reputation," and Esther loses hers in the Jarndyce household, where she is companion, spinster, hired friend, and surrogate daughter, under what name can the mother and daughter travel? Unspoken names follow them both: even the name Barbary, the adopted name of Esther's aunt, the woman who raises Esther in shame and silence, cannot be either uttered or dismissed. Although it is a false name, it appears in the legal documents that link Esther and Honoria to the Jarndyce and Jarndyce suit, and Lady Dedlock, asked by the clerk, Guppy, if she knows the names Hawdon and Barbary, agrees that she had "heard the name(s)" (362); and yet, Barbary is a name that John Jarndyce, who knew both Honoria and her sister years ago, did not recognize.[14] The name of Esther's father, Captain Hawdon, is never spoken in her presence and is only hinted at in a letter to her at the book's end[15]: Esther has only two meetings with her father's ghost, the first, when she receives a letter from the legal firm Kenge and Carboys in her father's handwriting (an association we can make only retroactively, when she sees the same hand in Nemo's advertisement for legal writing); the second, when she comes to Krook's warehouse to visit the mad Miss Flite, and feels a chill walking by the room of her dead father, where she heard "that there had been a sudden death there" (178). The Esther who writes "her portion" of *Bleak House* would know who had died there, and what his relationship was to her, but her prose registers that paternal loss only as proleptic chill ("I felt as if the room had chilled me," [178] she says, in a stunning displacement), another characteristically anachronistic shudder that runs across the text.

While the father's death cannot be narrated by Esther directly, her mother's death is told repeatedly, in a prognostic series of losses. Lady Dedlock's death is suggested not only by her name and by her prophetic absence from her daughter's life, but by the corpses that come before: the dead baby in the brickmaker's house; the death of Miss Barbary, while reading the biblical passage about the woman taken in adultery;

Ada's death to Esther, when she marries Richard and leaves Bleak House; the death of Esther's "identity" in the death of her beauty and her "old face." No less an authority than Lady Dedlock herself has warned Esther to regard her as already dead, and in her inability to explain clearly why she cannot abandon her frozen life and join her loving daughter, she has (it would seem) made herself, if anything, more dead: the scene of recognition and parting between the two women could be read as a typical scene of Dickensian negotiation, one in which (we might be tempted to pun) the two sides are literally deadlocked. As at the end of *Dombey and Son*, when Florence pleads for any continued contact with her "beautiful mama," so here, the adulterous mother resists the contagion of contact with her daughter, as if it were equally deadly to them both (as indeed, it almost proves in this novel); as if they could not exist in the same narrative space.

The meeting between them highlights the scripted nature of their relationship, and the importance that (secret) documents play in their haunted family. Esther narrates the meeting, which is framed by the scene of her illness and the scene of her reunion with her beloved Ada. If the illness removes the signs that linked her with her mother (scarring the face that is their chief connection), and her passionate meeting with Ada restores to her the love her mother denies her (as they cling to each other on the floor of her room), these bookends nonetheless frame a scene of reading and writing the mother–daughter plot that is worth attending to, one that moves us closer to an understanding of the property of maternal narrative in this novel. For in this scene, Esther performs a rare act of daughterly piracy: she meets with her mother, who throws herself at Esther's feet; both cry, both exchange stories of loss; and at the end, her mother (like other lost mothers in Dickens, most particularly Edith Dombey) hands her a manuscript – a manuscript we never see, a text that Esther describes to the "unknown friend to whom [she] write[s]," the reader, but promptly destroys (777); a story that goes nowhere, that (in *Dombey and Son*'s phrase) never goes about.

By the time Esther meets her mother, she is a shattered version of herself, having survived the illness that left her "a little beside myself, though knowing where I was"; that left her with a "new terror of myself" and a face "very much changed – O very, very much," so "strange" that Esther almost "started back . . . before it" (444–445). The process that began with her misrecognition of herself in her mother ("her face [was], in a confused way, like a broken glass to me, in which I saw scraps of old remembrances" [225]) ends with Esther's face itself confused, made crazy by the scarring and the misremembrances, confronted with the scraps of her mother's letter, which Esther burns, taking care to "consume even its ashes" (453). Given this powerful consumption, the fire that (like Esther's fever state) destroys all traces of the mother's love, what does Esther stand to inherit from her mother, the original of the face in the broken glass?

Honoria Dedlock cannot leave her daughter any property. The laws that governed married women's property in Victorian England, the laws of coverture, insist that a married woman can bequeath only personal property; any will she writes must have the approval of her husband, and that approval can be revoked at any time up until probate. Honoria seems herself to preclude bequeathing anything at all to her daughter: when she leaves Chesney Wold, fearing she is about to be revealed as a fallen woman, disgraced and the disgrace of the Dedlocks, she takes only the clothes on her back, and a watch with which she bribes the brick-maker into letting his wife change clothes with her. With no property with her, she begins her final wanderings, a fierce walk through the England winter – a walk that will mislead Esther and Inspector Bucket into following the wrong woman, until they double back to London, and "follow the other" (689), follow Lady Dedlock, only to arrive and find her dead.

That they find her at all, however, has to do with another curious document she leaves for her daughter. She has left a letter with Guster – a servant whose orphan status and name link her to Esther, and whose habit of falling into "fits" links her to the broader female habit of "falling" that the text identifies. The letter carries within it a chronology: it is written at three stages, as Lady Dedlock grows weaker and nearer death. It is folded roughly "like a letter," directed to Esther "at my guardian's," but it remains unaddressed: it begins "I came to the cottage with two objects," and goes on to recount her wish to see "the dear one" again; in the second fragment, "written at another time," she describes her wandering, and that "I have no purpose but to die." In the final portion, written "at another time . . . [says Esther]. . . . To all appearances, almost in the dark," she adds "I have nothing about me by which I can be recognised. This paper I part with now. The place where I shall lie down, if I can yet get so far, has been often in my mind. Farewell. Forgive" (710). In this last message, written in the darkness of near-death, the mother both makes a final plea, and parts with her paper, with a testimony that seems almost like a testament, one not of leaving possessions *to* anyone, but of having left all possessions behind. The property with which she parts is the paper itself, and the story that she has willed her daughter, as in the earlier autobiographical fragment she wrote, giving it to Esther with the warning to destroy it, for fear the traces of writing might disgrace them both. The mother's last words to her daughter, in short, are of the dangers of women's words.

In a novel obsessed with last wills and testaments (which reads wills not as ends, but beginnings) this "will" takes the place of the "end" of the Chancery suit, which never is resolved. The letter seems to point to a kind of writing the law *cannot* contain: these words are never "posted," but travel in texts handed on between women, from one fallen woman, we might extrapolate, to another. This last letter seems to offer yet another inheritance to Esther, seeming to undo the harshness of Honoria's last meeting with her daughter, at the same time that it bitterly announces the futility of any hope of a further reunion. The last inscription to "the dear one" seems to call Esther by some secret name, to make of the insistent secrecy of the rest of the novel, finally, a gift.[16] For to the extent that any story is property in this novel, Esther owns (or is owned by) the richest secret in the novel, both in what it is worth to others, and what it is worth to her. But its worth, in part, depends on her keeping it private – its real promise, to Esther, is to buy her (back) a mother; its danger, is that in spending (telling), she loses all. So, indeed, in the final search, she must whisper out to Bucket that Honoria is her mother; as if by magic, her mother seems to die with that breath, as if saying were spending after all. In the most materialist reading of the novel, with Honoria's death goes Esther's last link to that monetary inheritance that hangs over the novel like a promise; with it, as well, the promise of the mother's forgiveness for the sin of having been born. And with Honoria go other secrets as well, secrets that, in other novels, would demand a story. In *Bleak House*, exchange offers none of the usual rewards, pleasures, or even revelations: mysteries seem to travel under their own agency, and they have a particular interest in never seeing the light of day. So we might ask, given that code of silence, when Honoria writes her "secret" text to her daughter, encoding her, blanketing her in a silence as profound as the snow that falls over the cold and dead body, now covered only by the hair Esther's hands lift, what message is she sending? What is the maternal property the text wills on?

The answer to that riddle lies in Esther's own narration, in the word that provides the puzzle to the central narratorial question, of who tells the story of *Bleak House*, and why. In answering that question, we come closer to the heart of the novel: the "progress" the bastard daughter makes through the property plot to her own identity, an identity that she forms in the writing of the novel. The word that Esther uses for her own narrative is *portion*: "my portion," she writes, "of these pages." This is the verisimilar crux of the problem of the split narration: Esther seems aware of the third-person narrator, and of the submergence of her narrative within it. And as Robert Newsom has noted, the only way to account for this knowledge is that Esther both is aware of and *is* the third-person narrator. The "other" narrator is aware of her ("While Esther sleeps," begins Chapter VII, following Esther's going "hopefully to bed" at the end Chapter VI) but he does not tell her story; indeed, she attends far more to his concerns (repeating his events) than the other way around.[17] It seems to me entirely possible to read "his" text as "her" imaginings of those scenes from which she is absent: the fact that she refers to herself in the third person within ("while Esther . . .") can be no obstacle to a theory of absent-minded authorship, driven by a woman who is accustomed to thinking of herself as "Old Woman" and "Dame Durden." The third person is a short step from the dissociation that marks much of Esther's self-narration: its flatness, its coolness at moments of stress, its refusal to be the text of female desire we might expect.[18] In fact, one could postulate that in writing the other narrative, Esther has achieved what she claimed she wanted in her own: a text in which her little body will, in fact, "fall into the background."

But what, along either model of narration, is her "portion"? A portion can be, to follow the order of OED definitions, "the part (of anything) allotted or belonging to one person; a share": in that model, Esther's narrative is simply the number of pages she is given to fill, no more, and no less. The question of whether it is allotted or belongs is one we might leave for the moment, taking up the next definition: a portion is "a quantity or allowance of food allotted to, or enough for, one person." This definition is quite "Dickensian," conjuring up Little Dorrit's tiny dinners, or the meals allotted "the Infant Phenomenon" in *Nicholas Nickleby*: it raises even more powerfully the relation of allotment and belonging to, for it offers no guarantee (as, indeed, Esther's portion in life does not) that what is "allotted" is "enough." And if a portion is allotted, what is Esther's sufficient allotment, given that the next definition offered is of "the part or share of an estate given or passing by law to an heir," something we know Esther to be excluded from – as she is from the next, "dowry; a marriage portion." Given the poverty of Esther's hopes of either inheritance or property sufficient for a dowry, we might look with some bitterness on the final of these possible definitions: a portion is "that which is allotted to a person by providence; lot, destiny, fate." Is Esther, in writing "her portion," limited to writing only her destiny, writing only what she has been allotted, and must make the best of?[19] Or is she, following the maternal inscription, *re*writing her inheritance, her dowry, her destiny? Is that act of writing itself her inheritance, her dowry, her destiny?

The end of the novel makes the writing of identity seem even more perilous, and of a less solid nature. After Esther's mother's death, Esther's narrative pauses briefly for an illness that seems to break off authorship all together: after its resumption (Esther repeats herself, beginning twice: "I proceed to other passages of my narrative" [714]) the novel itself seems to have some trouble continuing, though event follows rapidly on event. But the mode of transmission seems to have changed; *Bleak House*, we might say, stutters to its close. As if the novel knows its characters will die, it tries to hold on to its every utterance, repeating itself, echoing itself hollowly: John Jarndyce's mournful repetition of the phrase "Bleak House must learn to take care of itself" (714); Richard's laugh that "had not quite left him . . . but it was like the echo of a joyful sound" (722); the "good night . . . good bye" which Esther makes Allan Woodcourt repeat when she dismisses his proposal (733); the confusion echoed in Esther's repetition that she never guessed Jarndyce's secret resolution to give her to Allan: "But I was never, never, never near the truth" (749). Its most poignant echoes are silent, like Ada's fingers playing restlessly above the piano keys, "going over and over them, without striking any note," fluttering above them in painful pattern (723). For the rest of the novel, it stammers through its hasty deaths, as if *Bleak House* (as John Jarndyce says of his home, Bleak House) is thinning fast. The bodies pile up, or rather, seem to decompose before us, as if hurrying to return to their elements: Lady Dedlock becoming an "it" of dampness and hair before the cemetery gates, "cold and dead"; Richard, defeated by the abrupt lack of closure the Suit offers as it withers away, no words in his mouth but the blood that speaks through him, his body racing (as if to drain itself) to empty itself out.[20] The body parts, elements, ooze that have haunted the novel (the slime that Krook returned to, becoming fog and smoke, an after-effect of "chops") return in the characters' hurried disembodiment, as they become bodily receptacles, empty of feeling. Characters in this novel, racing to some other judgment, die of exposure, and they die quickly: Honoria, within days of leaving Chesney Wold; Richard, within hours of leaving Chancery. Sir Leicester stammers out his last messages, then lives on, a wreck of himself; Phil Squod slimes his way across the walls of the lodge; Caddy Jellyby's baby signs her way into speech; even the houses have no choice but to repeat themselves (like Bleak House, magically doubled) or fade away (like the moldering Chesney Wold). The novel itself ends, halting, on a pair of dashes; *Bleak House*, too, fading away, melting away, "thinning fast."

"But its mistress remains," as Esther might answer, and *Bleak House*'s last word is Esther's – a word she notoriously does not speak, withholding the conclusion of her sentence, "even supposing – " (770). Esther's position as the final (non)speaker of the novel confirms much I have argued: no narrator figure resumes the tale, puts her "portion" in its place. Her power, at this moment, as narrator, is almost entirely unlike her powerlessness as *character*. Esther has been "given," almost literally, like a prize, to Allan Woodcourt, not only as proof of his virtue, but proof of her own, that she has come into what her guardian, at least, believes is her true inheritance: the "good that could never change in her," a "true legitimacy" that even Mrs. Woodcourt, with her talk of Morgan ap Kerrig, accepts with alacrity (752). Esther, now diminutized, is put in a doll's house version of the first "Bleak House," given "a willing gift" by John Jarndyce who asks, holding for himself the privilege of visiting at any time, "what do I sacrifice? Nothing, nothing" (753). Esther, it seems, has mastered the daughter's quest, inheriting the father's house while retaining the father's love; he gets to give away his house and keep it too, and she manages to double herself as well, solving the novel's problem of unstable female identity with an exact image of her perfect house, garden, tidy arrangements, and relentless duty.

But that Esther, happily doubling herself, a mother to everyone's children, including her own nameless daughters, would have no need to write this manuscript to a nameless friend; and it is (sticking with vraisemblance for a moment) a complicated manuscript, one that she cannot even claim (as does David Copperfield) to have written late on into the night. No spousal companion urges her on, or holds her pen, as David's various wives did for him; the manuscript bears few traces of writing, few scenes that assert "I remember," "I see," or even "as I write."[21] And yet, in her closing envoi to the reader, she sounds very much like DC – and perhaps even more like CD, imagining in the reader (as Dickens seemed to in his autobiographical fragment) the one friend he has never met; the companion he never had; the reader he would be for himself, if he only could.

It is a commonplace of Dickens scholarship that David Copperfield is simply too uninteresting to have written his own novel – more accurately, that he lacks the darkness we sense in Dickens, the urgency and loss that would have driven him to stay up into the night writing his story. A more likely fabulist, the convention goes, is Philip Pirrip, with his dreamy bitterness and heartbroken irony – Pip who ends his tale in business, making "a sufficient living," still alone. More of a defense can be made of David than this model allows – certainly if we ask the Dickens questions of him: did he ever tell all of his sufferings to anyone, even to Agnes; did the little boy he sees trudging a dirty road at the novel's end ever really come "home" – but a stronger case could be made for Esther Summerson, or Esther Hawdon, or Esther Barbary, or Esther Woodcourt, whose life has all the drama (and then some) of David's, who feels no less powerful a sense of loss than Pip, and who has as powerful a sense of language, of irony, of hopefulness, and of the sharp knife concealed within hope, as any Dickens narrator – or the Dickens whose resentment shines through as fiercely in his refusal to forget his mother's abandonment as does Esther's in her "autobiographical fragment."

Or does it? *Bleak House*, I have been arguing, forces on us a reading of the mother–daughter relationship as essentially scripted: the two women spend more time together through texts than they do through bodies; they speak together only once, and the face that links them (the currency of the novel-proper and the mystery-novel manqué) is destroyed halfway through the book. The Esther who writes to raise her mother's ghost is doing something more complicated than what a writer customarily does with ghosts, which is simply to bring them to life, and then kill them again. In *Bleak House*'s stuttering closure, the novel seems to kill her again and again and again: the death becoming like the birth scene the novel cannot (however fiercely the lonely child tries) bring to realization. Or perhaps it tells that story for a different reason: as D. A. Miller has written of all narrative, and of Roland Barthes in particular, fiction stages that moment in which "death is doubled when after the decease of someone I love, I suddenly comprehend that the person to whom in my grief I have thought of turning (he will know how to console me, remember with me) is the very person who has just died."[22] In some profound way, *Bleak House* cries out to be read as a letter to that dead, consoling, imagined mother, who is the "very person who has just died."

To write that letter, Esther must first tell her mother the story she needs to "remember with her": she must make of the novel the remembering that its scattered body parts cried out for. She does so not only out of the fragments of stories and secrets, the broken-down bodies, shoes, orphans, bags of hair, of which the novel has been made, but out of a thousand images of herself, the "pattern young lady" she is often called. In composing herself, and her text, she recomposes a whole world – a little world – a little "bleak house." No less than that third-person narrator she (or Dickens) imagines, the one who can fly with the crow and descend to the depths, she imagines a fully realized world: crowds and horses and street-sweepers and street-sweepings, all, in a sense, the children of "nobody," trying to find home. That the home the novel writes is a bleak house indeed might remind us of another connection made by D. A. Miller: that of Queen Victoria's statement, "I never feel quite at ease or at home when reading a Novel."[23]

To which both Dickens and Esther might reply, nor am I at ease when writing one. If this book is, as I am claiming, Dickens's most profound statement of authorship, it is a dark one, and it does not promise healing, or forgiveness, although it does promise its own (dark, warped, bleak, lost) version of love: a love that, if still accomplished (as is Esther's marriage) in the language of debt, exchange, and property, at the least promises that the self can be exchanged for what the self really wants (in Esther's case, Allan) even if that exchange costs the giver (John Jarndyce) a pain the text can hardly fathom: his denial of his sacrifice ("Nothing, nothing") rings hollower and hollower the older I grow. And Esther as novelist, romancer, moralist, detective? Does she write her mother's story, her own, her culture's? And at what cost?

Perhaps the best we can suggest is that she has come into her own inheritance, which was, simply, to wander, to scribble, to be secret, to seek for her own face in the wide world, and never, ever to hope of finding it again, on herself or on anyone else, for she (and the text) have killed off the one true double she had. For there can be no doubt, in the book's psychic economy, or in its textual one, that Esther has destroyed her own duplicate, destroyed the one woman whose story could drag her down (both by revealing her status and destroying her secure place in Bleak House), destroyed the woman whose abandonment left her in that wide world. There can be no doubt, once Esther survives her bout of heroine-disease, that her mother will die of it; that as much as Esther claims not to be seeking her mother, she is hunting her down; that Esther is the doom of the Dedlocks, the fulfillment of Lady Morbury Dedlock's curse; and that Honoria is destroyed by the resurfacing of her face on her daughter, and her daughter's destruction of that face, though it buys her time, cannot buy her life. Her life ends, at the gates of the pauper burial ground, when she herself has been reduced to nothing but a "face," an "it," for "it was my mother cold and dead," and her daughter leans over her, at once a heartbroken and a triumphant survivor.

This cannot be true, of course, for that last sentence ("And it was my mother cold and dead") is the most piercing in the novel; the book resounds most powerfully as the daughter's long cry of grief for the lost mother. Little comfort to say that Honoria was dead (as well as deadlocked) from the beginning, and the novel only a bizarre action of startling her into life, and returning her to the inaction of the frozen lady she was before reading her dead lover's living hand. The attempt to bring the mother back to life, to hear the words she never says to her daughter, is the most powerful motive for fiction in every Dickens novel from *Oliver Twist* to this one, and this novel is merely the one that gives it the most piercing voice. But it gives the daughter her most powerful voice as well, and it does so by giving her two voices: the one that longs for the mother, and the one that condemns her abandonment of the child Esther was; the one that inscribes her death, and the one that hunts down her murderer; the one that mourns her, and the one that kills her again and again.

This might form another answer to my initial question: not, why does Dickens write two novels (that is, write "his" and Esther's) but why does he write a novel in which one woman (Esther) writes two narratives. This returns us to the larger question of having a "will": the will to power that is the novelist's; the agency that is the character's; the power of Esther's investigations of all the scenes that she was absent from, the story her mother did not tell her, but that she (I speculate) recreates. The power of the narrator is, as narrative theory teaches us, the power to be "nobody," to imagine a vantage point that belongs to no single person, but to the consensus of *all* positions – the moment when the different perspectives that any novel conjures up come together, in the imagination of an author, or a more perfect perspective than any individual (character) can imagine. That position of "nobody" links Esther, of course, to her own father, who passes through the novel as "Nemo," and dies a death of the ages, "just as dead as Phairy!" (126). That narration of nobody, the dead narrator, seems opposed, initially, to the cry of the living daughter for the dead mother – but suggests again the blend of self-possession and self-annihilation that was always Esther's fate: the fate of the child "better . . . never born," or of her first, best reader, the doll to whom she told all her stories, and whom she comforted herself in believing that she could care for (19).

This reading of Esther's scene of writing suggests that writing takes the place of every form of care and every form of property: the love the absent mother does not give; the love Esther wants to give her mother; the anger at the enormous and incalculable absence that the universe (but an indifferent parent, as John Jarndyce says) presents at the bleak end of the novel. Think of Esther's last note of (seemingly obsessive) modesty at the book's end: she concludes her characteristic litany of the wonders of those around her with the phrase, "people even praise Me as the doctor's wife" (769). Esther Barbary Hawdon Summerson Woodcourt seems entirely to have disappeared again – as, of course, she did legally (and as her property would have done, had she managed to inherit it) under the laws of female separate property under which this novel is written. But this novel does not read as if it had been written by "the doctor's wife": rather, it seems more like the last will and testament of the woman Esther was *before* she became anyone's wife, and before she moved into the second Bleak House; before she lost, under common law, the ability to make a will of her own. For the range, the power, the *will* that both narratives convey (in their energy as well as their suffering) seems to me to go back to the powerful will of the earlier Lady Dedlock, pacing Chesney Wold; to Honoria, defying Tulkinghorn and walking off into the cold night bearing her own secrets; to the Esther who faced her own suffering, her disease, and finally, her own mother's death, in that coldest night of all.

The courage to write her testimonial seems to me the message she received in that last letter from her mother, for in the dead mother's will, the bequest to "the dear one," we see the mother's most powerful, terrifying, alien gift: to scribble, write, crease, direct, dictate; to devise and bequeath; to rewrite and revise; the courage not to *stop* that process of writing and rewriting that is duplicated in every reader's baffled reading and rereading of *Bleak House*. For in *Bleak House*, a text that manages to give the quiet daughter and the angry mother both their due and their opposites (to inscribe the daughter's anger and the mother's remorse), we see the daughter's most powerful revision of her mother's (literary) gift, and a text that refuses to stop its telling, merely briefly breaking off – promising, like the other wandering story tellers of the novel, to begin again elsewhere, and in the same place.

CHAPTER FIVE

Amy Dorrit's prison notebooks

Little Dorrit reads very differently from the other novels of Dickens's late career: it moves through a concentration of characters, of space, and of detail; it relies on a series of separate but oddly similar focal points (the prison, the Circumlocution Office, Arthur Clennam's labyrinthine search for his family history); and as Lionel Trilling noted, it bears an uneasy relationship to realism, depending on the abstraction of something that "is an actuality before it is a symbol."[1] But the feeling of intense concentration depends as well on constant reversals and inversions: formally, it seems to move through parable and paradox, for just as its characters seem to stand for more than they are, so, too, do they seem to embody contradictory positions.[2] The central contradictions of the novel circle around the confusions of persons and property, of having and owning, of possessing and being possessed – of property and love, which characters seem to treat interchangeably.[3]

The novel does the opposite: following the impulse of the daughter's plot from *Dombey and Son* on, it takes renunciation and dispossession as the condition of love, making social redemption as well as personal salvation a result of the daughter's choice of "nothing" as her portion. But it cannot carry further the plot of *Bleak House*, where the daughter's paternal disinheritance led her back to the mother and away from the father's word; it is as if Dickens saw a narrative dead end in the emptying out of John Jarndyce's bleak house, and sought to bring back the daughter's patrimony – but here, with a vengeance. Here, property leads back to the father, but to a recast patriarchy, one in which the daughter (unlike the disinherited and seemingly disloyal Florence Dombey or the bastard Esther Summerson) is legitimate; but still inherits as little as possible.

Amy Dorrit inherits twice, under two different wills, and she renounces her fortune twice. In a world profoundly shaken by the possibility of the wife's separate property, *Little Dorrit* plays constantly with the possibility of female inheritance, only to ask (equally constantly) of what property the self might be, in a world where property is always, if not theft, at the least debt. The novel points to the violence of owning, and to the perversion at the heart of the property plot; but (and here it follows on the narratorial experiments of *Bleak House* far more than critics have noticed) it points to writing as another form of property, one in which women might be able to claim ownership. Much as it plays with the will plot, with a variety of relationships to material property, so it plays with relationships to writing, to fictional property; it asks, everywhere, not only what is the daughter's portion, but how little does it take to create a self, and at what price?

Little Dorrit expresses everywhere its obsession with containment, and its narratives of female property (like those of the female self) begin in captivity. The story opens with three scenes of incarceration and one domestic scene (which is by far the most claustrophobic); the first scene takes place in the Marseilles prison where the murderer Rigaud tells the story of killing his wife for her money. Rigaud's account of her death begins with his character, which is, he says, not to "submit," but "to govern."[4]

"Unfortunately, the property of Madame Rigaud was settled upon herself. Such was the insane act of her late husband. More unfortunately still, she had relations. When a wife's relations interpose against a husband who is a gentleman, who is proud, and who must govern, the consequences are inimical to peace. . . . It has been said that I treated Madame Rigaud with cruelty. I may have been seen to slap her face – nothing more. I have a light hand; and if I have been seen apparently to correct Madame Rigaud in that manner, I have done it almost playfully." (49)

The central conflicts between Monsieur and Madame are over money – "Even when I wanted any little sum of money for my personal expenses I could not obtain it without collision – and I, too, a man whose character it is to govern!" (50) – but it is the reversal of power that upsets "governance," leading to the initial, parodic "playful" correction, and then to Rigaud's astounding account of his wife's death:

"Madame Rigaud grew warm; I grew warm, and provoked her. I admit it. Frankness is a part of my character. At length, Madame Rigaud, in an access of fury that I must ever deplore, threw herself upon me with screams of passion (no doubt those that were overheard at some distance), tore my clothes, tore my hair, lacerated my hands, trampled and trod the dust, and finally leaped over, dashing herself to death upon the rocks below. Such is the train of incidents which malice has perverted into my endeavouring to force from Madame Rigaud a relinquishment of her rights; and, on her persistence in a refusal to make the concession I required, struggling with her – assassinating her!" (50)

Rigaud presents his story as if his invention (that his wife killed herself) were merely an appropriate response to a deeper "perversion." He has cleverly inverted the story to fit the physical evidence that accompanied her murder at his hands, but the real "refusal" of facts lies in the perversion of a wife with interfering relatives, a mind of her own, and with her own property settled on her; that alone requires an unnatural narrative.

But the second anecdote of property, one that features a gentle daughter and a kindly prison guard, suggests as deep an anxiety about women, property, and persuasion. The turnkey of the Marshalsea Prison, best and earliest friend to Amy Dorrit, poses a similar puzzle over a woman's inheritance. The turnkey is attempting to find a way to leave his money to Amy without fear of it being swallowed up by her father. He puts the question to every lawyer leaving the prison:

"Supposing," he would say, stating the case with his key on the professional gentleman's waistcoat; "supposing a man wanted to leave his property to a young female, and wanted to tie it up so that nobody else should ever be able to make a grab at it; how would you tie up that property?"

"Settle it strictly on herself," the professional gentleman would complacently answer.

"But look here," quoth the turnkey, "Supposing she had, say a brother, say a father, say a husband, who would be likely to make a grab at the property when she came into it – how about that?"

"It would be settled on herself, and they would have no more claim on it than you," would be the professional answer.

"Stop a bit," said the turnkey. "Supposing she was tender-hearted, and they came over her? Where's your law for tying it up then?"

The deepest character whom the turnkey sounded, was unable to produce his law for tying such a knot as that. So, the turnkey thought about it all his life, and died intestate after all. (110–111)

In that "supposing she was tender-hearted" is the "heart" of *Little Dorrit* – both text and heroine – and the novel is deeply pessimistic about the possibility of "tying" anything up – its operating thesis would seem to be, first, that women are already tied up, and second, that on such "tying up" a decent society depends.

The novel seems possessed by the idea of willed female *dis*possession; more particularly, with the daughter's self-renunciation, her willed smallness. The earliest version of female property the book produces is, not surprisingly, food: "Little Dorrit," whose unprepossessing name marks her status as a day-worker in the Clennam household,[5] is a mystery to those around her, and the oddest element of her mystery is her insistence that she eat alone. When Arthur Clennam, newly returned from the East and curious about the phantom-like Amy, follows her home, he finds that her home is the Marshalsea prison, her father the prison's most famous debtor and longest resident (the "Father" of the Marshalsea, as well as of Amy, who was "born in that place"), and that the secret of Amy's dinner is that it is carried home each day to feed her father. The role of female property in sustaining men could not be made more explicit than in the fact that the heroine's eponymous smallness is caused by her daily deliverance of her supper into her father's mouth, an inversion of property relations made explicit later by the narrator's passionate explanation of her devotion as that of the "Roman daughter," who succored her father with the breast-milk meant for her infant; Amy's sacrifice, it seems clear, is not of her maternal function (she is the text's "little mother," with enough maternity for everyone) but of her sexuality, itself diminutized (to her great pain) in the eyes of almost everyone around her.

Amy's smallness, and the sacrifice of her bodily property to her father's needs, is carried through in an equally compulsive narratorial miniaturization. When she goes to tell her story to Arthur's old fiancée, Flora, she tells it simply, "condens[ing] the narrative of her life into a few scanty words about herself and a glowing eulogy upon her father" (333). Amy's more general textual function is to write things large, to render, as her father says elsewhere, "legible . . . what I desire to be blotted out" (532). But her own story can only be condensed, as she writes of herself in a letter to Arthur Clennam: "She [Pet Meagles Gowan] speaks to me by my name – I mean, not my Christian name, but the name you gave me. When she began to call me Amy, I told her *my short story*, and that you had always called me Little Dorrit. I told her that the name was much dearer to me than any other, and so she calls me Little Dorrit too" (607, emphasis added).

No reader of the many pages of this novel could argue convincingly that Amy Dorrit has a "short story"; but the work of expansion to make Amy's story into the book's takes an odd form, almost of hijacking her property and (to borrow another Dickens phrase) "blowing it up." The clearest outline of that story is Pancks's, when he appears as "Pancks the fortune teller":

He was so far troublesome that he was not at all wanted there, but she laid her work in her lap for a moment, and held out her left hand with her thimble on it.

"Years of toil, eh?" said Pancks, softly, touching it with his blunt forefinger. "But what else are we made for? Nothing. Hallo!" looking into the lines. "What's this with bars? It's a College! And what's this with a grey gown and a black velvet cap? It's a father! And what's this with a clarionet? It's an uncle! And what's this in dancing-shoes? It's a sister! And what's this straggling about it in an idle sort of a way? It's a brother! And what's this thinking for 'em all? Why, this is you, Miss Dorrit!" (334–335)

Pancks's account, with its implicit praise for Amy's almost narratorial care ("thinking for 'em all") is the novel's, and it is the move the book makes when it makes its two important shifts: the first, from Arthur's story, to follow Amy into the prison and recap the twenty-three years before the book's beginning, following her father's journey into the Marshalsea; the other, when Amy enters Arthur's room in Covent Garden for the first time, and the book declares, "this history must some-times see with Little Dorrit's eyes . . ." (208).

This shift seems to endorse Amy's vision – to see with "her eyes" – but it follows the conscious renunciation by Amy herself of her story: hers is to be condensed, that others may be "eulogized." In effect, Amy carries out through narrative exactly the renunciation the turnkey imagined: for another (say a husband, a father, a brother) she has given up ownership of her own story. Though the narrative is focalized through her, and though two long letters of hers form separate texts in Book Two, Amy seems reluctant to assume even what narrative authority is given her. Indeed, the move to Amy's "eyes" (literally, here staring at Arthur and his rooms) follows the text's introduction of her into the room: Arthur has been imagining his life as a "green tree," which has born him no fruit (207). When he asks what his life has led him to, a prophetic voice answers "Little Dorrit," and that ends the chapter: only with the begin-ning of the next, do we learn that the words were spoken out loud, by Amy herself, in a modest attempt to introduce herself. Here, as else-where, where she might be entering her own story, she is introduced as the key to Arthur's. It is as if the narrator himself did not want to embar-rass the modest heroine by forcing her to claim that her presence is central even to her own story.

But while Amy seems to express herself most fully by containing her story – even in her fairy tale, seized on by most critics as the expression of female desire in the novel,[6] the "tiny woman's" only possession is the shadow she keeps in a "secret place," a possession that dies with her – almost everyone else in the novel gains a self through a repetitive self-expression, an indulgence of the self's willingness to dilate and expand into narrative. Certainly, all the other heroines (like most characters in Dickens) exist in perfect, calm faith that they are at the heart of every story, and that all narrative roads lead to them. Of course, they are wrong (the novel is not named after them), but nonetheless they also control a great deal of narrative power: indeed, the narrative's own metaphor for its activity, one based on roads and prisons, comes from the novel's angriest woman, the illegitimate and passionate Miss Wade, who claims that "In our course through life we shall meet the people who are coming to meet *us*, from many strange places and by many strange roads . . . and what it is set to us to do to them, and what it is set to them to do to us, will all be done" (63).[7] What "will all be done," what comes to meet us, seems in this novel most clearly "set to" in the "will" plot itself: everything Amy sets herself to contain, to renounce, and to leave unnarrated, is set in motion by the plots of property and desire, which share only partially her anxiety about what it might mean to possess property, a self, and a story.

In *Little Dorrit*, as in Dickens's other fiction, the daughter's role is to secure collective memory: to make sure that past people and places are accorded the right weight; that they are put away in the right place. The daughter functions as a kind of narrative last testament: what she carries out is the distributive function associated with dying words. In this way, her work is the work of the inheritance plot as well. Wills exist in novels not only to get property into the right hands, but to get characters in the right place: the "aha!" of conclusion is that X-thing belongs to Y-person, but also that Z-person belongs to Y-person. A will plot makes narrative connections literal by carrying out the proper connections of people, places, and things, by the logic of inheritance, the dead hand of the past writing (if not righting) the present.

Little Dorrit certainly tries gamely to carry out that classificatory task, making the forms of the inheritance plot accord with the functions of character. It offers not one but two wills, the first, to grant "riches" to the Dorrit family, trapped in the catch-22 of the Marshalsea prison; the second, to reveal the deception that cost Amy her inheritance from the Clennam family, and to shadow her eventual marriage to Arthur by the symbolic connection of Amy's family to his proper mother. This plot carries out the psychic work Arthur has hoped for all along: that his guilt and Mr. Dorrit's imprisonment are related; that Amy can be blessed with a fortune, and with it, he can be blessed with forgiveness for a crime of which he is in fact innocent. It will make literal (or so Arthur dreams) what he saw metaphorically, the implication that Mrs. Clennam is imprisoning herself in her house to make reparations for Mr. Dorrit's imprisonment, saying, thus I make reparations; my freedom for his; he rots in his prison, and I in mine.

Arthur reads plot a little as if he were a petitioner in Chancery: aligning guilt, property, and right action will set him free, giving him (at last) the proper inheritance. But property does not follow so logical a path in this novel – at least not originally. It seems as if the aberration of separate female property that Rigaud and the turnkey's stories pointed to contaminated all of the book's proper (propertied) relations. At times, the confusion between people and things (desire and property) is merely comic. When Arthur meets his old sweetheart, Flora ("whom he had left a lily, [now] become a peony" [191]) she states that:

> Mr Clennam might not have heard that Mr. F had left her a legacy? Clennam in return implied his hope that Mr F. had endowed the wife whom he adored, with the greater part of his worldly substance, if not with all. Flora said, oh yes, she didn't mean that, Mr F. had made a beautiful will, but he had left her as a separate legacy, his Aunt. (198–199)

Mr. F's aunt, who is referred to as Mr. F's relict, is the novel's darkest comic success, following Flora around like a bitter shadow, making irrational comments to everyone and anyone, and making (most critics claim) little sense. But she both *is* property, and is herself obsessed with property: her first remark in Clennam's presence is, "When we lived at Henley, Barnes's gander was stole by tinkers" (199). And as the object of property, one "willed" to a woman herself seen by the text as an ornamental possession, her seemingly irrational anger is also associated with Flora's resentment at Clennam's defection, a rage Flora cannot express: Mr. F's aunt asks, frequently, the question "'What he come there for, then' . . . with implacable animosity" (200). This is a question Flora, with her clear sense that "I am not what you expected," might ask Arthur, who turns up in Flora's house only when he needs something from her. In the romantic heroine's plot Flora reruns continually in her head, the question might indeed be, what has Arthur come back for?

What is comic in the property plots of Flora and her surrogate is less amusing elsewhere in the novel. Flora's rage, to the extent that it can be surmised through Mr. F's Aunt, is unusual in that it seems not to have distorted her character; indeed, her enjoyment of Mr. F's Aunt's "liveliness" suggests a pleasure (part of the "comfort" with which Flora is associated – a fact enhanced by the fact she gives Amy her first good meal in the novel) that other characters seem not to take even in the property they hold. Most characters seem eager not only to claim the property of others, but to claim others as property, much as Pancks is possessed by Casby, his "proprietor" (322) or the indigent Mr. Dorrit claims Old Nandy, the pauper, as "an old pensioner of mine" (423). This proprietariness is hardly rare in Dickens; nor is an awareness, from everyone, of just how much property anyone else might have or claim. But this novel holds up the disturbing possibility that the self can be imagined only as a version of violent property relations: not only the general contagion of indebtedness in the novel, the resentment of characters like Miss Wade, Mrs. Clennam, Fanny Dorrit, and the more deeply repressed fury of Mr. Dorrit himself, but the weight of desire associated more generally with sexual relations, share this wolfishness. In this text, property and love can hardly be wedged apart.

For some characters, like the text's anomalous love-child, Miss Wade, property offers the only available version of a self. A woman seemingly set apart from "natural" relations precisely by her status as a natural child, a bastard, Miss Wade presents a puzzle of propertied relations. She is a woman of some education, dramatically attractive and passionate, angry and mysterious; she has enough money to travel freely but not enough to bring a maid or companion with her. She seems to stand in the novel for "singularity," both in her repudiation of others, and the intensity of her self-assertion: she is, she seems to announce, her own property, her only property, only her property. But her actual property is shrouded in a different kind of mystery: Pancks says to Arthur, "She is somebody's child – anybody's – nobody's. Put her in a room in London here with any six people old enough to be her parents, and her parents may be there for anything she knows." She "may make chance acquaintance of 'em at any time; and never know it" (595). Caught up in the mystery of birth is another of the text's mysteries of inheritance: as Pancks describes it,

"[Casby] has long had money (not overmuch as I make out) in trust to dole out to her when she can't do without it. Sometimes she's proud and won't touch it for a length of time; sometimes she's so poor that she must have it. She writhes under her life." (595)

The money here stands for family, indebtedness, servitude; it is also what allows Miss Wade some freedom from the life of governess, drudge, companion. But having it ties her to her own rage: Pancks says, "the wonder is to me that she has never done for my proprietor, as the only

person connected with her story she can lay hold of" (595). Money, property, violence, story, ownership; the same terms keep getting shuffled
around. And indeed, when Miss Wade does tell Arthur her story, she
does not account either for her money or for the "proprietor," who has
indirectly become *her* proprietor as well.

But the novel does hold up interesting examples of independent
female property – even if that property is oddly obtained. Miss Rugg,
the daughter of Pancks's landlord, has money gained in a breach of
promise suit from the baker, a "fiend in human form" (347); she puts up
some of the money for the search for Amy's inheritance. Flora seems to
have money of her own, given to her (in addition to the human relict) in
Mr. Finching's "beautiful will" (198), but she has nonetheless returned to
the maiden sanctity of her father's home, and is being introduced again
as "Miss Flora" – her separate property does not seem to be doing her
much good. The only woman who has money and operates (relatively)
freely in the world is Mrs. Clennam, who has inherited half of her
husband's business, and buys Arthur's share back from him; but by some
negotiated agreement, she seems to be running the business with her
servant, Flintwinch, whose constant rage at being under her control
seems paradigmatic of the resentment created by any separate female
property. This resentment permeates even the most ironic of characters:
when Henry Gowan's mother discusses his wife Pet's money, which
comes from her parents and supports the young couple, she claims:

> "On the death of the old people, I suppose there will be more to come; but how
> it may be restricted or locked up, I don't know. And as to that, they may live for
> ever. My dear, they are just the kind of people to do it." (443)

Property owned by women (restricted or locked up) is a cause of resentment, of anger, of curiosity – in short, a source of plot. But it further has
the power, in this late novel, of undoing Dickens's own most habitual
plots: in this novel, the bastardized (disavowed) daughter and the illegitimate (nonbiological, adulterous) mother of *Dombey and Son* and *Bleak
House* no longer speak to each other, but rather express only their own
"singularity." As Miss Wade and Mrs. Clennam suggest, the family
romance and the daughter's desire have come almost fatally unhinged,
meeting only in their obsessive need to repeat, *ad infinitum*, their own pro-
prietorship; their own self-storying.

The stories told by Miss Wade and Mrs. Clennam register as dis-
turbances in the narrative field. Miss Wade's narrative, the one thing she

claims outright in the novel, gets an entire chapter of its own. Labeled as "The History of a Self-Tormentor," a title she cannot have given it, the chapter serves as a self-contained narrative with no narratorial commentary, and with no sense of how its one intradiegetic reader (Arthur) reads it. In that sense, except for its rather condescending title, it seems to stand free – but it also seems to stand free of the work of plot, for while it provides motive and "background," it serves no clear plot purpose; indeed, it seems to have been added to the novel because one number-part ran short. However, Dickens made no move to cut it from the novel, as he sometimes did with such additions, and (in both its technical and thematic brilliance) it has remained a critical keynote, but only as a separate, bravura set-piece, as if it were a Browning dramatic monologue rather than part of a complicated fictional structure.

Miss Wade's narrative is almost perfectly the inverse of Amy Dorrit's; where Amy sees herself nowhere, Miss Wade sees herself everywhere. The text she offers tells the story of a woman, raised to be a dependent, cursed with an independent spirit, one who sees in kindness condescension, in affection, a trap. When she has a close friend at her "grandmother's" house, and her friend (who "had what they called an amiable temper, an affectionate temper") "distribute(s) pretty looks and smiles to every one among them" Miss Wade knows "that she did it purposely to wound and gall me!" When the girl takes Miss Wade home with her for the holidays, "Her plan was, to make them all fond of her – and so drive me wild with jealousy. To be familiar and endearing with them all – and so make me mad with envying them." Miss Wade's response is to reproach her:

"And then she would cry and cry and say I was cruel, and then I would hold her in my arms till morning: loving her as much as ever, and often feeling as if, rather than suffer so, I could so hold her in my arms and plunge to the bottom of a river – where I would still hold her after we were both dead." (726–727)

This expression of murderous passion, the confusion, again, of self and other, destruction and self-destruction, is hardly unique even in Dickens: it anticipates Bradley Headstone's desperate pursuit of Eugene Wrayburn, while the latter, in turn, leads him on. Like the other Browningesque moments of Miss Wade's extended dramatic monologue, this moment of the girl's "cry" suggests the cruelty of the woman who presents herself as sufferer. But it also conveys powerfully Miss Wade's suffering – that of the dependent, the impoverished, the proud. "I told my supposed grandmother that, unless I was sent away to finish my education somewhere else before that girl came back, or before any one of them came back, I would burn my sight away by throwing myself into the fire, rather than I would endure to look at their plotting faces" (727): the plotting woman's revenge against society, at this moment, can only be self-destruction, and it is not a happy alternative.[8]

Miss Wade's note of self-containment ("I resolved that they should not know [my value]," she says [731]), the key note of her narration, *fails* in view of the very act of narration: why is she telling her story? And why, of all people, to Arthur Clennam?

The narrative is not only the one thing she imagines that she owns: to her the very point of fiscal independence is that it allows her to tell her story her way. All her agency in the plot is similarly narratorial: all the crucial documents of the novel, we subsequently find out, have ended up in her hands; to resolve the plot, they must be stolen by Tattycoram, the Meagles's maid whom she has coaxed away to share her anger, and returned to Amy at the Marshalsea. But if Miss Wade is in the book to hold on to pieces of paper until the time for them to be released, freed to rejoin the narrative's progress, what sense can we make of *her* narrative, which seems to interrupt rather than further the book's progress, which has no legal or economic status, and which seems to float further, in its purity of self-expression, as an uncommented-upon commentary on Arthur and Amy's progress from "nobodies" to "somebodies."[9] Miss Wade, freed from parents, property, even a first name, seems to float similarly free – except, as her narrative (and the frame of its title) seems to suggest, that her story is as deeply constrained and conscripted, as little independent, as any in the book.

Miss Wade's narrative takes the position of a "portion" of these pages, as does Mrs. Clennam's and, in its turn, Amy Dorrit's: the most striking thing about *Little Dorrit* is the way it continually stops for women to tell their stories. But unlike the other novels, it does little work to reconcile these narratives, or to bring the women who tell the stories into any relationship other than that of shared purveyors of documents. Each of them, in its own way, seems to strike the key-note announced by Mrs. Clennam in the scene of *her* great revelation: "I will have it seen by the light I stood in" (843). If Miss Wade stands as a self-tormentor, Mrs. Clennam stands as the self-justifier, though her narrative, no less than Miss Wade's, is framed and commented on by its position in the text, here under Amy's somewhat stony judgments. But Mrs Clennam's narrative also, like Miss Wade's, provides its own counter-narrative – it is no less powerful or less tragic than Miss Wade's, and it casts as interesting a light on the problem of female self-possession that all the stories in the novel, not least of them Amy Dorrit's, are trying to resolve.

Not that Mrs. Clennam's story offers itself up easily for any kind of sympathetic reading, for Dickens's editorial hand is rather harshly in evidence as Mrs. Clennam tells her story. As she recounts her uncovering of Arthur's father's affair, her discovery of their child, her subsequent abduction of the child and sequestering of the mother, her language remains severe, biblical, condemnatory – hers is not her own narrative, but God's, realized in her life. Amy's questioning response is no less absolute: Mrs. Clennam has simply got hold of the wrong god, an angry god, and set herself in his place. Amy "recoils with dread from the state of mind that had burnt so fiercely and lasted so long" (860), and argues to Mrs. Clennam that "angry feelings and unforgiving deeds are no comfort and no guide to you and me. . . . Be guided only by the healer of the sick, the raiser of the dead, the friend of all who were afflicted and forlorn, the patient Master who shed tears of compassion for our infirmities. . . . There is no vengeance and no infliction of suffering in His life . . ." (861).

Mrs. Clennam makes no answer. With Amy's help, no reader could miss the obvious revision we are to make of this story: Mrs. Clennam, not Arthur's mother, is the sinner; and, like Miss Barbary before her and Miss Havisham after, Mrs. Clennam is to be condemned as much for her usurpation of narratorial authority as her defiance of God; Mrs. Clennam is guilty of trying to be an author. When she insists she will tell Blandois her story herself, Flintwinch replies "He knows all he cares about it"; what stands as the book's motto is Mrs. Clennam's response: "He does not know *me*." And echoing Miss Wade's favorite metaphor she concludes, "What! Have I suffered nothing in this room, no deprivation, no imprisonment, that I should condescend at last to contemplate myself in such a glass as *that*" (843).

But her narrative offers two significant points of departure from Miss Wade's, both of which suggest the very different power Amy's narrative will have. The first is that a story of pathos with its own shadows appears within her story, one that links her narrative to Amy's more benevolent desire. The most telling sadness is the love she feels was stolen from her by "a graceless orphan, training to be a singing girl" (848), the woman who was Mr. Clennam's mistress (and possibly wife) and Arthur Clennam's mother. Of her husband, she says, "What Arthur's father was to me, she made him. From our marriage day I was his dread, and that she made me." When she looks at her son, she can see only "him, with his mother's face, looking up at me in awe from his little books, and trying to soften me with his mother's ways that hardened me" (859). But her "softening" is evident in her longer description, to Amy, of her son:

"He never loved me, as I once half-hoped he might – so frail we are, and so do the corrupt affections of the flesh war with our trusts and tasks; but he always respected me and ordered himself dutifully to me. He does to this hour. With an empty place in his heart that he has never known the meaning of, he has turned away from me and gone his separate road; but even that he has done considerately and with deference. . . .I would not, for any worldly recompense I can imagine, have him in a moment, however blindly, throw me down from the station I have held before him all his life, and change me altogether into something he would cast out of his respect, and think detected and exposed." (860)

This is the other Mrs. Clennam, the one who kisses Amy (to the amazement of the watching Affery); the one who approaches Amy with a "great supplication that I address to your merciful and gentle heart" (858), that she not disclose the truth to Arthur until Mrs. Clennam is dead. It is Mrs. Clennam whose story reveals, more clearly for being so unexpected, that the language of inheritance and documents has the power it has only in a society that does not offer love: what she wanted was Arthur's affection; if she cannot win him from his "other mother," she will settle for taking the other inheritance. But the story she tells leaves little doubt that if she had more love, she would need less money – and fewer documents.

Even given that final example of the exchange I have been stressing, the exchange – or here, substitution – of property for persons, Mrs. Clennam's relationship to documents is of interest. That interest has to do with the other side of her story: that through the pathos, we see a hitherto unsuspected narrative of property, and her authority is linked to a usurpation of legality and the proper paths of property, an undoing of the usual causative narrative of inheritance. I say this knowing that in some way (secret wills, illegitimate births, illicit marriages) the plot machinery of *Little Dorrit* makes it appear an utterly conventional novel, one that breaks with realism long enough to yoke in the gothic machinery of missing or misplaced inheritances, and then returns to realist solutions. (Certainly, most critics have read the novel this way.) But this is not the conventional disruption of the "real" by the gothic, or of the proleptic of the bildungsroman by the analepsis (the "evocation after the fact of an event that took place earlier than the point in the story where we are") that inheritance always carries, for the simple reason that the property (and the inheritors) of this property are not conventional either.[10] If this novel were called *Arthur Clennam*, and the job of the narrative were to return this missing property and his birthright to him, the novel would be completely assimilable to the ordinary logic of property. Instead, the novel is called *Little Dorrit*, the money in question is Amy's, and all the "interruption" of the normal plot (the thing that kept the money from Arthur's uncle in motion, until it reaches Arthur at the end) is in the hands of women who serve as uncanny narrative agents.

For it is in Mrs. Clennam's story of the codicil and of the hiding of Arthur's mother, the missing singing girl, that the book carries out its most sustained engagement with both female writing and separate female property. The money Arthur's father's uncle tried to leave to Arthur's birth mother, and left (in a codicil to his will) if not to that woman, then to the youngest daughter or niece of her caretaker (Frederick Dorrit, Amy's uncle) is connected not only to Arthur's mother's disappearance and her death in a madhouse, but to the other set of papers in motion, her beseeching letters to Mrs. Clennam begging to see her son one last time. At this moment, all the documents seem part of a single inheritance, and ordinary inheritance (codicils, endowments, beneficiaries) seems as much like magic writing as these pathetic letters. Further, the revelation of all this (and of the property) takes place in a conversation between two women about the papers of a third – papers we learn have been held by yet a fourth woman, Miss Wade, and returned by a fifth, Tattycoram. And these women have more in common than their relationship to a small piece of missing property: all these heroines, like Arthur's mother, have no first name, and no clear autobiographical narrative to relate;[11] but they do have fierce desires, a passion for narrative, and an obsession with property.

Mrs. Clennam's story reveals that there are two sets of documents in furious motion in the novel: the first, the suppressed codicil of Gilbert Clennam's will, smuggled out by Flintwinch; the other, the sad, insane letters of Arthur Clennam's unnamed mother, the singer who dies in the captivity of Flintwinch's twin brother. The doubling of the keepers suggests not only the gothic doubling apparent throughout the novel, but the link between the two sets of papers: the one, legal inheritance; the other, the spiritual legacy of love that does not make its way to Arthur. We never see these letters, and have only Mrs. Clennam's description of them: what seems to take their place in the novel's circulation of documents are the two letters we do read, those by Amy Dorrit, which *do* reach their intended reader – Arthur Clennam, the man for whom Amy will renounce her fortune.

Dispossession, like property in the wrong hands, can lead only to narrative in this novel. Like Miss Wade, whose history circles around her deepest deprivation, her homelessness, and Mrs. Clennam, who walks across London (leaving her carceral home behind) in order to tell her story, Amy Dorrit must be without a home before she can write. The turning points of her narrative take place outside the Marshalsea: the scene when she visits Arthur's room; her "party," when she walks over London Bridge and sleeps in the church; the prostitute she meets on the street; the conversation she has with Arthur on the Iron Bridge, which becomes their private place in her mind. There is something harshly unsentimental about Amy's peregrinations: she must wander to escape the "little story" of her devotion to her father, but she has no solid identity away from the Marshalsea. She remains, as her sister calls her, a "prison child."

The paradox of Amy's identity is, of course, that as the only child to love the prison, she is the only one who is truly able to leave it: to leave the Marshalsea is to leave her father behind, but it is also to move into the romance plot, a plot that, for Amy, cannot be resolved until she has moved her lover (or the plot has) back into the prison. She does resist – and it is her only point of real resistance – her father's insistence that the prison story (his) and the love story (hers) are the same: the horrifying scene where he pressures her to marry John Chivery, whose successful pursuit of Amy will make her father's life more comfortable, is the only time she refuses to grant her father's wish, and the only scene where she admits that he is not what he pretends to be. As he storms that she has never seen him as her mother saw him, she can only repeat, sadly, after she stays with him until he sleeps, "No, I have never seen him in my life" (276). His inadvertently self-revealing monologue in which he invents the fiction of a fellow inmate whose "not the daughter, the sister – of one of us" (271) was loved by a guard, is Mr. Dorrit's most pathetic moment, and the only moment when he admits that he lives by the charity of others; the only moment when he acknowledges that his funeral will be in the prison ("it must be here, I know it can be nowhere else" [273]); the only moment when the narrator admits that the other prisoners are "laughing in their rooms over his late address in the Lodge" (273). It is at this moment that the narrator makes clear that the father's abusive love is her only inheritance:

Enough, for the present place, that he lay down with wet eyelashes, serene, in a manner majestic, after bestowing his life of degradation as a sort of portion on the devoted child upon whom its miseries had fallen so heavily, and whose love alone had saved him to be even what he was. (275–276)

This salvation has never seemed more like a mistake; and his love has never seemed less like an offering: "No other person upon earth, save herself, could have been so unmindful of her wants" (274). This "portion" has seemed to many readers the daughter's only self, the "duty" as Mr. Meagles will later sum up Amy's life, that is the lesson she represents to the world.

Amy, however, claims another portion, and it is not an accident that her letters, which take up two long chapters in the second volume of the novel, echo not her father's imprisonment but Arthur's mother's. Like the "tiny woman" who hides a shadow, the one thing Amy agrees to "own" (owns up to owning) is the secret of her love for Arthur – a secret, of course, kept from no one except Arthur. As Fanny Dorrit says, everyone has their subject, and Amy's seems to be love; even the soft-headed John Chivery knows Amy loves Arthur, and he must finally (after Arthur has disinherited himself, coming to the Marshalsea and choosing the "freedom" of having lost everything) physically touch Arthur to convince him that he is loved. Amy Dorrit writes to Arthur Clennam because she loves him: the letters are there to reveal the love that readers see, and Arthur overlooks, as he misses every question to which he might be the answer, in his desire to overlook himself. But they also claim a particular space for Amy, not only of romantic love but of self-possession: like the observations of Florence Dombey and Esther Summerson, they also carry out Dickens's characteristic social observation, a work the daughter in love is particularly poised to inscribe. Only Amy, the prison child, can see the poverty around her; only Amy, who knows that Arthur offers a different kind of emotional haven, can notice the pervasive uprootedness, the displacement, of all the rag-tag refugees she meets in Europe.

The letters begin with Amy's own sense of displacement: she writes because "everything in my life is strange, and I miss so much" (521). Writing to the absent beloved – as well as back to the England she misses – is to attempt to create a center for herself, a self outside of the Marshalsea and away from Arthur. At the same time, what Amy writes is an absence, one even more palpable than that of the other female texts: every event (meeting with Pet, learning foreign languages) is referred back to Arthur, and events have meaning (one imagines) only when they are conveyed to him. The letters can only be written through a familiar act of self-negation. Amy attempts to explain why she does not describe "all these new countries and wonderful sights":

They are very beautiful, and they astonish me, but I am not collected enough – not familiar enough with myself, if you can quite understand what I mean – to have all the pleasure in them that I might have. What I knew before them, blends with them, too, so curiously. For instance, when we were among the mountains, I often felt (I hesitate to tell such an idle thing, dear Mr. Clennam, even to you) as if the Marshalsea must be behind that great rock; or as if Mrs. Clennam's room where I have worked so many days, and where I first saw you, must be just beyond that snow. Do you remember one night when I came with Maggy to your lodging in Covent Garden? That room I have often and often fancied I have seen before me, travelling along for miles by the side of our carriage, when I have looked out of the carriage-window after dark. We were shut out that night, and sat at the iron gate, and walked about till morning. I often look up at the stars, even from the balcony of this room, and believe that I am in the street again, shut out with Maggy. It is the same with people that I left in England. (522–523)

The note on which the passage ends, the missing phrase ("especially you") which so goes without saying, is in many ways the dominant note of the passage: "dear Mr. Clennam, even to you"; the room "where I first saw you"; looking up at the stars in the street ("your lodging") in Covent Garden, looking up "even from the balcony of this room" at the stars of *that* street, *that* room, *his* room, the room which travels "for miles by the side of our carriage." The passage ought to work – though there is no evidence it does – to jar Arthur's smug recollection of the past: only here does she reveal that she slept outside the gate of the Marshalsea all night, kept out by her visit to him. Arthur shows no eagerness (until his own imprisonment) to re-examine the past Amy is so intent on studying here; the past that travels along beside her. But the deeper sense of disconnection that marks this passage (the sense that the past travels with her) is what not only Arthur but the rest of her family cannot see: Amy's letter marks the vanity and stupidity of the other Dorrits in imagining that they can leave the Marshalsea behind, that it is not traveling alongside their carriage. The rest of the family would be surprised to wake up, still in the Marshalsea: despite her miniaturized travel-narrative ("that great rock"; "just beyond the snow"), Amy knows she is always traveling in the past.

Amy's persistence of memory (her ability to embody memory for her family – precisely what they resent her for, as they resent the prison garb she cannot leave off wearing, and in which she will greet Arthur when she visits him in the Marshalsea) is deeply bound up in the depths of her love for Arthur, and her refusal to forget that. Amy's insistence on repopulating the world through gratitude ("It is the same with the people I left in England"; "I think it would be ingratitude in me to forget") is not so different from Miss Wade or Mrs. Clennam – or from Arthur's mother, who worked the message "DNF" ("Do not forget") into the beads on Arthur's father's watchpaper, prompting the quest for resolution ("Your mother," says Mr. Clennam, pointing at the watch and confusing his son [74]) that gives Arthur his "will."

Amy's memory similarly conjures up the dead mother: the dreams she recounts in her letters look back to a past before the novel began:

I have always dreamed of myself as a child learning to do needlework. I have often dreamed of myself as back there, seeing faces in the yard . . . but, as often as not, I have been abroad here – in Switzerland, or France, or Italy – somewhere where we have been – yet always as that little child. I have dreamed of going down to Mrs. General, with the patches on my clothes in which I can first remember myself. I have over and over again dreamed of taking my place at dinner at Venice when we have had a large company, in the mourning for my poor mother which I wore when I was eight years old, and wore long after it was threadbare and would mend no more. (609)

The dream is what her father will act out when he welcomes Mrs. Merdle's guests to the Marshalsea in the middle of Rome; but it is also the only account of Amy's mother the book offers other than her appearance and death in the Marshalsea, and the only time Amy mentions her mother in a book almost totally dominated by her father. But it also looks forward to Arthur's mother (like Amy's, unnamed) and her heritage of letters: the texts Mrs. Clennam has kept from him that travel the female narrative-circuit of the novel. The mourning Amy wore for her mother ("long after it . . . would mend no more") must also be the mourning Arthur is wearing, the "empty place in his heart," as his mother says, "that he has never known the meaning of" (860).

If this embodiment of maternal mourning suggests the ways Amy will in time restore Arthur's (other) mother to him, the way she will fill that empty place with meaning, her letters also look forward to that moment of embodying, and the ways Amy will herself become property, and become the fulfillment of Arthur's lack, as she earlier became the "Roman daughter" who nurtured her father. As she closes the final letter, she describes her dreadful homesickness: "so dearly do I love the scene of my poverty and your kindness. O so dearly, O so dearly!" (610). Every element of the book's resolution is here: the "dearness" that is realized through love – a love that can take place only through Arthur's kindness, and Amy's impoverishment. For Amy to be the "fullness" Arthur needs, she must empty herself of her property – return, in a sense, to what she remembers his calling her, his "poor child." For Amy's story to end properly, she must renounce that fortune once more. It is not for nothing, we might remember, that Amy begins her letter to Arthur by telling him he cannot write back: for all that these letters conjure him, and their love, so powerfully; for all that they invoke so powerfully her confusion, her intelligence, her generosity of spirit, they cannot invoke – indeed, they interdict – a response. And with property, as with letters, Amy cannot imagine, cannot hope for, indeed cannot quite tolerate, getting anything "in return."

But the fact that Amy is so aggressive in her renunciatory fervor, so quick to claim poverty, both of expression and of worldly goods, ought not to encourage us to move so quickly from the substantial property she possesses, at various times in the novel. For all her modesty, her letters claim a space of *self*-possession as powerful as that of Miss Wade, or Mrs. Clennam; for all her quickness to shed it, she is the beneficiary of all the lost wills the novel uncovers; for all her narratorial meekness, she is the only character to speak, uninterrupted, for two chapters, and to make so powerful a claim for herself and her way of seeing. And indeed, for all that her romance has to do with abasement and denial, she makes two marriage proposals in the course of the novel, and the second is accepted: given the book's economy, the fact that Amy has only to lose a (monetary) fortune to gain a romantic and a spiritual one makes her the book's clear winner. She has, in the book's relentless passion for exchange and transformation, traded up – indeed, gotten what every other letter-writing, story-telling woman in the novel would be happy to get: her heart's desire. If the reader feels some pang for the (now imaginary) financial fortune that has been shadowing Amy's path for so many pages, that reader has not quite learned the novel's lesson: that there is no property that cannot be "come over" or that can be properly "tied up," and it might not only be better to give than receive, but better never to have been given at all. At the plot's end, Amy gives Arthur the codicil to burn, asking him to speak a "charm" ("I love you" [893–4]) as he burns the secret of how his family stole her fortune. But Amy's final view of that inheritance is far from charming – it is as savage as anything in the novel. As she cries out to him,

"I have nothing in the world. I am as poor as when I lived here . . . O my dearest and best, are you quite sure you will not share my fortune with me now? . . . I never was rich before, I never was proud before, I never was happy before, I am rich in being taken by you, I am proud in having been resigned by you, I am happy in being with you in this prison . . . I am yours anywhere, everywhere! . . . I would rather pass my life here with you, and go out daily, working for our bread, than I would have the greatest fortune that ever was told, and be the greatest lady that ever was honoured." (885–886)

What might, elsewhere, pass as merely the ideological trappings necessary to prove that pride and riches go before various falls, and the best heart is a simple one, seems in this novel a terrible confirmation of the book's darkest message: that there is nothing that cannot be taken, and to be "yours" may be the only way of truly being one's own. Amy says to Fanny, "If you loved anyone, you would no more be yourself, but you would quite lose and forget yourself in your devotion to him" (648); such loss and forgetfulness, in a novel fascinated by the perverse possessions of property and memory, may be the most secure holdings of all.

What, though, of the slippery property that has been moving with the stealth of documents, codicils, and whispered secrets for the many chapters of the novel? It has gone back to the realm of secrecy – and with it, it would seem, that most secret property of all, the wife's separate property. But it is worth taking one last look at that promised, much-battered property – and at its role in one last economy, the economy of writing, which the novel puts forward.

In keeping with *Little Dorrit*'s prizing of constraint, the novel reaches an excessively sober conclusion, as if it were drawing its forces back in toward a single figure. Amy Dorrit, says the narrator late in the novel, is the book's "vanishing-point" (801), the imaginary space towards which all lines of perspective converge – the point that implicitly locates *our* perspective (as it explicitly does Arthur's) and pins us to the novel's readings; the point that will confirm that we have successfully completed the novel and achieved some satisfactory release from its wanderings. But Amy remains the book's vanishing point in other, less comfortable ways as well: so small she is in danger of disappearing, she seems almost to have no view of her own, as, by the end, she has no property. If Arthur does, indeed, take all she has, what is the blessing she expects to receive? What is the blessing the book's conclusion will confer? And will she be present, in any material form at all, to receive it?

The Dickens daughter, we are always being reminded, is no material girl; in that way, Amy, who grows up in the "shadow of the Marshalsea" and tells a story in which a shadow is the only property, is the only

possible site of value for so dark and so late a novel. There are characters still smaller; still more pitiful; still more beyond the reach of the
inheritance plot. Maggy, a step below even Amy in the book's property
hierarchy (and a character easily dismissed as a sentimental sign of
Amy's compassion), seems to suggest that even Amy's renunciatory (self-
negated) personhood is an achievement in this harsh world. Maggy, after
all, has an even shorter narrative to tell than Amy's, one that lacks even
grammatical connectors. Asked to tell her story, Maggy says: "'Gin.'
Then beat an imaginary child, and said, 'Broom-handles and pokers'"
(143). Maggy's conjuring of her abusive grandmother, and her own subsequent retardation at the age of ten, her fantasy of the perfection of
"hospitals" and "chicking," presents an even barer fantasy than Amy's,
one that no debate over separate property will touch. Maggy cannot get
anything like a fairy-tale ending, for even in her imagination, hospitals
and chicking cannot undo whatever was once done to her: like the many
bustling strangers jostling Arthur and Amy after they are wed, she
cannot have anything like full subjectivity restored to her, even if, like the
questing Arthur, she wants "to know" – and she wants to have – more.

Amy's quest is to have just enough, and no more. She proves that she
is worth an inheritance by rejecting one over and over and over – but
this novel, unlike other Dickens texts of fathers and daughters, actually
takes her at her word, and takes away all her money. She and Arthur
begin their life together with nothing beyond the "works" of Doyce and
Clennam; Arthur's family house has collapsed, Mr. Dorrit's money followed him and the disgraced Merdle into the grave, Mrs. Clennam's
fortune goes unmentioned. For Amy, as for Arthur, going "down into a
modest life of usefulness and happiness" (895) is portion enough.

The voice asking for more in this novel is Miss Wade's, for she rejects
all that Amy represents, all fantasies of material renunciation and spiritual gain, as nothing other than a swindle. For Miss Wade, every generous offer is a trap; every sacrifice she makes a power-play; to eat the
scraps at the table becomes for her, as it never is explicitly for Amy, the
assertion of her own identity. For a modern reader, bent on self-expression as self-possession, Miss Wade's seems the more powerful gesture:
she seems to speak for everyone in the novel, in her assertion of her own
misery. In the view of Miss Wade, who has, as she reminds us, the mis-
fortune of not being a fool, Amy is the novel's chief fool, and the relent-
lessness of Amy's apotheosis at the novel's end makes Miss Wade's view
almost a welcome relief. Miss Wade's resistance weighs in against the
force of Dickens's passion, which makes Amy's sacrifice of her own food,

her offering up of her own body, the most moral act of the novel – a perspective that makes Dickens curiously akin to the Dorrit family, whose sin is not that they feed off Amy's generosity, but that they never remember to say thank you. As Dickens reads it, that is, the world needs Amy not to eat on behalf of others.

Miss Wade's resistance is, in part, ours; it is hard to read Amy's desire for nothing as anything other than a disguised wish for something in another form. It is hard, that is, to accept renunciation as anything but another move in a complicated game, and it is all too easy to rationalize away Amy's desire to free herself from fortune. There are any number of such theories implicit in the novel: Amy is in it for herself, and getting her own pleasures out of "service," winning love to herself rather than goodies for herself;[12] Amy is a child of duty, and merely offering herself up to a higher account book; Amy, in short, remains self-interested. Even the most perverse of readings, one always available to a Dickens reader, that Amy is simply a masochist, makes Amy yet again someone in it for herself. Much as Dickens wants to believe that Amy has taken herself out of the vicious relations of the novel's food chain, she remains within it. The masochist does not reject the law of the market; she merely wants, as does anyone in a market world, to determine the terms by which she is to be consumed. As Walter Benn Michaels has memorably summed up, in what he calls the "masochist's contract," "If the masochist's desire to be owned is perverse, it is nevertheless a perversion made possible only by the bourgeois identification of the self as property . . . The masochist loves what the capitalist loves: the freedom to buy and sell, the inalienable right to alienate."[13] Such a reading allows us to pathologize both Amy's response and Dickens's dependence on it – though paradoxically, it also lessens its possibility for critique of property relations.

Before we race to do so, we might take the path Michaels took to get to that insight: following the psychoanalyst and writer Helene Deutsch, he argues that for women, conventional femininity looks so much like masochism as to render the latter term near useless as a diagnostic tool. In one case from Krafft-Ebing that Michaels cites, Case 84, the speaker "says that she sometimes fancies herself the slave of the man she loves, but then notes bitterly that 'this does not suffice, for after all every woman can be the slave of her husband.'"[14] Given these propertied relations, what woman, in culture, is not a masochist?

Such might seem the perspective of *Little Dorrit*, which seems to argue that in a world without separate female property, sacrifice is common sense: women can acquire power *only* by giving up what they *already* don't own, themselves. That it is a purely negative power is confirmed throughout the novel – by Mrs. Clennam's self-enclosure in her wheel chair, "like Fate in a go-cart" (330); Affery's marriage to Flintwinch, which she describes as "a Smothering instead of a Wedding" (79); Flora Finching's drinking, rattling on, and self-willed permafrost at the age of seventeen; Fanny's decision to throw herself away on a booby to revenge herself against Mrs. Merdle's condescension; and, of course, Miss Wade's rejection of everyone she might have loved, including the fiancé who offered her the Cinderella plot of class advancement, romantic fulfillment, and an end to her bitter narrative. In its vicious revision of *Jane Eyre*'s class fantasies and erotic empowerment, *Little Dorrit* seems to offer only the darkest empowerment, one of renunciation, debasement, and transformation: "*take* all I have, and *make* it a blessing to me" (828: emphasis added).

And certainly the novel's end allows so dark a view of property *and* of power – though its conviction is slightly undercut by the novel's most insidious insight: that Miss Wade's anger makes her considerably more unhappy than does Amy's subservience. We could read Amy's "gift" (her choice of "nothing" as her portion) as the novel's vicious recuperation of the daughter, a triumph of paternal plotting, the end of separate female property – or separate identity. But here *Little Dorrit*'s closural anxiety re-enters the discussion, for the process of the daughter's subsumption is less easy than ever in this novel, and the questions we have been considering throughout this chapter unnerve it further. We might wonder if, at this moment in his career, Dickens hasn't begun to think seriously about what happens if the daughter decides to fight – or to bite – back. The nature of that fear becomes considerably clearer in *A Tale of Two Cities*, with the invention of the guillotine, "Dr. Guillotin's daughter." But in *Little Dorrit*, the daughter's gift (of food, narrative, the body) is being read through a system other than political revolution – that of the inscription of property relations.

In this way, Dickens's novel (for all its involvement in what the turnkey would call "coming over" women; encouraging them to renounce one fortune after another) registers a deeper anxiety about relations between society and individuals, as well as between men and women. The debate over women's separate property called up just such an anxiety in the culture: as one MP, a Mr. Massey, in the debate over the provisions of the Married Women's Property Bill argued, changing these laws "might disturb the whole of the relations of married life, and revolutionize all the principles which applied to the rights of property in this country."[15]

The novel's own revolutions (its inversions and perversions of people and things) register a similar threat: how are novelistic exchanges to be carried out, how is novelistic value to be assigned, in a world in which relationships are so completely "disturbed"?

This anxiety offers us another way of reading Amy Dorrit's renunciation, and the readerly perspective that the "vanishing" of her property is to ensure. Amy Dorrit's sacrifice works to anchor our perspective only if, after the text's property reversals, we imagine that the reversals have stopped, that "proper" closure is doing its work. And yet, the novel offers far less resolution than we might expect: the end of the book's several wills is not truth; the mother's manuscript never reaches the son; nor does the novel carry on *Bleak House*'s work of restoring mothers and daughters. In many ways *Bleak House*'s fantasy of female property (and female writing) is here abandoned into the darkest of Dickensian enclosures, when Arthur and Amy go out, into that middleness that is the end of all proper Victorian fiction, "in sunshine and shade, [as] the noisy and the eager, and the arrogant and the froward and the vain, fretted and chafed, and made their usual uproar" (895). The property that floated around through the novel (Arthur's uncle's, his father's, his mother's, Merdle's, Mr. Dorrit's, even his real mother's imaginary property) has all gone unclaimed, and no one, in this novel, has more than enough.

But it is not so clear that all property goes unclaimed, for what of the ultimate fantasy property, the novel itself? Brian Rotman, in his discussion of the introduction of zero into the European accounting, aligns the "signifying" of nothing in mathematics with the introduction of perspective ("the vanishing point") in art and of paper money in finances: as he memorably puts it, "money required a system of writing . . . to enable it to function as an international medium of exchange."[16] In *Little Dorrit*, a novel with letter-writing daughters and will-lacking sons, Amy seems to encapsulate these functions; and it is through writing that she is able to claim a different kind of identity, a "separate" form of property, for herself.

At the book's close, Amy Dorrit signs her name for the last time, and disappears – into the novel's conclusion, and into the nothingness of her husband's name. She is now "Mrs. Clennam," and her separate story, like her separate property, would seem to end with that signature. This wedding, however, does not seem to be a smothering, for Amy's last signature has considerable power: in fact, it "signs" for the novel, for the novel and the church's books have been linked all along. Early on, Amy rested in the church in which she is later married, with her birth recorded in one book, her head on the "burial volume," asleep on "that sealed book of Fate, untroubled by its mysterious blank leaves" (220). At the novel's end, she signs the middle volume, the marriage book, as if, by magic, the novel had replaced the usual progress (birth, marriage, death) and could thus keep its characters alive forever, by marrying them off.[17] And at the wedding the registrar mete fictionally invokes this mystery.

"For, you see," said Little Dorrit's old friend, "this young lady is one of our curiosities, and has come now to the third volume of our Registers. Her birth is in what I call the first volume; she lay asleep, on this very floor, with her pretty head on what I call the second volume; and she's now a-writing her little name as a bride, in what I call the third volume." (894)

The reader, too, has come now to the third volume; the death of the novel marked by the final writing of "her little name." It is from that magic-writing that Amy and Arthur go "down into a modest life of usefulness and happiness," but also, that the book goes down as *Little Dorrit*, its "curiosities" resolved in its own three volume completeness and death.

This sense of Amy's power over the novel's conclusion might calm some of the storm raised by many readers about the marriage that ends the book, for far more than Esther Summerson, submerged into "the doctor's wife," does Amy seem still a writing (plotting) presence at the end of this novel – and certainly the sense of relief when Arthur finally embraces Amy is more powerful (perhaps because of the terrible tension of so much of the book; perhaps because of the directness of Amy's desire) than any such feeling in *Bleak House*, where the marriage plot seems written as much by John Jarndyce's desire as any other. Perhaps the book's willingness not to finish its other stories (or rather, to suggest that they can only finish as they have begun) seems to give more agency to Amy and Arthur's last steps out of the novel, out of the garden, into the world. But perhaps it is simply a reflection of the revolution it conjured and, like Amy with Arthur's speaking of the "charm," made disappear: the revolution Mr. Massey feared seems to have become instead a revolution in fiction, as material property, as well, dissolves into writing; to have the power of writing is not to be "nobody" after all.

For Amy's doubled inscription raises again the written and writerly quality of female property in this novel: that for all the novel's renunciatory urgency, it seems to present itself as female property, as a text that belongs (like all true narratives, at least in this book) to women. And the book is present, not as Amy's imagined short story, but as rather a long story, and a story with a woman's little name on it. Only the novel holds all the stories, all the secrets, all the properties; for all that the novel urges renunciation to us, it gives little up in return. Amy (in her three-volume form) may stand as the perfect image of property, propriety, and sacrifice, all in one perfect bundle; inheritance may be yet once more dissolved into the paternalist moral tales of duty and guilt the novel tries to assert – nonetheless, the book, with its dependence on female property and its desire to "come over" us, suggests, as Amy writes her little name, that the novel itself may be the wife's best separate property.

PART FOUR

A violent conclusion

CHAPTER SIX

In the shadow of Satis House
The woman's story in Great Expectations

After the various experiments in narrative form and perspective in the novels that directly precede it, *Great Expectations* might seem a return to more conventional narrative gestures for Dickens, a return to the boy's autobiography (and its requisite story of identity) that we seemed to leave behind after *David Copperfield* with the immersion in the wider-ranging social fiction and novelistic experiments of the 1850s. Adept Dickens readers might note the specifics of the reprise: the return of Dora and Agnes in Estella and Biddy; the splitting of the bosom friend, Steerforth, into Herbert Pocket and Bentley Drummle; the careful regret and hard-won wisdom of the first-person narrator and the romance of maturity. Where, after the intervening years, is *Bleak House*'s pain of self-creation; Amy Dorrit's searing self-renunciation; the return to history and self-annihilation in *A Tale of Two Cities*, the novel that precedes *Great Expectations*, and whose terrors and fantasies the novel of identity might seem to elide? But note the other returns that *Great Expectations* makes: to the violence of coming to consciousness that *Oliver Twist* and other novels suggested; the darkness of the prison fiction and the revision of the Newgate story; the snaky convulsions of the inheritance plot, of the dead father's will and the mother's seeming perversion of the son's story. And in its revisiting of that son's coming to consciousness, property, and story-telling, *Great Expectations* offers yet another new twist to the same old story: a different version of the daughter's coming to consciousness and inheritance, and a powerful revision of the son's always question-able authority.

For of all Dickens's fantastic accounts of boys' lives, all of them alter-nately fairy-tale and horror story, none more insistently plays with the story of the fairy princess, or more insistently rewrites that story's darker side, than does *Great Expectations*. Pip casts his own story as a romance, with Estella as at once the beautiful, cold, distant "light" of his existence and the reward for his trials; as he carefully positions her (the star by which he can navigate), so she must remain for his story to have coherence. We, too, mark our positions by her distance: to the extent that we are ironic readers of the novel, we will focus on her unsuitability and Pip's obsession; if we choose to value Dickensian sentiment, we will emphasize her changed heart and her altered form, and we will, with Pip, look for no "shadow" of a further parting. The Estella who has been "bent and broken" will in either case monitor our progress and wisdom and our assessment of Pip's growth.

But one of the persistent problematics of *Great Expectations* – the real shadow that haunts its ending – is not whether Pip ever marries Estella, but whether Pip ever *sees* Estella: does he ever free her from her fixed place as the guiding light of his existence? This question matters as an emblem not only of Pip's maturity, but of Dickens's relation to his hero – his narrator – throughout the novel. Pip, as everyone knows, is an insufferable young man, but fewer readers have commented on the ways in which he remains insufferable to the end of the novel. No character points out his shallowness throughout more effectively than Estella, questioning and teasing him, mocking his efforts to be his own hero. But more to the purpose here, no character so writes her own novel, escaping Pip's monomaniacal obsession, than Estella, who throughout is wiser, sadder, and funnier than Pip – and who is the character most entirely "bent and broken" by the novel into another form.

What Estella's story offers – particularly when it is read in concert with the novel's fascination with female plotting and the indirections of female inheritance – is a retelling of the story of inheritance, guilt, and masochism we have been attending to since the "prison narratives" of the opening chapter. For Estella, unlike Florence, Esther, or Amy, there is no return to the father's house, no reconciliation with the lost mother, indeed, no home left at all. But reading for the inversions of Estella's story also "retells" what seems to be *Great Expectations'* own account of itself. To try to read Estella's novel – with its bitter realism and its own change of heart – through Pip's narration is to illuminate not only the way Dickens constructs narratives-within-narratives, the way autobiographical narrative is always questioning itself, but to question again the nature of narratorial closure that *Little Dorrit* examined so precisely. Reading for Estella's "end" is to make of the famous "second ending" of *Great Expectations* two quite different endings, suggesting that Dickensian closure – like Dickensian "art" – writes itself through (the fear of) the woman's story.

Though not a novelist, Pip is one of Dickens's greatest fabulists, and his favorite story is that he is designed to marry Estella, and she him. She, however, is his most critical reader: from her initial valuation of him ("what coarse hands") through her most honest moments ("Do you want me, then, to deceive and entrap you?"), she has the ability to put him off balance, to begin his story again.[1] More disturbingly, she questions the notion of autonomous heroics his story depends on, reminding him that "We have no choice, you and I, but to obey our instructions. We are not free to follow our own devices, you and I" (285). Her tone, he recounts, was "as if our association were forced upon us and we were mere puppets [and it] gave me pain; but everything in our intercourse did give me pain" (288). In fact, though, Estella is right, and they are both puppets: if Pip's tragedy is his assumption of authority where none exists, Estella's is her knowledge that she is powerless and her realization that knowing this will in no way change her story.

Pip's story, like most critical accounts of it, begins with him alone, trying to trace out of linguistic fragments his own history, probing the "authority of tombstones" in order to generate out of them a family, a personality, a past.[2] Facing the emptiness of the marshes and himself, a "small bundle of shivers growing afraid of it all and beginning to cry" (36), he is grabbed, shaken, tumbled upside down, released prematurely from his examination of "the identity of things" (35) and set loose in the world which Dickens describes as that of the "accoucheur policeman" (54) ready to abduct people for the effrontery of having been born. Pip, that orphan, seedling, blossom, who has been "brought up by hand" (39), "Ram-paged" upon (40), "dosed" (44) and "fixed" (57) will spend the rest of the book trying to escape the world he has been abandoned into and to fill in the pictures behind those words in the graveyard, for without those words he is empty and might as well, as Mrs. Joe wishes, have been buried in the graveyard. Having "called myself Pip and [having come] to be called Pip" (35), he must write himself a story and find his own way out of the marshes.

This version of Pip's story is one often rehearsed by critics, in part because it is a readerly explanation. What Pip sees as the way out is suggested to him in the first chapter: it is primarily linguistic, for he can read the tombstone; he can invent his lost family; he can "give it mouth!" as the convict orders (36). But that narrative of linguistic self-creation is linked to human recreation: Pip's quest for the "beginning(s)" of his cry becomes one with his quest for love and fulfillment. Out of the pristine and terrifying loneliness of that initial scene, of reading identity through tombstones, comes a desire to read and be read, to find another to give meaning to the story of self that Pip is trying to create. Pip's erotic journey is, for him, a method of perception, his creation of a self linked to speech and desire. But in this model romantic desire is the primary vehicle for the self coming to consciousness: the young boy "becomes" himself by seeking an object for desire, and by absorbing that object into himself. This romantic consciousness partakes of fulfillment and mastery at the same time; Pip can call himself into being (realize his "expectations") by achieving the object (here, by winning the girl) he has identified as his own.[3] But Pip's expectations are not only of "calling himself Pip" and of winning the girl, but of winning everything associated with her. In pursuing a princess in the tower, one difficult to capture and hard to hold on to, Pip will fulfill his economic expectations as well, running together romantic desire, class anxiety, and the promise of happiness – all conveniently presented in one figure, that of the heroine of the romance, who will become the contested site of "value" in the novel.

Dickens obviously links these worlds of language and desire in the descriptions of how Pip comes to love Estella – or at least in Pip's accounts of them. But I want to trace a different account of identity, one that begins before Pip ever sees Estella: in Pip's attempts to learn to write, his cross-examination of Joe Gargery, and his first trip to Satis House. That story tells a different version of what Pip's "mastery" will mean. It is linked to violence and victimization, and it offers a different kind of home for identity.[4] In that story, if Pip's transformation begins when he learns to read, his real education begins when he learns why Joe cannot.

Pip's early efforts at reading land him amidst a tangle of economics, criminality and anxiety: he struggles "through the alphabet as if it had been a bramble-bush; getting considerably worried and scratched by every letter"; when he goes on to the numbers, "those thieves, the nine figures," they "seemed every evening to do something new to disguise themselves and baffle recognition" (75). But Pip wants to read only in order to "make" something of himself, and "at last I began, in a pur-blind groping way, to read, write and cipher, on the very smallest scale" (75). The small "scale" is in keeping with Pip's repeated anxiety about size in general: he himself is, as Joe remarks, "oncommon small" (100), and he seems to fear this is his only sign of remarkability. But his hope is that it is writing that will make him uncommon, and his first literary activity is to write a letter to Joe – for which "there was no indispensable necessity . . . inasmuch as he sat beside me and we were alone" (75). The sense that "alone" and "beside" coexist is key to this novel, and the aloneness of their togetherness is accentuated when Pip learns Joe cannot read except for the most rudimentary picking out of "J-O." Joe, like Pip, looks in texts only for what he can find of himself.

But Joe's account of his inability to read connects literary knowledge with sexual domination. When Pip asks why Joe cannot read, he tells a story of his parents: his father, when he was "overtook with drink . . . hammered away" at Joe's mother, and, whenever Joe and his mother ran away, his father "were that good in his hart" that he came with "a most tremenjous crowd" and "took us home and hammered us." "Which were," Joe says, "a drawback on my learning" (76–77). His story further explains how he became acquainted with Pip's sister, and "the talk how she was bringing you up by hand." Her kindness in taking the boy is part of how he comes to propose to her, and to propose that she "brings the poor little child" to the forge; it also becomes part of the reason why he must now be careful to learn "on the sly," for "your sister is given to government" (79). While Pip is "startled, for I had some shadowy idea (and I am afraid I must add, hope) that Joe had divorced her in favour of the Lords of the Admiralty, or Treasury," Joe only "mean[s]tersay the government of you and myself" (79). And while he feels that Mrs. Joe "would not be over partial to my being a scholar, for fear I might rise," his explanation of why he doesn't "rise" reinvokes his mother's suffering: "I see so much in my poor mother, of a woman drudging and slaving and breaking her honest hart and never getting no peace in her mortal days, that I'm dead afeerd of going wrong in the way of not doing what's right by a woman, and I'd fur rather of the two go wrong the t'other way, and be a little ill-conwenienced myself" (80). Joe's fear of "not doing what's right by a woman" is constituted in the face of the "hammering" that his father does, a kind of sexual labor that is almost constant in this novel; the novel offers as an explanation both of Joe's goodness and his inability to protect Pip from the violence his father did to his mother. More ominous in terms of Pip's anxieties about his education, however, is Joe's assertion that it was male sexual violence that has kept (and keeps) him from learning to read: to read, Joe stresses to Pip, is to be "like a sort of rebel."

But Pip's own sense that it is better to suffer than to strike back is only reinforced by Joe's example: Pip's progress into narrative will be through a story he tells himself about "slaving and breaking [his] honest hart," a story that identifies being "ill-conwenienced myself" as the principal way to identity. The novel offers one of its most powerful metaphors of the loneliness of identity, one linked imagistically to the book's opening on the marshes. Pip goes on:

Joe made the fire and swept the hearth, and then we went to the door to listen for the chaise-cart. It was a dry cold night, and the wind blew keenly, and the frost was white and hard. A man would die to-night of lying out on the marshes, I thought. And then I looked at the stars, and considered how awful it would be for a man to turn his face up to them as he froze to death, and see no help or pity in all the glittering multitude. (80)

Pip's ability to imagine the "awful" fate of this man suggests his willingness to see himself in the same position. It is as if he is choosing his future by choosing his perspective, choosing to live out the role of solitary victim, defined by those things more distant, contemplating his own contemplation of them and his inability to reach them or even read them. At this moment, he is a boy looking for a glittering star; he is looking to freeze to death.

What comes in from the cold in this scene is Mrs. Joe and Uncle Pumblechook, bearing the news of Pip's coming visit to Satis House. When he goes there, Miss Havisham ("so new . . . so strange, and so fine – and melancholy" [89]) sends him to the door to call Estella, where he finds only more coldness and more strangeness: "To stand in the dark in a mysterious passage of an unknown house, bawling Estella to a scornful young lady neither visible nor responsive, and feeling it a dreadful liberty so to roar out her name, was almost as bad as playing to order. But, she answered at last, and her light came along the dark passage like a star" (89). Pip plays on the starlight of Estella's name here as if he could make it literal – as Miss Havisham has made literal her broken heart; Magwitch, his desire to "make" a gentleman and revenge his conviction – but Estella's scorn (like that of the distant, uncaring stars) *is* her attraction. For Pip, looking to create the torment he can name and hope to master, Estella's invisible, unresponsive self becomes the light that will guide him both in and out of "a mysterious passage of [the] unknown." Pip's whole identity will circle around that light; he makes her instantly "the embodiment of every graceful fancy that my mind has ever become acquainted with" (378).

This instant instantiation of Estella with meaning is one that persists throughout the novel: late in the book, Pip will tell Estella she has been a part of "every prospect I have ever seen" (378), and at every moment throughout (as he works at the forge; when he is "rescued" by Jaggers from his apprenticeship; when he learns to be a gentleman) his only question is, will this help me win Estella? But romantic love goes further for Pip, until he cannot tell the difference between himself and Estella, or between Estella and his "fancies" about her. But as he learns perfectly,

as Miss Havisham urges, to "love the smiter" (261), it is his own vision
that he finally loves – his own narcissistic image, frozen on the marshes,
that he turns to. Like any Philip to any Stella (from Sir Philip Sidney on),
he loves in Estella the image of his own expectations, the image of his
own desolation, the image of his own destruction. Pip will go on, near
the novel's end, to tell Estella that she "cannot choose but remain part
of my character" (378): as Freud suggests, "At the height of being in love
the boundary between ego and object threatens to melt away. Against all
the evidence of his senses, a man who is in love declares that 'I' and 'You'
are one, and is prepared to behave as if it were a fact."[5] For Pip, the "I"
and "You" are always the "I": there is no Estella, and yet there can only
be a Pip if he is in love with something he calls Estella.

Pip's story is given unity by his faith in the oneness of their identity
and in their eventual union, but the narrative discourse's remarkable
tightness of imagery is equally dependent on this imagined union. We
get some sense of this in the powerful rush of images when Herbert
Pocket suggests that Pip try not to love Estella, that he "detach [himself]
from her": "I turned my head aside, for, with a rush and a sweep, like the
old marsh winds coming up from the sea, a feeling like that which had
subdued me on the morning when I left the forge, when the mists were
solemnly rising, and when I laid my hand upon the village finger-post,
smote upon my heart again" (271). Pip can only be "smitten" once more;
all the identity he has ever had (mists, village fingerposts, the sea, the
forge) is suffused – fused – with Estella; there can be no subjectivity here
without his utter subjection to Estella; no (novelistic) language without
the images that subdue him again and again. It is his own "embodiment"
he creates through his "graceful fancy" of her and his own fancy of
loving the smiter.

The novel, then, posits a self that realizes itself through violence,
through abusive sexuality, by being "smitten" and loving the smiter. Or
rather, this is how it seems to posit male subjectivity. The problem of the
feminine, or of female subjectivity, is more vexed. In some ways, there
can be no freestanding, narrating woman because Pip views himself as
the woman in the text: Pip has chosen to identify himself with the fem-
inized, and all subjectivity in the novel, all sentiment, all narration, is
female – or rather, the victimized, battered, self-emasculated male. Joe's
story offers a clear choice, and Pip, like Joe, chooses to be a mother, not
a father; a wife, not a husband; a girl, not a boy. He will "play" a hero's
part, but he feels himself to be the passionate, abused heroine; it is for

that reason, perhaps, that he has so much trouble telling the difference between Estella and himself.

But these differences exist, and they are registered along linguistic and psychological axes: what they point to is a different relationship of power and of volition in the novel. What Pip cannot see is that to the extent that he is forcing Estella to abuse him, he is in turn an abuser. His identification of her with "the smiter" is as much a victimization of her as his (elected) identity as smitten is of him. The difference between them becomes clear in their relation to the violence that marks this novel: where Pip seems to choose pain, out of guilt, out of doubt, Estella seems only to tolerate it – until her marriage, when she seems to embrace it. When Pip asks if she has chosen to "fling [her]self away on a brute," she answers, "On whom should I fling myself away? . . . Should I fling myself away upon the man who would the soonest feel (if people do feel such things) that I took nothing to him? . . . I am tired of the life I have led, which has very few charms for me, and I am willing enough to change it" (377). Estella's "fling" is into a world of violence: as Pip recognizes "in despair," Drummle is "such a mean brute, such a stupid brute." But she replies, "Don't be afraid of my being a blessing to him . . . I shall not be that" (377). Lost, like Pip, in a world of "mother(s) by adoption," Estella has no self that is a "blessing": her self, like Pip's, seems made ("formed" or "forged," in the novel's terms) to be thrown away. What Estella's "flinging" herself away does in other ways, though, is to subvert the exchange value mentality in the novel, the ways in which all emotional relationships take place in the world of the "cash-nexus," a world in which people have value only insofar as they can be exchanged, or bring profit. In that view, Estella is herself a commodity, an attraction, someone who "uses" others – as Miss Havisham begs her to do – only to find herself "used" in turn. To throw oneself away is no longer to have any price: it is a costly gambit, but it is one way to regain value for one's self.

A psychoanalytic reading might argue that if Pip's victimization suggests male narcissism, Estella's reflects in part what Freud and subsequent feminist theorists have argued of female narcissism. Mary Jacobus, following Sarah Kofman, has referred to the world of narcissistic women as "a lost paradise of narcissistic completeness, [which] leaves the [woman's] lover forever unsatisfied": applying her language to Estella, we might claim that what Estella has kept is the "self-sufficiency" of loving only herself.[6] As Freud argues, while love for men has the effect of "an impoverishment of the ego as regards libido in favour of the love-object," narcissistic women can love only themselves "with an intensity comparable to that of the man's love for them," and in fact they have "the greatest fascination for men not only for aesthetic reasons . . . but because . . . another person's narcissism has a great attraction for those who have renounced part of their own narcissism and are in search of object-love."[7] This essence of woman, as Sarah Kofman theorizes it, represents to men the lost "part" of their own narcissism, their fascination with their own double; but to do so it must involve a woman who is not defined in terms of loss, a woman who does not "need" men. Like Freud, Dickens seems at moments to fear, to "run from," the narcissistic woman; but, like Freud again, Dickens also raises the question of what the woman who is a projection for a man has for herself. We can know what the attraction is for the man; what can we know of the woman who possesses fully (only) her own status as enigma?

In this novel, questions of self are always questions of (self-) possession and the material world, and Estella, a child who is abandoned and bought, a jewel who is brought up to display the jewels of others, is the savviest economist in the novel. In her early scene with the Pocket family, as they gather around the funereal birthday table and Camilla recounts how she, valuing the "credit of the family," forced Matthew to buy funeral weeds, it is Estella who asks the important question: "*He* paid for them, did he not?" " 'It's not a question, my dear child, who paid for them,' returned Camilla, '*I* bought them' " (110), but Estella learns early the difference between buying and paying. The emotional language of the novel is similarly rewritten as economic exchange: in the same scene, Estella slaps Pip's face, and asks, "Why don't you cry again, you little wretch," to which he replies, " 'Because I'll never cry for you again,'. . . Which was, I suppose, as false a declaration as ever was made; for I was inwardly crying for her then, and I know what I know of *the pain she cost me afterwards*" (111, emphasis added). But Pip's knowledge of "costs" is retrospective, while Estella's of "payment" is immediate: one might argue that Pip will learn what things cost in part at Estella's expense. At the end of this scene, Estella beckons to Pip, saying, "Come here! You may kiss me, if you like!" When he does, he explains, "I felt that the kiss was given to the coarse common boy as a piece of money might have been, and that it was worth nothing" (121). To ask what it was "worth," again, is not to ask what it "costs" Estella to give; "the Estella," as he calls her later, was created to "give" kisses, but not, as Estella will remind Miss Havisham, to feel love. She is a kind of instructive prostitute here, giving a sentimental education – breaking Pip's heart and forming it, precisely because she is unable to feel herself anything but "worth nothing." She is Pip's prize, but she possesses nothing of value, only the value accorded her by others.

To argue for Estella's value apart from Pip's valuation of her, to argue against his casting of Estella as the bewitching princess who batters and wounds him, is to argue against his vision of his story – and that of most critics. Her value, like that of the narcissistic woman Freud imagines, has always existed only in Pip's idealization (and our potential denigration) of her. To imagine valuing her differently might seem a deliberate perversity; within the novel itself, however, it is Estella who most often critiques Pip's vision, who points out to him the folly of his obsession and the unnecessary heartbreak he has written for himself. When she asks Pip if he wants her to deceive and entrap him, and Pip responds by asking if she deceives and entraps Bentley Drummle, she answers, "Yes, and many others – all of them but you" (330). Earlier, "seem[ing] to pity me," she asks,

"Pip, Pip . . . will you never take warning?"
"Of what?"
"Of me."
"Warning not to be attracted by you, do you mean, Estella?"
"Do I mean! If you don't know what I mean, you are blind." (319)

Pip imagines a range of conventional responses ("I should have replied that Love was commonly reputed blind"), but he does not make them, he claims, because he thinks her unable to answer, "pressed" by Miss Havisham's orders; but certainly, he is as much impressed by his vision of himself as a lover. He is, as Estella calls him, a "visionary boy." Imagined from Estella's perspective – precisely the way this scene encourages us to see – "courtship" looks very different. Miss Havisham hired her, as a child, to break hearts; the one person she could hope would know better, around whom she could be something other than "the Estella," refuses to free her from that role.

Pip himself seems to see her function in economic terms – and what he resents most is the reminder that he is economically, as much as erotically, bound to her. While her value is always in both her cost and the value she carries with her, what he fears is the economic reading of his "enslavement," which might otherwise look merely like ambition. His most detailed denunciation of her suggests that he both knows – and resents – any analysis of who "pays":

I suffered every kind and degree of torture that Estella could cause me. The nature of my relations with her, which placed me on terms of familiarity without placing me on terms of favour, conduced to my distraction. *She made use of me* to tease other admirers, and she turned the very familiarity between herself and me, *to the account of putting a constant slight on my devotion to her.* If I had been her secretary, steward, half-brother, poor relation – if I had been a younger brother of her appointed husband – I could not have seemed to myself, further from my hopes when I was nearest to her. (318–9, emphasis added)

Pip is exactly those things he fears being: a secretary, a steward, half-brother, poor relation. And when he goes on to describe how "maddening" she is, one can read again how maddening *he* is. In her "slighting" of his devotion, we hear her voice, saying to him as directly as she does before marrying Bentley, "Pip, don't be foolish" (329): it is only in Pip's mind that she is leading him into the flame; only in his mind that he has any "hopes"; only in his mind that what he calls "my trials" exist.

These are, of course, the trials of romantic love, and Pip's most moving statements encourage us to read Estella as his visionary mistress, his star, his expectation. Pip's authorship is so strong as to make Estella's story almost disappear, to make Estella almost disappear. When Pip says, "You are part of my existence, part of myself," he takes her away from herself, swallows her up, makes her into his story. As he himself says to her, "Estella, to the last hour of my life, you cannot choose but remain part of my character, part of the little good in me, part of the evil" (378). Where in this equation, with its careful partitioning, is Estella's character – and where is her choice?

In some ways, it is surprisingly easy to reimagine *Great Expectations* as Estella's novel, as a successor to *Bleak House* and *Little Dorrit*. In that scheme, it is Estella who is a revision of David Copperfield – or rather, of "Betsey Trotwood Copperfield," the (imaginary) double of David whom Aunt Betsey planned to rear, raising her to fear and distrust men. If we were to read Estella as the natural heir to Florence Dombey and Amy Dorrit, Pip would become not the obvious hero of the novel, but the equally obvious revision of a series of absurd, "foolish" boys with silly names. In that version of the novel, Pip is just another Toots, following his idol around, or Guppy, wooing Esther Summerson and unable to tell the difference between his love and his ambition, or (most ironically) another version of John Chivery, passionate and poetical, dreaming of Amy Dorrit, and writing pathetic tombstones for himself. That novel is not so hard to construct out of the various pieces of this one.

But to read Estella's character back into the complicated and aggressively coherent first-person narration we are given, to separate her story from Pip's subsuming of it, is a different kind of activity, and it takes us in two directions: into a discussion of plot and into a discussion of metaphor. On the level of plot, Estella's story is one with a pattern of disruptive plotting, disruptive to Pip and his expectations, throughout the novel. It is remarkable, in his dealings with Estella and elsewhere in the novel, how many of Pip's mistakes are connected to confusion about female plotting, both the plots women are spinning and the stories women are made a part of. He assumes, consistently, that Estella intends to flirt with him; he assumes, almost fatally, that Miss Havisham intends him for Estella; and he assumes, pathetically, almost to the novel's end, that Biddy will wait for him to choose her. Other men, more powerful readers of female plots, similarly build expectations on them: Jaggers, after all, "made" his career on Molly's trial, the trial that brought him to Miss Havisham's attention, and which prompted her to ask him to bring her a child; more movingly, it was the love of his lost daughter, Estella, that caused Magwitch to respond so powerfully to the orphan boy Pip and to vow to make him a gentleman. Women and the violence directed against them seem behind much of the plotting, overt and covert, in the novel; but female plots have unexpected kicks and quirks in them, and they tend here, as elsewhere in Dickens, to turn against the men who think they read women so well.

To learn that Magwitch, looking at Pip, really sees his lost daughter, Estella, is to see Pip, unexpectedly, as a "daughter after all." It is to think our way back into Miss Havisham's dark house, and into Pip's sister's home as well – to think ourselves back into the daughter's plot, and to do so, as with Estella, *through* Pip's version of his story. For the Miss Havisham who so terrifies Pip is also a daughter after all: still living in her father's house, and reaping the revenge he sowed for her.[8] Her story, as Herbert Pocket tells it to Pip, is caught up in her father's ambitions and anger, and the legacy he left her:

"Miss Havisham, you must know, was a spoilt child. Her mother died when she was a baby, and her father denied her nothing. . . . Well! Mr. Havisham was very rich and very proud. So was his daughter."

"Miss Havisham was an only child?" I hazarded.

"Stop a moment, I am coming to that. No, she was not an only child; she had a half-brother. Her father privately married again – his cook, I rather think."

"I thought he was proud," said I.

"My good Handel, so he was. He married his second wife privately, because he was proud, and in course of time *she* died. When she was dead, I apprehend he first told his daughter what he had done, and then the son became a part of the family . . . He turned out riotous, extravagant, undutiful – altogether bad.

At last his father disinherited him; but he softened when he was dying, and left him well off, though not nearly so well off as Miss Havisham." (203–4)

This minibiography calls up not only female plotting but female inheritance – and its relationship to the plot of *masculine* inheritance we have been tracing. The "secret marriage" between father and cook suggests the cross-class rape of *A Tale of Two Cities* and the cross-class romances of *Our Mutual Friend,* and adds an odd edge to the relationship between Jaggers and his once-violent, now-tamed housekeeper, Molly; its story of the riotous, exiled son suggests as well the interloper Heathcliff, wreaking havoc on the world of Wuthering Heights.

But in the father's passion, his second family, and his favoring of his proud and imperious daughter, lie the seeds of the daughter's tragedy: she will inherit more money than her brother Arthur, and he, in his resentment, will design the plot that will lead her to offer her considerable affection (and much of her fortune) to her brother's wastrel friend, Compeyson. When Compeyson leaves her, devastated, at the altar, she will destroy all around her, making a ruin of her father's house, making a mockery of the idea that "whoever had this house, could want nothing else" (86). As Estella herself says to Pip, when offering him this free translation of Satis House ("Greek, or Latin, or Hebrew, or all three – or all one to me – for enough") "They must have been easily satisfied in those days, I should think" (86). But the inference is clear: the "satisfaction" of the father (the secret marriage, the false pride and violence hinted at in his final union) will lay waste to the daughter's inheritance, leaving her with far less than enough. As Estella goes on to say of "Enough House" and its "curious name," "it meant more than it said."

Earlier Dickens novels have been haunted by the inability of the daughter to inherit the paternal house – her inability to have, in the risky world of female property, "enough house." Here, the nightmare takes a different form: the daughter's inheritance becomes, in the reversal of Amy Dorrit's plea to take her wealth and make it a blessing to her, a paternal curse. The daughter who lives in the father's house of sufficiency is described almost entirely in terms of what she lacks: the dress, flower, and bride "had no brightness left but the brightness of her sunken eyes"; the dress "had been put upon the rounded figure of a young woman, and . . . the figure upon which it now hung loose, had shrunk to skin and bones" (87); everything has lost its "lustre." The only "weird" glow left to Miss Havisham, the fire behind the sunken eyes, is the desire to spin out plots, to punish her relatives, revenge herself on the world, and (indirectly) to torture young Pip – to find a human boy on whom to practice and "play." Much of the energy of the novel is caught up in Pip's attempt to read Miss Havisham's mind – to find the plot that inspires her, and that (in turn, as he imagines it) inspires and inspirits him. The book's larger construct encourages a reading of Miss Havisham as trapped in the ruins of sufficiency; only in Pip's mind is she the fairy godmother, appearing in ruins to tempt him on to riches.

That is to say that at some level, the book is obsessed with what Pip perceives as a world of plotting women – beginning not only with Miss Havisham, but with Mrs. Joe, "my all-powerful sister" (46). That world of phallic mothers – best illustrated by the pins in Mrs. Joe's apron, against which she holds the bread she is slicing and buttering for Pip and Joe – offers Pip (in the same contradictory gesture of Satis House) both terror and reward, and seems to hold all the plots together. But here we must begin to pull the novel away from Pip's earliest constructions of it. The most obvious gap we must open is between the early, weirdly powerful Miss Havisham and the pathetic creature Pip must come to forgive – in that reading, her "bright eyes" become one with the other wounded children in the book, with Pip himself, and with the infant Estella, whose father, Magwitch, sees those eyes in the young Pip. But that charity might extend itself to another of the text's orphans, Mrs. Joe herself, whose name and identity have been submerged into her husband's, smothered, as she feels herself, under the apron she can never take off.

Generations of readers have asked, along with Pip, why she couldn't just remove the apron, but the delicate class and power relations *Great Expectations* delineates so carefully suggest the lack of freedom Mrs. Joe might feel: Mrs. Joe seems (although Joe has the more powerful uncle, Mr. Pumblechook) to have come from a higher class than her husband; the attachments of finer living that cling to them (the parlor, the second entryway) seem hers rather than her husband's; it was she who could read and write, and who has moved "downward" in the marriage. This loss of class perhaps inflects less ironically the "fine figure of a woman" Joe continues to see in her, and while the novel, like other Dickens texts, mocks women's social pretenses when they fly in the face of their husbands' realism, it is important to note here that Pip shares his sister's social shame at the "realities" of the smithy and its world of muscles, fires, and grime. But despite the familial residue of lost status, Mrs. Joe seems (like Pip) entirely alone in the world: no mention of any other family surrounds her, and Pip's sense that she must have forced Joe to marry her seems shared by everyone else as well.[9] Yet the very attributes Pip scorns (too much of bone, her redness of skin) in other characters (most notably Peggotty in *David Copperfield*) are viewed affectionately; somehow, the force of "my all powerful sister" leaves no space for Mrs. Joe but the monstrous, and the comic excesses of Peggotty are refigured as the female grotesque. But at the same time, in Pip's account of Mrs. Joe's marriage, male violence is refigured as comic and hence unimaginable: though Joe himself, in the fable of violence against his mother, suggests his wife's possible vulnerability in the face of this "gentle giant" of a man, Pip sees only the violence directed at him.

And why shouldn't he; but the novel conjures up, in Mrs. Joe's image, a series of what Estella will call "mothers by adoption": women who offer needles instead of a maternal bosom; bone instead of gentleness; blows instead of compassion. What these women share (and if Mrs. Joe is the first of them, Estella is the last) is that they themselves lack mothers. The one mention of Mrs. Joe's name reminds us of this, when Pumblechook tells Pip her "name was Georgiana M'ria from her own mother" (484) and conjures up the maternal affection she, as well as Pip, has lost. The image suggests, briefly, Mrs. Joe herself crouching over her parents' tombstones; as when Estella, much later, claims "I have a heart to be stabbed at or shot in . . . and if it ceased to beat I would cease to be" (259), the image hints at the heartlessness that greeted these women in the wide world, as well as the heartlessness they seem to spread around them. The roles available for mother and daughter have (in ways reminiscent of the concentration of plotting in *Little Dorrit*) collapsed further in on each other: this is not the world of *Dombey and Son*, where Edith could be Florence's "beautiful mama" even if acquired through marriage; in some ways, the nightmare bond between Miss Havisham and Estella seems a terrible playing out of the possibility of the damaged mother and the vulnerable daughter, leaving behind a world of battering and possessive men. But the stretch of imagination it takes to imagine Estella as the good daughter falling under the shadow of the angry, beautiful woman (to imagine Miss Havisham into her earlier vulnerability and passion) is to notice once again how the gentle daughter's powers have dissipated into her unstable, seductive opposite, have themselves been weirdly "adopted" by the witches this novel constantly invokes.

The power of these "mothers by adoption" seems singularly like that of the "accoucheur policeman," arresting people for the temerity of being born: here, it is a kind of cannibalism enacted by willful mothers on starving children; an effort to make the children rewrite the mothers' plots. (This is not, of course, so very different from what Magwitch endeavors to do with Pip; this is not the least of the reasons Pip and Estella seem so admirably, if painfully, appropriate for each other at the book's end.) Estella's calm critique of Miss Havisham describes concisely the inscription of the mother's story on the daughter's life:

"If you had brought up your adopted daughter wholly in the dark confinement of these rooms, and had never let her know that there was such a thing as the daylight by which she has never once seen your face – if you had done that, and then, for a purpose had wanted her to understand the daylight and know all about it, you would have been disappointed and angry?

"Or . . . – which is a nearer case – if you had taught her, from the dawn of her intelligence, with your utmost energy and might, that there was such a thing as daylight, but that it was made to be her enemy and destroyer, and she must always turn against it, for it had blighted you and would else blight her; – if you had done this, and then, for a purpose, had wanted her to take naturally to the daylight and she could not do it, you would have been disappointed and angry? . . .

"So, I must be taken as I have been made. The success is not mine, the failure is not mine, but the two together make me." (324)

The language of "making" is pervasive in the book, and is no less present in Pip and Magwitch's interwoven stories: the question of who's to be maker is as powerful as who's to be master.[10] But the language here, in particular, of the mother who raises the (adopted) daughter to fear what the mother represents suggests the daughter's vulnerability to female plotting, one that Pip shares. Miss Havisham, in rebuking Estella for her failure to love, says,

"O, look at her, look at her! . . . so hard and thankless, on the hearth where she was reared! Where I took her into this wretched breast when it was first bleeding from its stabs, and where I have lavished years of tenderness upon her!" (322)

Miss Havisham's language veers from the maternal ("reared") to the sado-masochistic ("bleeding from its stabs") into an erotics close to that of Miss Wade and Tattycoram: "Years of tenderness [lavished] upon her!" All in all, this seems a fairly large arsenal to bring against a small child.

But Estella's response offers a different way out of "the hearth where she was reared," one that recapitulates both Estella's clarity of vision and the limitations her upbringing has placed on that vision. For she responds not with affection, familialism, or erotics, but with inheritance and legality:

"At least I was no party to the compact . . . for if I could walk and speak, when it was made, it was as much as I could do. But what would you have? You have been very good to me, and I owe everything to you. What would you have?" (322)

That question is at the heart of every parental exchange in Dickens's fiction, the question the Frankenstein "child" shoots back to the world: you have made me, and I owe you everything, but what do I owe you? When Miss Havisham responds "Love," Estella can answer, calmly, "You have it," but the novel supplies the missing answer: she can never know what that kind of all-giving love would be, precisely because she has never had it, and to respond to claims for it would be both empty and hypocritical. The language of contract Estella speaks – "I was no party to the compact" – suggests with precision the limits of what she can return: the love written into the adoptive mother's plot is always that of the compact, never the fiercer love Miss Havisham thinks she wants, or the more tender love Magwitch offers at the novel's end. It is as if the plot of maternal love, like that of the daughter's inheritance, were asking, again and again, what would be enough? What would it mean to be satisfied?

The novel, in terms of plot, can never serve up "enough"; can never quite explain, logistically or legally, what a sufficiency would be – the closest it comes is when Pip says, at the book's end, that he makes a "sufficient living." Instead, it offers more than enough in its linguistic and metaphorical excesses, as in its excessive redundancy of plots – so many fathers, so many rivals, so many angry mothers. In lieu of sufficiency, what it offers is an eternal *return*, essentially, a freedom from debt. This release from obligation, a way out of the "compact" of sufficiency, is connected with the only form of female writing in the novel, something very different from the self-inscription in the novels we have been examining. But the thematic work these textualizing moments offer is essential: repeatedly, these "mothers by adoption" model for Pip the writing of forgiveness, the writing that will make up the specific textual strategy of this novel.

After Mrs. Joe is struck, violently, by Orlick, and lies stricken and paralyzed, she uses Pip's slate to communicate with Pip, Joe, and Biddy. "Again and again and again" she produces a curious hammer-shaped character shaped like a "T," which only the clever Biddy can properly interpret as a symbol for Orlick (150). When her attacker is produced, Mrs. Joe appears eager to propitiate him, smiling and humbling herself, Pip says, "as I have seen . . . a child towards a hard master" (151). Everything in this story is consistent with Pip's larger story: Mrs. Joe is, as others will be, humbled by being beaten; Biddy, who was Pip's first teacher and always ahead of him in his lessons, must tell Pip what he cannot read for himself; it is his own slate that Mrs. Joe uses, rewriting his story to include the violence of Orlick, and the appearance of various wonderful signs and mysteries, which he cannot read. That "slate" will reappear when Miss Havisham has been burned and scarred, after Pip's story has humbled her, and she returns repeatedly in her fever to the ivory tablet about her neck, echoing her request that he "take the pencil and write after my name, 'I forgive her!'" (415). Pip's story, in its widest resonance, is a form of writing forgiveness, of writing the proper end to the story of others – but he gets there, we might argue, only through the continuous misreading of the writing of women.

But Miss Havisham's return to the plot of forgiveness, her abandonment of her own vain quest for authorial control, comes in an astonishing moment, one that offers in its place a quest for *maternal* forgiveness: she has knelt down, before asking him to inscribe his change of heart, at Pip's feet, "with her folded hands raised to me in the manner in which, when her poor heart was young and fresh and whole, they must often have been raised to heaven from her mother's side" (410). That scene, of the daughter at the mother's feet, seems to suggest a wholeness the novel does not offer anywhere else – and one that is pointedly absent from the plot of another abjected female, Estella.

The final and necessary twist of Pip's story is his quest for Estella's mother, and for the relationship between the now-tamed Molly, who had told Magwitch she was prepared to kill their child (and who may have attempted to do so before Jaggers rescued the child and brought her to Miss Havisham to be raised), and his own story of tangled origins, desires, and plots. For Pip, the plot "proper" begins at the moment of Molly's maternal rage (if Molly had not taken Abel Magwitch's daughter, Magwitch would not have conceived the idea of making the boy Pip, who reminded him of the lost girl, his own heir and gentleman-in-the-making – in short, Pip would have no plot); further, Pip's *understanding* of his plot begins at the moment he can tell the complete story of Estella's life. For Estella, the limits of her self-knowledge end where Pip's begins, for that is a story she can never get whole.

This point is worth dwelling on, for it is the moment when the digression I have taken through female inscription and the writing of forgiveness returns us to female plotting, and the deep connection *Pip* makes between his own plot and Estella's – and suggests again that reading the novel from Estella's (imagined) perspective places Pip's story in a very different perspective. Pip makes the recovery of Estella's history the central mystery plot of the novel, and the necessary return of any mystery novel (to revisit sites once of ignorance, now of knowledge) is here the journey Pip makes in piecing together's Estella's lost (or stolen) memory. As he pieces the story together (from Herbert's narration; from Magwitch's; from his questioning of Miss Havisham, and his interrogation of Jaggers) he thinks of the act of recovering Estella's history as forming part of his own: he will find out her origins, and she will love him. One of the book's many dramatic ironies is, of course, that while Pip is turning himself into a gentleman for Estella, he is learning that she is the child of a convict and a murderess. For all that he fears the prison dust and the "Newgate cobwebs" on him when he meets Estella, she *is* the Newgate novel at this romance novel's center. Indeed, *Estella, Girl of the Streets*, as her story would have been had Jaggers not rescued her, would have been a tale much more like *Oliver Twist* than like *David Copperfield*, and would have fulfilled the destiny Mrs. Joe always imagined for Pip: that men in the Hulks always begin, as she warns him mid-question, "by asking questions" (46). Pip's questions seem to be those of the Oedipal plot (who am I, who is my father, how did I get here?) but the more powerful version of them in the novel is Estella's – and it is a plot he never reveals to her. In this novel, the daughter's real inheritance is the guilt, violence, and shame the hero has been fantasizing all along – and his role is to discover them, and protect her from them. Estella never learns she has a living mother or a dying father; Pip's last gift to Magwitch is the knowledge that he has a daughter ("she is a lady and very beautiful and I love her" [470]), information that binds them the more deeply together but leaves Estella alone and unknowing.[11]

In this scheme, the daughter is powerless to write her story, for she cannot ever completely possess it. All that she does know she learns through the plot the hero has imagined for her – in this novel, the plot in which she is bent, broken, and asks only for forgiveness. The only texts daughters control are trivial and, often, destructive (Mrs. Pocket's use of the book of baronets, which she ponders while her children trip over her booby-trapped skirts and "are to be nutcrackered dead . . . into their tombs" [217]); the only writing women do is equally trivial (Estella's matter-of-fact notes to Pip; the illegible notes Mrs. Joe tries to leave for Joe and Biddy); the only stories women tell are of regret, violence, and pain.

And yet, this does not seem quite true to the feeling of the book, particularly not to the work of the novel's language. For what women do seem to control somewhat (and this, too, is related to Miss Havisham's weird control over plotting, one that remains psychically powerful long after Pip realizes that it was Magwitch who actually wrote the plot that held him prisoner) is the power of language and image-making: from

Miss Havisham's invention of the wedding-day museum to Estella's heart-breaking invocation of her own heartlessness ("if you had taught her . . . [to] turn against [the sun]" [324]), women seem linked to the world of metaphor as well as the world of plot. But this, too, seems to take a different shape when we hold up against each other what we might call "Pip's novel," and "Estella's."

The second way in which we might revise the novel beyond Pip's misreading of Estella, then, is through a reading of novelistic language, and the relationship of imagery to desire. Here we rejoin our discussion of Pip's romantic identity and Estella's place in it, for at the heart of his view of romantic love (and I think it is Dickens's critique of Pip that speaks here) is the violence of Pip's metaphorical subsuming of Estella. This might seem in contradiction with Pip's earlier self-presentation, in which he is the masochistic victim of the cold, distant woman, but it suggests the deeper pleasure Pip received from the story he told of himself as victim, the pleasure he takes in what is essentially a fantasy of control in which he gets to have it both ways, to be both smiter and smitten, narrator and character. Within his story, Pip never sees himself as violent, pushing most of his aggression onto the more plausible figure of Orlick, but where Estella is concerned, he maneuvers his violence onto Bentley Drummle – whom he sees, not incidentally, near the village, with a man whose "slouching shoulders and ragged hair" remind him of Orlick.[12] It is, of course, Orlick, come back to the village, but it is not an accident that these two figures have been pulled together: Orlick avenges Pip by beating Mrs. Joe; it is Bentley who will accomplish Pip's metaphorical ravishing of Estella, marrying the woman who doesn't truly love him, then literally beating her into submission and (until the novel's end) silencing her voice.

When Pip dines with Mr. Jaggers just after Estella's wedding, Jaggers announces that Drummle ("our friend the Spider") has "won the pool." As I have suggested, it is impossible to discuss women in this novel without economic metaphors; there are no women who are not to be paid for, except those who can be "won" from others.

"He is a promising fellow – in his way – but he may not have it all his own way. The stronger will win in the end, but the stronger has to be found out first. If he should turn to, and beat her – "

"Surely," I interrupted, with a burning face and heart, "you do not seriously think that he is scoundrel enough for that, Mr. Jaggers?"

"I didn't say so, Pip. I am putting a case. If he should turn to and beat her,

he may possibly get the strength on his side; if it should be a question of intel-
lect, he certainly will not . . . A fellow like our friend the Spider . . . either beats,
or cringes. He may cringe and growl, or cringe and not growl; but he either
beats or cringes." (402)

Pip is "burning" (always a significant word in this novel) because this is
a "painful" subject for him, but there is a weird excitement here – in
Jaggers's telling of the story, in Pip's listening, in the certainty of the
ostensibly vague "putting a case." The reader might ask, what, then, is
Pip's "case"? And will Pip, in turn, "beat or cringe"?

The novel has certainly heretofore been more concerned with beating
than cringing, and the violence seems only to escalate after this conversation. The scene is followed by Pip's recognition of Estella's face and
hands in those of Molly, Jaggers's murderous, tamed housekeeper; it
takes place in a nexus of violent sexuality everywhere in the novel. In
Orlick's threat to rape Biddy, in the incestuous violence of Clara's
"gruffandgrim" father, in Miss Havisham's pounding of her own heart
("broken"), we, like Pip, are constantly initiated into scenes of dark
passion, "secret" loves and (de)formed bodies. The end of the novel is a
series of visions of violated women: Magwitch tells both the story of
Arthur Havisham's death, haunted by the apparition of Miss Havisham,
and the story of Compeyson's wife Sally, "which Compeyson kicked
mostly" (362). Pip envisions Miss Havisham "hanging to the beam" (94)
and then (in a dangerously sexual scene) he smothers her in blankets
"like a prisoner" (414) while she burns.[13] Herbert tells Pip the story of
Molly strangling another woman, then swearing she has strangled her
own child. The novel in both versions ends, almost comforted, with the
story that Estella *has* been beaten by Drummle, who "used her with great
cruelty, and who had become quite renowned as a compound of pride,
avarice, brutality, and meanness" (490–491). "Suffering," Estella says in
the second ending, "has been stronger than all other teaching, and has
taught me to understand what your heart used to be. I have been bent
and broken, but – I hope – into a better shape" (493). The beatings that
Drummle has given her, in short, have transformed her into a woman
who can love Pip.

But this is Pip's view of Estella: once again, as readers, we play out the
differences between the Estella whom Pip sees and the one who moves
free of his vision. Moreover, we focus on the fiercely transformative
power of his vision: if she is his "fancy," he can remake her as he pleases.
His doing so, however, depends on her silence, her passivity, her fixity as
object. His doing so, then, on one hand echoes accounts of violence

against women in the period (ranging from rape trials, in which women were refused the right to testify, to cases of wife abuse, in which women had no legal status from which to bring charges).[14] On the other, it is linked to the work Dickens is doing in the novel, the work of metaphor-ization: Estella "is like"; she never "is." The novel is pointing to some-thing cannibalistic in its own acts of metaphorizing, something Dickens plays with constantly in highlighting the *constructedness* of the metaphors that hold the novel together so tightly.

This attention to metaphor is crucial to the novel's story of identity: in the speech in which he links Estella to "every prospect I have ever seen," Pip both gives a story of origin for his own imagination and reveals that imagination as a self-conscious construct. Estella has been "in every line I have ever read" (and, one imagines, in every line he has ever written, a key revelation for the autobiographer); she has also been "in every prospect I have ever seen since – on the river, on the sails of the ships, on the marshes, in the clouds, in the light, in the darkness, in the wind, in the woods, in the sea, in the streets" (378). At this moment, she becomes not only a part of writing and of vision, but also – and again, this is Pip's version, but it points to the process of metaphor-cre-ation in the novel – "the embodiment of every graceful fancy that my mind has ever become acquainted with." As he says, she could move "the stones of which the strongest London buildings are made" as easily as she could displace her presence and influence to him. Estella is both *embodied* solely in metaphor and *represents* the embodiment of metaphor for Pip. How could she, indeed, escape this process, inevitable and random, powerful and fanciful, as it seems?

Virtually every metaphor in the novel works in this way, playing up its own literalness *and* its arbitrariness. It is all simply too obvious: Miss Havisham, like any hysteric, has turned her body into its own sign; she is the symbol of her own grief, and it hardly surprises us when she turns up in someone else's dream with that metaphor made literal: when her brother sees her, there is blood on her chest, "where you [Compeyson] broke it," exactly as she prophesied when she first told Pip, "gleefully," that her heart is "Broken!" It is her metaphor, and it is only right that others "see" it. Moreover, we "see" her symbolic structures being repaired: in the scene after Estella and Miss Havisham quarrel, and Estella takes her only extended leap into metaphor in her speech about the sun, we, with Pip, watch Estella sitting at Miss Havisham's knee, sewing the tatters on her dress. And Estella is literally fixing the tatters, not the dress – the dress must remain in a permanent state of collapse;

it must always be repaired to stay in disrepair, so that the spectacle Miss Havisham presents, one Pip originally compared to "waxworks" and to a "skeleton in the ashes of a rich dress," can continue (87). The metaphor is at once natural and created: like Pip's allegorizing fantasy of Estella, it can both be seen and seen through, for it constantly gives itself away.

To argue that rape and metaphor share a common structure in this novel and that both depend primarily on a male narcissistic fantasy of female fixity is also to return us to the terrifyingly unfixed world with which the novel begins. Pip, when turned upside down by the convict, prefers to see (believe) the church standing on its steeple; Miss Havisham, abandoned before her wedding, on her birthday by her bridegroom, prefers (needs) to see that abandonment as the birth of a new, creative (if monstrous) self. If it is the fabulist self that these characters create, it is still a divided self that these fables reflect. These are fantasies of necessity. Like Pip's story of "the Estella," they give the unstable self an object towards which to move, but like Pip's story of Estella, they also enforce silence on the other.

But as the self smites others, so it is smitten itself. If Pip's anger has been acted out by a series of violent surrogates, its excesses have stayed with him: in his own hysterical dreams, he "confounded impossible existences with my own identity; [dreamed] that I was a brick in the house wall, and yet entreating to be released from the giddy place where the builders had set me; that I was a steel beam of a vast engine, clashing and whirling over a gulf, and yet that I implored in my own person to have the engine stopped, and my part in it hammered off" (471–2). Pip has divided himself nearly fatally here, "implor[ing] in my own person to have . . . my part . . . hammered off," and yet the end of the novel recreates the utopian (narcissistic) dream of having "no shadow of another parting" (492), reunifying the self through union with Estella. No wonder, then, that he, too, hopes Estella has been bent and broken into a "better shape."

The end of this novel, however, does not easily unite these "parts," but maintains the distance between Pip's and Estella's fictions. To the very end, Estella says one thing and Pip hears another; while he insists he sees "no shadow of another parting," she says they "will continue friends apart." The plotting of sexual violence I have been tracing generates yet another set of "two endings" to perplex us, and it raises questions of Pip's precarious hold on authority. This is not to argue that Pip's linguistic enclosure of Estella is a form of wife-beating or that his abrogation of her "end" is a literary murder, but rather to point to the consistent violence of language around sexuality, a violence in which Pip participates. Such a reading also suggests that the novel at central moments, and again at its close, separates itself from this pattern of abuse and usurpation, of violent re formation. Even if we read closely the famously ambiguous passages of the "second ending" (the purportedly romantic revision Dickens made of his bleak tale at Bulwer Lytton's suggestion), that ending does not choose between Pip and Estella's endings: rather, it points to the difference between them, and it allows that difference to stand.[15]

In part, these characters' versions of "the two endings" reflect the generic differences within the novel. Estella, as always, is the realist: whereas in Dickens's first ending, she read Pip's state erroneously, thinking him married, with a child; in the second, she is, again, as always, painfully attentive, curious, responsive, but decisive. She is further linked to the realism of real estate: the land is the "only possession I have not relinquished," "the subject of the only determined resistance I made in all the wretched years" (492). The child who always knew who paid has become a woman who has retained a piece of maternal inheritance, a house that is "enough," property that ("At last") can be built on. Pip's novel, however, remains a mistier romance: he is still entranced by her beauty; more, he maintains, eleven years later, "you have always held your place in *my* heart" (492), still reproaching her, subtly, for not always having accorded him a parallel place. The fairy princess and now successfully embourgeoised pauper still seem to be in different books; he is still trying to get her to agree to his "fancies."

The second ending is almost always read as Dickens's attempt to satisfy his "romantic" readers – and perhaps his secret, romantic self – at the expense of the grim realism this novel had, uncharacteristically for Dickens, aspired to; it has, in short, been read as trying to unwrite itself. But the second ending, unlike the first, might merely allow Pip to believe once again in his own expectations. Despite its misty ambiguities, Pip reads this ending as allowing for no partings – something a trail of scholarship suggests we might have more difficulty doing. The second ending actually accomplishes something else: it gives Estella back her voice. The line that had previously concluded the novel was Pip's, as he searches her face for certainty: "I was very glad afterwards to have had the interview; for in her face, and in her voice, and in her touch, she gave me the assurance that suffering had been stronger than Miss Havisham's teaching, and had given her a heart to understand what my heart used to be." In the first ending, Estella has said nothing of herself except "I am greatly changed"; her face, voice, and touch are what "assure" Pip, and the distance of his reference to "what my heart used to be" gives us a false assurance that Pip's education is complete. But in the second ending, when Estella *says* suffering has been stronger than all other teaching, has taught her to understand what his heart used to be, and that she has been bent and broken, she concludes by saying, "Be as considerate and good to me as you were, and tell me we are friends." At this moment she is asking for what Pip has always been incapable of – the friendship that would give her a separate existence, a "parting," an existence in which she is not a "shadow." This novel is haunted by shadowy women, half-women, victimized women, women whom Pip cannot see clearly, women who hide from the light. Estella seems to step out from the mists here into the "broad expanse of tranquil light," the "expanse" suggesting the "expense" she has escaped, a way out of the cash-nexus, out of violence and self-abuse, into a self she never quite owned, a self who wants only "to continue friends apart."

The most effective shading of the slippery second ending and of Pip's unspoken response ("*I* saw no shadow of another parting") is the question with which we are left: has Pip escaped the realm of romance and fantasy, satisfied with "a sufficient" living, or is he still drawn on, a moth to the flame? Has he really left the "old place," or is he still the "visionary boy," still "abroad," still visiting the ruins "for her sake," lost in the "poor dream," lost in his own "expectations," unable to see even (with another emphasis) the "*shadow* of another parting from her"? The second ending turns the question on us: on our desire to see those dreams continue, at the same time that we want to be "satisfied" at last, to see the novel truly end, with nothing else to want.

What the conclusion does make clear – and it is what is most frightening and most moving about this novelist who knows the secret ways to get at a boy's heart – is that the novel, to *be* a novel, must share Pip's expectations. My own reading of the novel is that it deliberately leaves us without a guide, without a monitor, without a star to follow, that ambiguity is its final lesson. But however critical of its own tradition it may be at moments, and wherever its misty ending leaves us, like Pip, *Great Expectations* could not "be" without the prospect of Estella. It is the desire for "vision" that creates this novel; it is its creation of its own counter-vision that gives it the depth that at once challenges and rewards other expectations.

CHAPTER SEVEN:

Our Mutual Friend *and the*
daughter's book of the dead

Many of the stories we have been telling in this book reach a bitter end in *Our Mutual Friend*. The attempt to locate value in the golden heroine; the attempt to win the daughter a portion of her own; the attempt to free the novel from the darkest toils of the inheritance plot – all, in *Our Mutual Friend*, notoriously come to dust. Not surprisingly, the end of the novel has garnered as much opprobrium as the conclusion of any Dickens novel, and reflects the problems of closure these final chapters have been tracing: what would be enough; who profits; who renounces; and what is to be done? All problems of closure – value, reward, and the promise of future happiness – seem concentrated in this novel, and seem, moreover, to topple unpleasantly on readers' heads, like so much matter in a finally overfull closet.

The novel begins in an equally concentrated way: a father and a daughter row a small boat across the Thames "In these times of ours"; behind them they tow the body of a drowned man.[1] The plot will expand from these central elements, but it will not add to them: in the course of the novel, two daughters will choose between two fathers and pledge absolute loyalty to them; two daughters will cross the water to find happiness; and two daughters will marry men who have been drowned and found dead. They will find happiness through labor, but they will neither speak nor write their own plots – in contrast to all the other legacies of Dickens's oeuvre, theirs will come through death and not through reading. But the novel will find its true inheritance by turning these daughters into wives: the proper end of this novel is to bring a dead man to life by teaching him to say one magic word, and that word is "wife." The daughter, in this book, has no word of her own, and only by renouncing plotting can she fill her place; only by becoming property can she inherit; only by the absolute alienation of property can any be held on to; and only by the deepest distrust of the magic of fictions can Dickens write his last novel.

178

The plot of turning daughters into wives is a property plot in this novel. That plot begins before the novel opens, with one of the heroines, Bella Wilfer, willed to the hero, John Harmon, "like a dozen of spoons" (81). His father's will states that Harmon must marry Bella (whom he has never seen, and whom his father has seen only once, when she was in a childhood tantrum) to inherit the profits from the dust mounds that brought the family fortune; it is to escape that mercenary romance that John Harmon has agreed to stay dead, to play along with the fiction that he met a watery demise. Bella, too, seeks a way out of the mercenary romance plot, out of her status as property, but can do so only by willed immersion in another business proposition: she will marry well, acquiring rather than being wealth, and that plot will win her another degree of happiness.

Our Mutual Friend's other daughter seems, initially, to be playing a very different fantasy, one more closely allied to the good daughter plot of *Dombey and Son* and *Little Dorrit*. Lizzie Hexam, the daughter of the water-rat who dragged the false John Harmon's body back to shore to claim the coroner's fee (and who probably robbed the dead body of its wealth) wants to stake out a plot where she can stay true to her father while disowning his ill-begotten wealth. While Gaffer Hexam's robbery has sparked one of the novel's liveliest debates, if anything can "belong" to the dead, Lizzie is already anticipating a plot in which "she has set her heart upon the dead": she wishes to be without property, to turn herself into a gift (and into nothing) and will herself out of paternal inheritance altogether. Unlike Bella, who sees in herself wealth in the making, Lizzie claims only her labor as her own, refusing to seek any other plot.

Like earlier Dickens novels, this one must bring its heroines together for their mutual instruction: in this case, Bella takes an interest in Lizzie because of their connection with the dead man; each is intrigued, however, by the other's strength and beauty, and they share fascinating scenes of conversation by the fire, where Dickens dreamers inevitably cluster. But unlike most domestic versions of the heroine (the beautiful, delicate, passive angel who must play off against her darker, more sexualized, more hostile opposite), Bella Wilfer offers the novel's more powerful critique of romantic relations. She goes to live with the Boffins, the couple who served Old Harmon and, in default of his son's appearance, inherit the dusty wealth; once there, she meets Boffin's secretary, John Rokesmith, who is John Harmon in disguise. Harmon, who studies her to see if she is worth loving (if, in essence, she is worth coming back to life for) comes to love her; she scorns his affection with a passion that can only suggest her eventual succumbing to his charms. But her rebuff is made in the name of a larger rebuke of romantic relations:

"I have heard Mr. Boffin say that you are master of every line and word of that will, as you are master of all his affairs. And was it not enough that I should have been willed away, like a horse, or a dog, or a bird; but must you too begin to dispose of me in your mind, and speculate in me, as soon as I had ceased to be the talk and the laugh of the town? Am I for ever to be made the property of strangers?" (434)

Bella's speech points to a double conversion into property: the first time as inheritance; the second as speculation, as a property that will out of itself develop new assets.[2]

This is entirely the structure of *Our Mutual Friend*: the novel is imagined as a test of the heroine, a proving of her inner quality that will generate new goodness and new wealth in her. In this plot, Bella will not win riches for herself through marriage, but will prove to be a richness in herself: she will be (and offer) the "true golden gold" of female, wifely devotion, and become the gold-standard heroine the other novels held up so proudly. But Bella resists this plot heroically and resolutely: indeed, she reclaims the language of heroines like Edith Dombey or Estella Havisham, insisting that by knowing her own value she will at least sell herself intelligently in the marriage market.

This is the language Noddy Boffin will adopt in his efforts to convert Bella from the pure market economics she espouses – in his efforts to "espouse" her to someone of true value and remake her in the form of an equally true value. Boffin, in one of the novel's somewhat queasy uses of fictions, pretends to be a miser to wean Bella from her appetites; in his efforts, he too claims to embrace spousal economics. As Boffin says to John Harmon, when he pretends to reject the latter's bid for Bella,

"This young lady was lying in wait (as she was qualified to do) for money, and you had no money. . . .This young lady was looking about the market for a good bid; she wasn't in it to be snapped up by fellows that had no money to lay out; nothing to buy with." (654)

But as the novel parodies and criticizes this version of marrying-up, it carries out the same plot twice: both Bella and Lizzie marry men with more money, men won to them by their own higher values; both men make "a good bid" for a valuable commodity.

Bella's sense of herself as a commodity ("the willed-away girl" [586]) is at once humorous and penetrating – and one of the things it skewers is Dickens's own customary assortment of terms for his female angels, dolls, pets, and prizes. Describing herself to her father, Bella says "If ever there was a mercenary plotter whose thoughts and designs were always in her mean occupation, I am the amiable creature" (376), and in her retention of her ironic "amiable" we are to see the essential harmlessness of her schemes – the deepest danger is to herself, and not (as might seem to be true with Edith or Estella) to the men she seeks to charm. But Bella also sees her own status as pet: in one scene with Lizzie, she compares herself to an impressive menagerie, saying "I have no more of what they call character, my dear, than a canary-bird, but I know I am trustworthy" (587); "any one should tear me to bits before getting at a syllable of it – though there's no merit in that, for I am naturally as obstinate as a Pig" (591); "I look in the glass often enough, and I chatter like a Magpie" (592). The plot's problem – what it hopes to award her if she passes its moral examination – is to raise Bella from a pet (a doll) into a fully conscious human being; unfortunately, it can never quite overcome its sense that Bella is both to be rewarded and to be a reward. When her father says to Harmon, "she brings you a good fortune when she brings you the poverty she has accepted for your sake and the honest truth's" (673) we recognize the familiar Dickensian note: Bella has traded in a far better market; she is also a product that reveals far better workmanship.

Lizzie Hexam proves herself as a heroine not by being a product but by being a producer – in essence, by being a good worker. What she seems to offer, by way of contrast with Bella's beauty and dimples, is a sense of autonomy through labor: when threatened by the novel's other hero, the decadent and delightful Eugene Wrayburn, she draws on that autonomy as a sense of vulnerability: "I am removed from you and your family by being a working girl. How true a gentleman to be as considerate of me as if I was removed by being a Queen"(761). But when she resists the approaches of Bradley Headstone, Eugene's rival for her affections, she is even more adamant, and draws on her life of labor as a form of authority:

With much of the dignity of courage, as she recalled her self-reliant life and her right to be free from accountability to this man, she released her arm from his grasp and stood looking full at him. (456)

In a novel obsessed with account books and profits, that dignity and self-reliance offer Lizzie what few characters possess: the courage to look "full at" another character and to stand free.

Female freedom in this novel, however, serves best to allow women to

alienate themselves freely, and it is this renunciation of self that Lizzie is
to teach Bella. When the two women exchange romantic histories by the
fire, Lizzie tells not how she fears Wrayburn (who seems clearly bent on
seducing, if not raping her), but how she fears *for* him; when Bella asks
if it would not be better to "wear out" her love for a man who doesn't
deserve her (if she wouldn't gain "in peace, and hope, and even in
freedom"), Lizzie asks "Does a woman's heart that – that has that weak-
ness in it which you have spoken of . . . seek to gain anything?" (590).
That question is "so directly at variance with Bella's views in life" that
she asks herself, "There, you little mercenary wretch! . . . Ain't you
ashamed of yourself?" (590); but when Lizzie goes on to describe what
she sees in the fire – "a heart well worth winning, and well won. A heart
that, once won, goes through fire and water for the winner, and never
changes, and is never daunted" – each names the other as "the figure to
which [that heart] belongs" (592).

The plot will serve up a similar symmetry of fate, as each heroine loves
on in spite of danger ("fire and water") and in spite of mystery; it is at
the end of this scene that Bella begins to soften towards John Harmon
(still Rokesmith) and that the narrator, speaking for him, wishes that he
"had but the right to pay your legacy and to take your receipt!" (594) –
here, the "kiss for the boofer lady" (386) that the infant replacement
"Johnny" Harmon has left for Bella, but more profoundly (and eventually, more accurately) the legacy left for John Harmon, the family fortune
and the fortunate female who accompanies (and guarantees) it. The
novel goes to painful labor to teach its heroine and us that wealth cannot
bring happiness; that riches make misers and misers mean misery; that
the truest heart is an empty pocket – but in light of its eventual dispensation of wealth to those same true hearts, it is worth asking, what do the
heroines have to prove to acquire the happiness their hearts merit; what
is the test they pass and what the reward?

For both heroines, the real test is not "fire and water" (relatively easy
obstacles for the women to overcome, though both John and, in particular, Eugene are considerably battered by the elements) but the
renunciation of the quest; for both, they must learn not to want, and not
to be curious. Bella makes this point explicitly when she marries John
Rokesmith and promises not to inquire into the mystery surrounding his
presence at John Harmon's inquest: "A married sphinx isn't a – isn't a
nice confidential husband" (815) she says, but while John doesn't reveal
"confidences" he is certainly (indeed, almost smugly) confident that she
will come through his test with honors. Bella goes further, invoking one

of Dickens's favourite marriage narratives, calling him "In earnest, Blue Beard of the secret chamber" (815); Rokesmith "confess[es] to the secret chamber," but to nothing else, leaving his wife unaware that she is herself the wife in the chamber, having married her dead fiancé unawares, through a trick designed to maneuver her into his waiting (if still probing) arms.

For Lizzie, the challenge is not only to give up plotting but to teach Eugene narrative theory. His friend Mortimer Lightwood continually asks him, "what do you intend?" and he can never answer; he must substitute for his own aimlessness Lizzie's confidence in him, and must learn from her abandonment of agency how he is to desire. It is women in the novel who know how to desire, but where for other heroines (like Esther or Amy) desire is linked to writing, in this novel the inscription of female desire is the scene of mockery: female desire exists to be abandoned, not described or even sublimated. The novel's one scribbling woman is the teacher at the school that adjoins Bradley Headstone, and she receives one of the novel's most incisive (if painfully ironic) imaginations of writing:

[Miss Peecher] could write a little essay on any subject, exactly a slate long, beginning at the left-hand top of one side and ending at the right-hand bottom of the other, and the essay should be strictly according to rule. If Mr. Bradley Headstone had addressed a written proposal of marriage to her, she would probably have replied in a complete little essay on the theme exactly a slate long, but would certainly have replied Yes. For she loved him. The decent hair-guard that went round his neck and took care of his decent silver watch was an object of envy to her. So would Miss Peecher have gone round his neck and taken care of him. Of him, insensible. Because he did not love Miss Peecher. (268)

Part of the mockery is the idea of Bradley (a nightmare vision to the equally class-ambitious Dickens) as an object of adoration – his very "decency" marks him as unworthy for the narrator, though that fragment "of him, insensible," is not without pathos.[3] Lizzie does not get any similar expression of desire; indeed, although she learns to read in the course of the novel, she is never imagined writing.

For Bella, progress in writing is also linked to the abandonment of agency. At the novel's beginning she is the one woman in the novel still capable of signing a contract. True, when she is first seen writing, it is in the mode of diminution and eroticizing that accompanies her through the whole novel: John Harmon signs his rental agreement with the Wilfers, and Bella, "looking on as scornful witness," signs her name. But the erotics of writing here are part of an independence of spirit.

[John] looked at her stealthily, but narrowly. He looked at the pretty figure bending down over the paper and saying, "Where am I to go, pa? Here, in this corner?" He looked at the beautiful brown hair, shading the coquettish face; he looked at the free dash of the signature, which was a bold one for a woman's; and then they looked at one another. (83)

At this moment, although the hair and face are the center of his vision, she is allowed a free dash of a signature; by the end of the novel, all this "boldness" has disappeared. After she leaves the Boffins's house she visits her father, "Rumty," in his office, and sits at his desk, holding his pen, "laying her round cheek upon her plump left arm, and losing sight of her pen in waves of hair, in a highly unbusiness-like manner" (675). John Rokesmith still "seemed to like it," but this is a far cry from the earlier scene: no remainder of the dash or the freedom of "business" remains, and the possibility that the heroine could look back seems equally unthinkable.

The erotic energy and self-possession suggested by that bold, dashing signature is redirected by the text into the heroine's renunciation of property: at the moment when Bella is converted by the Boffins into true economic value (hearts, not hides, in the language of *Dombey and Son*) she begs, "If you could but make me poor again! O! Make me poor again, Somebody, I beg and pray, or my heart will break if this goes on! Pa, dear, make me poor again and take me home!" (661). Like Uriah Heep on a rampage, she not only wishes to be poor but to make everyone else poor as well: Mr. Boffin, she explains, "would be a Duck [as a bankrupt]; but as a man of property you are a Demon!"(662) – and such is the impulse of the novel, that property is demonic, and to be a member of the Wilfer menagerie is to be redeemed and redemptive.

Bella's moral education is widely echoed in the novel. What this means in (relatively) practical terms is that women will achieve happiness (or Duckliness) only through renunciation; only by the self-alienation such rejection of property and property-love implies in a Dickens novel can anyone escape the demonic possession that property brings. When Bella leaves behind the wealth the Boffins promised her, and dresses again in the clothes she brought with her to the "Harmony Jail" (as their house is known), she is truly set free – like Amy Dorrit wearing her Marshalsea garments, she is saved by dressing herself down; or, as she puts it after her transformation, "Now, I am complete" (666). Her completeness can come only after self-dismissal: she calls herself a "worldly shallow girl"; she sees herself in a "poor and pitiful light"; she is "sordid and vain" and full of "conceit and folly" and "a girl [who was] unable to rise to the worth of what [John Harmon] offered her" (662) – and we can recognize her degree of self-loathing from her willingness to refer to herself in the third person. Only by separating herself from herself – from returning to her earlier, ill-clad self and imagining herself "like a little child" – can Bella free herself from the worldliness she fears will make her a monster; once she is free of it, she becomes a real treasure. To John, she is "a most precious and sweet commodity that was always looking up, and that was never worth less than all the gold in the world," and she becomes this by "wanting nothing on earth" (750). Far from offering women a separate property, this novel's apotheosis of female identity is to offer to separate them from any identity at all, to imagine themselves already sordid posses-sions, hoping only for redemption by someone more "worthy;" someone willing to "make [them] poor" and, hence, finally, "complete." Not writing, we might hypothesize, but erasing, will bring identity worth having in this novel.

The daughter is not alone in her dispossession. There is alienation aplenty in this novel: one need look no further than the novel's subplot, where the dwarf-daughter Jenny Wren lives with the noble Jew, Riah, who serves as one of the many fairy-godfathers – or in his case, as his ambiguous sexuality (seemingly linked for Dickens to his Jewishness) makes possible, fairy godmothers. Through much of the novel Riah must also play (not terribly convincingly) the part of the Jewish money-lender, only to be revealed as not a usurer but a front for one; Dickens, famously, is rewriting his earlier anti-Semitism in portraying Fagin by here rewriting (with only marginally less racial self-consciousness) the Jew into the truly "Christian" gentleman, Fagin into Brownlow – or, more accurately, Shylock into wedlock. But in this, Dickens is carrying out a dangerous game, playing with England's most literary aliens (the always-outside Jews) to rewrite the market plot into the marriage plot; and he lays himself open to the same critique of this move that *The Merchant of Venice* has drawn from one of the play's most astute critics. Marc Shell has written, memorably, that Portia – "the champion of mar-riage," as he calls her – cannot easily rule against Shylock. As Shell sum-marizes the play's problem, "The absolute ownership of another person through institutions like debtors' prison, slavery, and execution for debt may be abhorrent, but it is a necessary basis for the marriage Portia seeks." Nor does the marriage plot, in Shell's reading, escape the alien-ation of persons these institutions imply:

If Balthasar-Portia were to rule that the bond between Antonio and Shylock was illegitimate – arguing, for example, that all contracts seeking to take a human life have always been regarded as void, or that no man can rightfully contract to give to another his person under any circumstances or conditions – she would, by the same argument, be ruling away the possibility of marriage, which involves an equally extreme alienation of person and is, for Shakespeare, the only real solution to the problem of property and person that *The Merchant of Venice* depicts.[4]

Our Mutual Friend poses a similar problem of "property and persons"; like *The Merchant of Venice*, it hopes to find its solution in a marriage plot (an "extreme" and self-willed alienation of person) but perhaps even more than Shakespeare's play, Dickens's novel is profoundly aware of the extremity of its solution, and the violence against persons (in particular, against daughters) that marriage carries out.

In David Brion Davis's classic account of the problem of slavery, the slave has three defining characteristics: "his person is the property of another man, his will is subject to his owner's authority, and his labor or services are obtained through coercion." But Davis goes on to add an interesting proviso: "since this description could sometimes be applied to wives and children in a patriarchal family, various writers have added that slavery must be 'beyond the limits of the family relations.'"[5]

Our Mutual Friend makes this point far more economically: at a crucial plot moment, a minor character, Sophronia Lammle, describes her attempts to trick a wealthy young woman into a marriage plot, saying she is about to be "sold into wretchedness for life." This language is not new to Dickens: it was the key-note of Edith Dombey's attack on Dombey, that "I will be exhibited to no one, as the refractory slave you purchased" (748); that "He sees me at the auction, and he thinks it well to buy me" (473). But that novel managed to save its central, redemptive marriage from so scathing a critique: that safety valve is not possible in *Our Mutual Friend*, where, to borrow again from Marc Shell, "Marriage cannot avoid the alienation of persons that these institutions imply but can only work its way up through (in order, perhaps, to transcend) it."[6]

For *Our Mutual Friend*, marriage may not always be a state of being sold, but it is virtually always a state of being bought, and the purchase-price varies from moral to monitory to monetary. The novel's most explicit marital contract is made by Sophronia Lammle. Alfred and Sophronia have married each other under false pretenses, on the urging of the Veneerings, who tell each that the other has a fortune. In fact, they are both impoverished mercenaries, now locked in a parody of the perfect marriage. They swear vengeance on the society that has wronged them (and particularly on the Veneerings) but their only real connection is the cash bond between them: "We owe each other money, you know," Mr. Lammle says to his wife (190). They enter into the whirl of social deception, perfecting the art of living on nothing at all, and enter upon a life of total temporariness, renting houses that are too small while looking for the perfect house; never paying servants; living off the social generosity of others more pretentious (as well as more propertied) than themselves. The plan they hope will enrich themselves and impoverish others is to win the friendship and the heart of Georgiana Podsnap, and wed her to their unscrupulous, money-lender friend, Fascination Fledgeby. But suddenly, with little preparation, Sophronia Lammle breaks her contract, confides the plan to the baffled gentlemanly Twemlow, and saves Georgiana from the hell to which she herself has been condemned. Her only explanation: "I was a poor little fool once myself" (686).

This little plot suggests much of how *Our Mutual Friend* works: it is fiercely abbreviated, taking only a few scenes to sketch, and concluding even more quickly than that. It might almost serve as a microcosm of the world of all Dickens women: it plays on some buried notion of female goodness (Sophronia is not exactly like, but somehow kinder than Alfred), and also on notions of female masochism. Sophronia will risk her husband's rage to save another; she also feels in common with Georgiana a vulnerability (probably sexual) to male power, and "breaks out," briefly, to protect her. It also carries within it an almost parodic playing with the limitations of the legal language of husband and wife: as the laws governing coverture had it, a husband and wife cannot be convicted of conspiracy, because they are one person in law. Sophronia is both hiding behind her legally approved inability to plot (skating within the law) and breaking that deepest covenant, playing (in their favorite metaphor) a secret game against her husband. Just as her name calls up an earlier, more independent Dickens heroine (Sophronia Sphynx, the "marchioness" of *The Old Curiosity Shop*), her mockery of her own goodness and rebellion ("I was a poor little fool once") suggests a newer, deeper contempt on Dickens's part for the poor excuses for plots allowed heroines, who are allowed only irony, pathos, and an innocence the text comes near to mocking. In the bitter conclusion to this plot, the Lammles finally do go bankrupt, and only Georgiana stays true to them, escaping to the Boffins to offer her few pieces of jewelry (and a promise of her future inheritance) to bail out her (false) friends. The choices, as the novel outlines them, are simple and absolute: be a villain, or be a "poor little fool."[7]

This puts tidily what Dickens has long thought: better to be a fool and poor than wealthy and worldly-wise. But here, the foolish Georgiana retains her wealth; she shows herself virtuous when she attempts to give her baubles for the Lammles, but doesn't even lose those, for they are returned by the all-knowing Boffin, reconveyor of appropriate wealth. To be willing to sacrifice is to gain all; to alienate oneself is to win the reward of a true self. How can Lizzie and Bella hope to resist such a prize-structure?

Only one woman in the novel seems deaf to the siren-song of the marriage plot and its rewards, and that woman is the novel's most recalcitrant daughter. She is the unpleasant Pleasant Riderhood, daughter of Rogue, the betraying partner of Gaffer Hexam, Lizzie's father. Gaffer steals from, and probably murders, the sailors who then float up by the shore; he is a drunk and abusive; his only redeeming quality is the resentment he shows on behalf of *his* daughter: he repeats belligerently, as if in the name of all characters who are "minor" in spite of themselves, "Ain't I got a daughter?" (109, 202). Pleasant is in many ways an undaughterly daughter, cranky and ill-favored, but she does (for no apparent reason) love her father; when he is near death, almost drowned, she is frantic, wringing her slatternly hair and winning sympathy from passers-by – sympathy that holds until her father returns to unattractive life.

Unlike many of these daughters, however, Pleasant does have her own property, which she not only retains but multiplies: Pleasant is a small-time usurer herself, keeping a pawnshop bought with money that was left to her by her mother.

> Miss Pleasant Riderhood had some little position and connection in Limehouse Hole. Upon the smallest of small scales, she was an unlicensed pawnbroker, keeping what was popularly called a Leaving Shop, by lending insignificant sums on insignificant articles of property deposited with her as security. In her four-and-twentieth year of life, Pleasant was already in her fifth year of this way of trade. Her deceased mother had established the business, and on that parent's demise she had appropriated a secret capital of fifteen shillings to establishing herself in it; the existence of such capital in a pillow being the last intelligible confidential communication made to her by the departed, before succumbing to dropsical conditions of snuff and gin, incompatible equally with coherence and existence. (406)

The shop enters the novel when John Harmon, now John Rokesmith, enters it, looking for traces of "George Radfoot," the sailor with whom he had exchanged identities, and who he suspects was killed by Pleasant's

father, Rogue; Pleasant is part of the exchange of characters and identities at the novel's core, part of the mystery plot. But she also presents
yet another parody of Dickens's earlier versions of devoted femininity:
her story begins, like Florence Dombey's or Oliver Twist's, with a maternal kiss and a deathly secret, even if this last "confidential communication" is prelude to incoherence and death; unlike other abandoned or
motherless daughters like Esther Summerson or Amy Dorrit, she
receives a material inheritance she can turn to good use.

The pawn shop gives Pleasant not only "some little position and
connection" in the community, but some narratorial power: she carries
out (again "upon the smallest of small scales") the exchange the rest of
the novel depends on – the circulation of goods, trusts, debts. She is even
linked, in her sympathy with John Harmon *against* the interests of her
father, to the novel's most complicated work of exchange, the resurrection of the dead and the substitution of dead men for living ones. A
"leaving" shop, is, in a sense, a good name for the novel – things are left
for dead, "when found, made note of," and redeemed much later. It also,
however, gives Pleasant the means to resist the marriage proposal she
refuses till the novel's conclusion: that of Mr. Venus, the "articulator" of
dead animals. Pleasant "do[es] not wish to regard [her]self, nor yet to be
regarded, in that boney light" (128). Interestingly, Pleasant writes her
refusal – "in her own handwriting" – and in this way poses an interesting
contrast to Lizzie Hexam, whose father resists his children's literacy; in
fact, later in the novel when Rogue Riderhood visits Mortimer to
attempt to make money out of the Harmon murder (and out of his own
near-drowning), he carries a letter. Asked about it by Bradley Headstone,
he says "it's wrote by my daughter, but it's mine" (611). Although her
father lays claim to it, Pleasant is one daughter who possesses the power
to write.

And this daughter possesses the power to say no: Pleasant's resistance
to Venus is part of a larger vision of human nature, one fostered by the
bitter irony of a mother who gives a woman with so difficult a life so
unnatural a name ("Pleasant she found herself, and she couldn't help it.
She had not been consulted on the question . . ." [406]), the unasked-for
gift of a "swivel eye (derived from her father)," and a rather jaundiced
view of the world, cultivated by her dark business dealings.

All things considered, she was not of an evil mind or an unkindly disposition.
For, observe how many things were to be considered according to her own
unfortunate experience. Show Pleasant Riderhood a Wedding in the street, and
she saw only two people taking out a regular licence to quarrel and fight. Show
her a Christening, and she saw a little heathen personage having a quite

superfluous name bestowed upon it, inasmuch as it would be commonly addressed by some abusive epithet: which little personage was not in the least wanted by anybody, and would be shoved and banged out of everybody's way, until it should grow big enough to shove and bang. Show her a funeral, and she saw an unremunerative ceremony in the nature of a black masquerade, conferring a temporary gentility on the performers, at an immense expense, and representing the only formal party ever given by the deceased. Show her a live father, and she saw but a duplicate of her own father, who from her infancy had been taken with fits and starts of discharging his duty to her, which duty was always incorporated in the form of a fist or a leathern strap, and being discharged hurt her. (406–407)

Pleasant's view of the world takes on the character of Dickens's *Sketches by Boz*, a world of considerable violence (little personages "shoved and banged out of everybody's way") which would only perpetuate itself ("until it should grow big enough to shove and bang"); a world of meaningless death (funerals are "unremunerative ceremon[ies]") and even more meaningless love (a wedding is a "regular licence to quarrel and fight"). The source of this misanthropy is her own father, whose only duty to his progeny (and that dispensed only in "fits and starts") is hurting her with "a fist or a leathern strap."

One of the mysteries of the novel is why the gentle (and rather moral) Mr. Venus loves Pleasant so, but she holds a certain fascination for Dickens as well, and she is given not only the right to exchange secrets, write letters, and move property, but a view of the relationship of romance to realism: a view strangely sympathetic to the novelist's:

All things considered, therefore, Pleasant Riderhood was not so very, very bad. There was even a touch of romance in her – of such romance as could creep into Limehouse Hole – and maybe sometimes of a summer evening, when she stood with folded arms at her shop-door, looking from the reeking street to the sky where the sun was setting, she may have had some vaporous visions of far-off islands in the southern seas or elsewhere (not being geographically particular), where it would be good to roam with a congenial partner among groves of bread-fruit, waiting for ships to be wafted from the hollow ports of civilization. For, sailors to be got the better of, were essential to Miss Pleasant's Eden. (407)

"Miss Pleasant's Eden" might make a fine title for a novel – but it would be a far cry from the "reeking street" and bitter realism her story speaks of. The gesture is familiar, that of seeking the visionary amid the diurnal, the pastoral in the urban, looking skyward like heroines from Amy Dorrit on, but the possibility of escape – and certainly, of escape from "trade" – is nonexistent. But the harshness of the vision is not that far from Dickens's own – just as Pleasant's view of the world rises from the mean streets Boz once walked. Pleasant's sharpness of vision seems an expansion of the daughterly vision elsewhere allowed, and one that allows the novel's gritty realism to exist with an almost Wordsworthian romance: Pleasant, here, is Wordsworth's "poor Susan" looking homeward; at the same time she is the prisoner of the reeking streets around her. Her vision (and here again, she seems almost an allegory for the novel's vision) is tied not to the romantic side of familiar things but to the material side of exotic things, the leaving-shop superimposed on the tropical isles.[8]

All the daughters in this novel work, their romance never separable from their labor or their alienation. Pleasant Riderhood has her shop; Lizzie Hexam works for her father, in the pub of Abbey Potterson, and finally in a factory owned by kindly Jews; Jenny Wren, to whom I shall return later, walks the streets finding clothes for the dolls whom she dresses and sells. Bella Wilfer proves she is a good wife by mastering the "Complete British Family Housewife," a guide to domestic labor; even Sophronia Lammle is shown laboring at the work of making money out of her unhappiness. But the novel must work similarly hard, making the testing of the heroine its affective labor; turning the dust-mounds of human detritus into the redemptive fictions of the novel's end through the "pious fraud" of make-believe plotting. The daughter must be turned into gold, redeeming the excremental vision of the streets: she must be persuaded into the productive self-alienation the novel has been tracing.

But why must the novel make its way through alienation? And why must readers share the experience of disenfranchisement? For the pious fraud that converts the heroine has long proven a sticking point for readers, suggesting some deeper uneasiness about reading, seduction, and education; about our implication in the heroine's alienation. This fraud works on us in peculiar ways. No one can doubt that Bella Wilfer and John Harmon will marry, but the machinery that brings the wedding about (Noddy Boffin and his wife conspiring with John Harmon to delude Bella into thinking them new-made misers; proving to both lovers how much Bella loves John) is hard to accept.[9] Dickens prepared for this surprise by having an open secret, that "John Rokesmith" and "Julius Handford" are the same person, and are John Harmon. As with the collapse of the Clennam household in *Little Dorrit*, and a series of other openly performed tricks in earlier novels, Dickens did not expect readers to be much fooled by this; rather he knew that, as in any narratorial con game, because readers had penetrated one secret they expected to be ahead of the plot, and were less likely to guess the other. As is true for the heroine, our very cleverness catches us up in the novel's deceptive instructions.

The novel has other secrets (chief among them the will that Boffin has hidden, Venus's betrayal of Wegg, and the trap Boffin lays for the lame merchant), but they have raised fewer readerly hackles. Nor do these shenanigans much concern the characters, for they involve moving back and forth the (always imaginary) fortunes of characters whom we fully expect to be prosperous, so many counters in the moral exchange that makes up the finances of the novel. But the plots against Bella *do* concern us, because (unlike the Wegg trickery) they are tricks played on a character with whom we identify – and through whose eyes we see – through much of the novel; indeed, given Dickens's habit of connecting moral growth with the heroine's progress, the novel will succeed only if we identify with her. The novel claims to trick "us" just as it must its characters: for our own good, and through the very medium of exchange on which it depends, narrative. This leads, as others have noted, to some confusion of morals (if the Boffin trick is to play the miser, and so convince Bella that riches corrupt, the very fact that Boffin is "playing" a miser proves the opposite for no corruption has taken hold here), but also to a not uncharacteristic confusion on the part of the Dickens-narrator/author figure, about what the "good" of fiction is.

More than that, though, it is a trick played on a woman by her guardian and her beloved – a trick the husband is particularly unwilling to abandon, because she is doing so well under the "test" of difficult circumstances. This is no John Jarndyce preparation of a different house, abandoned quickly for the pleasure of pleasing the beloved; this is a deception about her husband's identity, about her own material circumstances, about the moral disposition of two people very dear to her, and it is carried out (for her own good) over hundreds of pages – while the heroine (whose only crime was a little vain wilfulness) proves herself over and over the "truest gold." It is a plot that makes the heroine doubly a dupe: of her husband, and of her own unexpected goodness – which suggests the other reason we might cling to Sophronia Lammle, who carries out the text's only successful counter-plot, even if that plot is one that ultimately serves every "moral" aim of the marriage plot and its devices. Bella has no counter-plot, for her resistance to the plot is the plot's point. The heroine, like the reader, must be confused in order to be saved; the reader must be dazzled by fraud; fortunes must be renounced to be restored; daughters must be alienated to be redeemed; we are all happiest when we are "poor little fools."

Just as Dickens asks readers to renounce authority over knowledge, so the daughters (and the sons) spend the novel trying to renounce their inheritances. Lizzie works throughout the novel to return to its true owner the property she thinks her father has stolen; Bella tries to free herself from being a form of property "like a dozen of spoons"; John Harmon and Eugene Wrayburn try to will themselves into plots of their own, freeing themselves from the fictions of "My Respected Father," as Eugene puts it. Yet all these fantasies of (self-) reclamation take place against a backdrop of such property inequities that the plot cannot begin to imagine an unalienated self. The novel is littered with pub crawlers, pawn shops, deceptions, deals, and deadbeats – the terror of the poor house and the desolation of the river. How, amid such an absence of warmth, is anyone to become an unalienated person? In the text's most efficient summary of the self-in-society, Silas Wegg, the itinerant ballad-seller, goes to visit his own amputated leg in the articulation shop. As he expresses it, "I should *not* like . . . to be what I may call dispersed, a part of me here, and a part of me there, but should wish to collect myself like a genteel person" (127).[10] Wegg's desire to "account" for himself suggests again the class limits of disposable selves, that he literally cannot afford to collect himself again, but what of the gendered implications of such dispersals and dispossessions? Pleasant Riderhood finally wins the right *not* to be regarded in a boney light (Mr. Venus agrees not to work on female skeletons), but in the world of alienation known as coverture, a married woman did not own her jewelry, her clothes, or her own hair; there is no reason to assume she owned her own bones, or could maintain title to them at the moment they were profitable to her husband.

But the novel's promise to recollect people, to gather the fragments into a "genteel person," seems to suggest it will overcome death, alienation, dispersal, to manufacture an authentic person. This is remarkable in a novel that has some difficulty staging the human: its fantasies of animation (women in menageries, wives in dolls' houses, invitations to "come up and be dead") return eternally to Riderhood's question ("can a dead man own property?") and to its own (can a woman be property?) and to the question that follows: can property have a soul? But if its central proposition is that the alienated daughter, who by becoming a wife assents cheerfully to her own status as property, proves the system's heart, then estrangement becomes the cost of consciousness; partiality the condition of wholeness; dispersal the enabler of collectedness.

Marriage, in itself a powerful legal fiction (particularly under coverture), thus proves a central element of both consciousness and fiction: the wife's emergence from the daughter becomes the sign that persons emerge from purses; that the novel's exchange of people and property has been successfully "gone through" and "transcended" at the same time. But how can any such idea survive the novel's savaging of marriage? Even its images of marital unity are bound up in property and violence. When Sophronia and Alfred Lammle plot their revenge and she interrogates him about their finances, he insists on their marital solidarity:

> She was resuming, "Have you nothing – " when he stopped her.
> "We, Sophronia. We, we, we."
> "Have we nothing to sell?" (620)

Her refusal to accept the pathetic trinkets offered by Georgiana Podsnap, and her insistence that the Boffins return the jewelry and the money to the frozen-cheeked girl, are among the book's moral highlights – and are also her last acts of resistance to her husband. But she illuminates her own state when she describes what will happen to Georgiana if she marries Fascination Fledgeby:

"She will be sacrificed. She will be inveigled and married to that connexion of yours. It is a partnership affair, a money-speculation. She has no strength of will or character to help herself, and she is on the brink of being sold into wretchedness for life." (476)

This is what seems to be realism in this novel: the critique of marriage; the assessment of property rights; the "boney light" in which Pleasant refuses to be seen.

But marriage remains more complicated as a model of authenticity in the novel. True, the Lammles are locked together in deceit: they wear "the shamed air of two cheats who were linked together by concealed handcuffs"; they are two people "weary of one another, of themselves, and of all this world" (717). When Sophronia and Alfred are plotting Georgiana's sacrifice, they do not even need to exchange a glance: their silent communication is "all done as a breath passes from a mirror" (184). This seems a vicious parody of the idealized communication between two souls that breathe as one – but the intimacy of that shared breath, the impossibility of knowing when breath fades and where mirror begins, suggests some longing for dissolution of self into other, some deeper sense of marriage (and indeed, the Lammles's is that) where secrecy and loneliness give way to (a too perfect) knowledge.

This is not exactly romance, though it does carry an odd wistfulness for the aging Dickens, a man who has left his wife, fallen in love with another woman, and can never call her by that magic word, "wife." And

the sense that loving Lizzie saves Eugene from a demonic and unnecessary sense of his own wastefulness is as powerful as the idea that Bella,
against all the odds of trivial and mercenary girlhood, becomes capable
of sacrifice, patience, and imagination. The power it has as a fantasy is
of overcoming that absolute alienation the novel begins with: the
absolute isolation of the figures on the river, the silence of the mercenary heart.

So Dickens's sense of realism seems to bounce back and forth between
the "romance" of the redemption of the heroine's bond, and the "realistic" depiction of the slave relationship any "bond" proffers. The legal
fiction of marriage (coverture), like the fiction of the "pious fraud" (that
misers lose their souls when they love their money), is at once necessary,
and beyond belief. But just as questions of realism and romance have
blurred into each other from the beginning of Dickens's career, so questions of authenticity and fraudulence are equally hard to reconcile, or to
keep separate. Perhaps questions of alienation and self-possession are
best approached from the other side: that in these plots Dickens is toying
with a number of versions of what it means to be a person; that this is
at the heart of the strategic deployment of fictions. The question is not
of an authenticity recaptured through self-alienation (as it seems to be
in *Little Dorrit*), but the possibility of transcending some far darker alienation, of finding some tolerable imitation of humanity. When Boffin
stages his plot against Bella, attacking John Harmon to force her to
defend the man she loves, he does so by reducing the language of sentiment to animal noises:

"Win her affections and possess her heart! Mew says the cat, Quack-quack says
the duck, Bow-wow-wow says the dog! Win her affections and possess her heart!
Mew, Quack-quack, Bow-wow!" (660)

To become a heroine, Bella needs to return to human speech, resist the
devolutionary progress of the novel; she also needs to recognize what
was already inhuman in the mercenary plots she was spinning.

The unnatural is the realm of most plotting in the novel, and it is what
Dickens must engage and reject. Most characters who "plot" with
fictions tend to dehumanize them: Silas Wegg has imagined a family
living in the house into which the Boffins move, so that he can dress up
his own self-pity as sadness on their behalf; the Lammles pretend a sympathy with Georgiana to make her a tool for their plots; Fascination
Fledgeby creates Riah, the Jewish money lender, in the image of his own
wolfishness, so he can disavow his own villainy – indeed, the fiction

allows him to behave worse than he would otherwise. Everyone who creates an "imaginary friend" in the novel makes the person they invent into a badly marred version of themselves, reducing the authenticity of others and destroying themselves in the process; the novel leaves available very little room for any plotting.

The only good plotters, and the only good plots, are those that plot with the dead. Lizzie solves John Harmon's murder, then fantasizes that the dead man has solved his own crime; Mrs. Boffin conceives the plot of bringing John Harmon back to life and winning Bella for him when she sees Rokesmith sitting like the ghost of the young John Harmon; when Mrs. Boffin wants to introduce Bella to the young (adopted) John Harmon, the real John Harmon (not at all dead, of course) recoils and says "how can you show her the dead?" (157). Even the Lammles die and come back better characters, dismissed by Boffin for their evil schemes and by the narrator, who claims the novel will never see them again. After this narrative death, they (unexpectedly) re-enter, as if to surprise the omniscient narrator, so that Alfred can beat Fascination Fledgeby into a bleeding mess, carrying out posthumously the novel's necessary revenge and saving goodness for characters who will need it in the following chapters. Only characters who have met their demise can do the novel's dirty work.

But all the novel's work is dirt: turning the dust mounds into the proper inheritance; turning Eugene's corpse into a husband; turning Bella's base nature into "the truest gold." The human (like the authentic) occupies a small space, shares it with the dead, and hovers just around the corner of the filthy, paper-swept streets. To get a life of labor and consciousness is in many ways already not to share in the deepest of alienations that the novel proposes, to be no better than your own amputated leg. Wegg laments, viewing his lost limb, that he doesn't think he ought to have to buy the leg back from the articulator, since it is still his. Venus asks in return, "Do you think so, Mr. Wegg? I bought you in open contract," but Wegg's reply is absolute: "You can't buy human flesh and blood in this country, sir; not alive, you can't. . . . Then query, bone?" (351). This novel is remarkably less certain about the status of flesh, blood, and bone; in its reprise of Shylock's contract, it finds very little not for sale or at least for exchange. And as Dickens has noted since at least *Nicholas Nickleby*, and Ralph Nickleby's discovery that it is his own son he has been hunting since the book began, to be a usurer is to begin by lending with interest only to strangers; it is to end in a world of no tribes, no families, no forms of union at all.[11]

In that world, marriage does not escape the alienation of strangers, but can only hope to add something to that phantasmatic contract. These are all haunted contracts, staged in the knowledge of death: when Eugene attends the Lammles's wedding, it is "with a pervading air upon him of having presupposed the ceremony to be a funeral, and of being disappointed" (165). Much the same disappointment, of course, marks his own wedding at book's end, where he swears that his best gift to his bride would be his own death. A similar sense of the presumption of living, or daring to live on, pervades much of the novel's fiction: Bella and Lizzie are both somehow better off marrying dead men, for all will soon be dust anyway.

The sense of things coming quickly to consumption, of Dickens's own weariness of fiction-making, is at war with our sense of the novel's redemptive quality: somehow, marrying a man you think is someone else, or a wealthy man who has been battered beyond recognition, convinces readers as well that life can transcend what Pleasant memorably thought of as the "reeking street"; one might be forgiven for traitorously thinking it a good thing that Pleasant can at least continue to bilk sailors in her leaving shop, dreaming of bread-fruit and raunchy deals in idyllic settings. The novel seems to be offering us the opposite: the deal is transcendence, but you have to get rather mucky, and renounce a fair bit of knowledge to achieve it, just as you will achieve consciousness only by giving yourself away. Interest, unlike in Pleasant's shop, will not accrue.

Dickens's fictional energy seems to partake both of this futility and a sense of something piquant just beyond the horizon; some strange fictional novelty. This is the other way in which Dickens is intent on restaging the human, and in this case it takes the form not of the heroine's gold-standard, but the eccentric heroine's revisiting of the doll's house. In this final fictional move, it is the eccentric daughter who gets to be fully a person, and who invents the new model of subjectivity to which Dickens comes, unexpectedly, at the end of his career.

Henry James famously hated *Our Mutual Friend*. For him, it marked the demise of any literary powers in Dickens: as he claimed, "the fantastic, when the fancy is dead, is a very poor business." James's emphasis on business is strange enough, suggesting an aesthetic distaste at both the marketing of the Dickensian and Dickens's own painful industry in finishing this most difficult novel, but it is not James's central point of attack: that point is the notion of Dickensian character. He says, "It is hardly too much to say that every character here put before us is a mere bundle of eccentricities, animated by no principle of nature whatever."[12] This is not a new critique for Dickens, and has as much to do with James's attempt to create a newer, more psychological realism for himself as with anything "really" in Dickens, but James's point of entry into the eccentric is worth noting: it is with Jenny Wren, for, as he asks querulously "What do we get in return for accepting Miss Jenny Wren as a possible person?"

For James, Jenny Wren, the text's "dolls' dressmaker" and "sharp little person," is not only a unique violation of *vraisemblance*, she is one of:

[Dickens's] pathetic characters . . . she is a little monster; she is deformed, unhealthy, unnatural; she belongs to the troop of hunchbacks, imbeciles, and precocious children who have carried on the sentimental business in all Mr. Dickens's novels; the little Nells, the Smikes, the Paul Dombeys.

And he goes on:

It were, in our opinion, an offense against humanity to place Mr. Dickens among the greatest novelists. For, to repeat what we have already intimated, he has created nothing but figure. He has added nothing to our understanding of human character.

The way Dickens reconciles us to "what is odd," James concludes, "conveys a certain impression of charlatanism."

It is worth noting the degree of James's indignation, as if he had in some way been taken in by the text. This brings back the points of critique I articulated earlier, the way the text's surprises bewitched and annoyed readers. James's cry (that Dickens adds *nothing* to our understanding of human character; that he reconciles us to the "odd"; that Jenny Wren cannot be accepted as a "possible person") adds up to a complaint about the fictionality of fiction; that to the extent Dickens reminds us this is a novel, he is inhuman, a nothing-adder, a charlatan.

But more notable still is that the sign of fiction, for James, is the female eccentric. He is quite wrong about Jenny Wren: she is not a "precocious child," a hunchback or an imbecile; she is crippled (not, probably, deformed, except by labor); she is indeed unhealthy, but that is precisely what marks her as neither unnatural nor at all sentimental: she has been made unhealthy by her life in the streets of London, and she is a product of a nature against which Dickens has been inveighing since his fiction began.[13]

In that sense, Jenny stands for a certain kind of realism: she is a sign for Dickens's fiction because she is a sign of a social fact, but she is also a sign for the fiction because she is linked to all sorts of "fancies" in the novel. Most interesting for our purposes here, she is a sign for fiction because she is the weird return of the uncanny daughter through whom Dickens early invented his fictional assurance. Just as Bella Wilfer and Lizzie Hexam recreated the blurring of fair and dark heroines that *Oliver Twist* located in Rose Maylie and Nancy, so Jenny Wren recapitulates the tiny, freakish heroine represented in Nell, Little Dorrit, Esther Summerson, and a succession of little, marked figures, who were at once "little mothers" and deprived daughters.

But both the novel and the heroine claim a slightly different space. Neither the narrator nor any other character is sure what to call Jenny Wren: her real name is Fanny Cleaver, but no one ever uses it; her profession ("the dolls' dressmaker") blurs into her father's identity ("Mr. Dolls") and her own; her size and age and shape vary from description to description. The narrator first calls her "a child – a dwarf – a girl – a something" (271). When her friend Riah, the Jew, introduces her to Miss Abbey Potterson at the nearby pub, Miss Abbey asks Mr. Riah, "Child, or woman?"; he replies, "Child in years, woman in self-reliance and trial" (498). When the odious Charley Hexam, Lizzie's brother, meets her, he describes her as "a little crooked antic of a child, or old person, or whatever it is" (278). In his description, she loses all age, all gender, everything but her crookedness.

Jenny introduces herself very differently. When Charley comes to call, she announces, "I can't get up . . . because my back's bad, and my legs are queer. But I'm the person of the house" (271). Charley, characteristically, cannot accept this – she does not fit his idea of a proper person – so he asks her again:

"Who else is at home?"
"Nobody's at home at present," returned the child, with a glib assertion of her dignity, "except the person of the house." (271)

The narrator might seem to be toying with Jenny's sense of herself (he knows she is a child) but he doesn't deny her dignity, however glibly she asserts it: for the first time in a Dickens novel, a daughter is the person of the house.

But what kind of person, to return to James's critique, can an "antic" daughter be? In some ways, she is another devoted daughter: she thinks herself her father's mother, and her father, a poor, wicked child. This is not an unusual reversal in a Dickens novel: the child for the parent, the daughter the father's guide and savior.[14] But here the reversal is so violent that the daughter treats the father with singular viciousness; she threatens him, rebukes him, and denies him money. More than that, she herself is a parody of that devoted daughter: the Little Nell figure nearing puberty; or Amy Dorrit, already a woman, though small. Her maturity sits so uneasily on her, that no character can be sure where she is as regards age or sexual development. In a novel of loving but distrustful daughters, she has the least to gain from being a child ("I know their tricks," she keeps saying), and is the farthest from achieving real maturity, kept back not just by size and age, but by physical immobility.

But Jenny is a figure of enormous imaginative power in the novel, and her fantasies are strong enough to make other people distrust their sense of reality. That uncanny sense of "a child – a dwarf – a girl – a *something*" (emphasis mine) enters as well the descriptions of Jenny Wren's creations, the fashion-model dolls she creates, but which she refers to alternately as people, as dress-making dummies, as wax objects. She walks the streets, forcing ladies of fashion (unknowingly) to pose for her dolls, lessening her own physical discomfort by imagining them pushed about as she forces them into postures. But this is almost incoherent in the text, and it is possible (as with the initial description of Jenny herself) to read for some time before the text *settles* the description of the "dolls" and the "dolls' dressmaker." The text's tendency to treat grown women as dolls does nothing to relieve this textual queasiness; nor does its confusion of Jenny Wren with the dolls she creates, as in Wrayburn's continued habit of calling her father "Mr. Dolls," or in Jenny's own gesture, when Miss Abbey admires her hair, of pulling out the whole "golden stream" of it, only to have Miss Abbey remark on it, saying "what lovely hair! . . . enough to make wigs for all the dolls in the world" (498). The reckless animism of *Bleak House* and its cluttered warehouses come together with the golden-haired doll's spectacle of *A Tale of Two Cities* – but here, even when confronted with what it clearly wants to mark as "a human character," *Our Mutual Friend* plays the same tricks of objectification, reification, reversal and animation.

Jenny plays them as well. Although she is realism's daughter, linked to those reeking streets, far from gardens and fancy, she smells imaginary flowers throughout the whole novel. She carries on long conversations with and about imaginary people, most noticeably "Him," the fiancé she imagines appearing, disappointing her, and bearing the marks of her displeasure. She sees dream children, who are unlike the mocking children of her horrible childhood, but beg her to come up and play with them; to "come up and be dead." That is to say, she fictionalizes in much the way Dickens does: she fills imaginary gardens with flowers that defeat "mere" realism; she gives imaginary people no-names that sound like Dickens's, as "Him" (her unknown beloved) resembles Dickens's "the man from nowhere" and "that popular character whom the novelists and versifiers call Another". Like Dickens, she turns horror into comic relief and unexpected blessing, for Dickens cannot stay any longer than Jenny with misery, but must, like her, move between the visionary and the infernal.

Not that Jenny has narrative autonomy. Her life story is written by the incessant and draining labor her father's drunkenness commits her to. When she briefly regrets the violence she directed at him, she conjures up her own life:

"How can I say what I might have turned out myself, but for my back having been so bad and my legs so queer, when I was young! . . . I had nothing to do but work, and so I worked. I couldn't play." (801)

So, too, does she echo Dickens's transcendence of his own childhood when she recollects the children's mockery and transforms it into the dream-children:

"They were not like me; they were not chilled, anxious, ragged, or beaten; they were never in pain." (290)

The beaten (and beaten down) daughter, like the grim Pleasant, or like Dickens himself, has only two escapes: more work, and more fiction.

Jenny's imaginative gifts seem linked to her connections to the death-plots. She came to her friendship with Lizzie Hexam because of her own grandfather's fate: she is the granddaughter of "The terrible drunken old man, in the list slippers and the nightcap" (65, 277) whose picture was on the Hexam wall.[15] She is linked both to the angry father and the dead man towed behind: like Lizzie watching the fire "like the ghost of a girl miser" (116), she speaks to the dead; at the novel's end, she comes in to interpret for Eugene, speaking to him as if he were dead and could only whisper to the living. It is Jenny, of course, who guesses the magic word, "wife," that will save Eugene's life, make reparations to Lizzie, and transform him into a true gentleman – and her into a recognized lady; it is also Jenny who marks throughout the novel's intermingling of marriage and death. She conceives the design of a surplice after her father's funeral, and creates a doll's wedding – which of course subsequently comes true. Here Jenny's vision and the novel's come together again: like Jenny, the novel conflates dolls and heroines, weddings and funerals, death and completion; it, too, wants to "come up and be dead."

Certainly, Dickens did: this is the novel he wrote after he himself almost died, and it bears the marks of that posthumousness everywhere. For *Our Mutual Friend* is in every way that counts his last novel: it is written when he (and his daughters) are old; when his marriage is over; when his health is failing; indeed, in the middle of it he was in a terrifying railway accident, in which he might well have died, and which haunted him afterwards. The postscript of *Our Mutual Friend* makes clear that Dickens thinks of himself as a dead man after the Staplehurst train accident, the incident in which he survived a crash, and then walked through the shattered train carriages rescuing travelers, trying to help the injured and dying. As he described it in a subsequent letter, he was shaken "not by the beating of the carriage, but by the work afterwards of getting out the dying and the dead" – that sense of walking amid the "dying and the dead" informs not only the near-fatal lethargy of *Edwin Drood*, a novel with more grave-haunting than *The Old Curiosity Shop*, but the sense of *Our Mutual Friend*, which he had in partial manuscript at the time of the crash, as a novel that came back from the dead – that came up to be dead. He recounts his rescue of Mr. and Mrs. Boffin ("in their manuscript dress") from the train-wreck, "much soiled but otherwise unhurt," and accounts for where they and other characters were at the time – their progress through the manuscript. But he then reports on his own progress: he adds that he himself never expects to be closer to death than he was at that moment, until they write "against my life, the two words with which I have this day closed this book: – THE END." "The End" of the novel thus coheres with his own imagined death scene, the punning on closure no less powerful than it was in the last sentence of his first novel, the already (and eerily) "posthumous papers" of the Pickwick Club, when he referred in the final sentence to the "steady and reciprocal attachment [between Pickwick and Sam Weller] which nothing but death will terminate."[16] But the connection with death and reading in this later novel (from Lizzie's contemplation of the corpse-notices to Wegg's of the "Decline and Fall off the Rooshian Empire") suggests again Dickens's memorialist art, and its fallout: his sense of his own as a dying art.

The ambivalence of that belief seems to me to have shaped critical response to the novel, not just in its sensitivity to the material from Shakespeare's last play (itself a "romance" of drowning, daughters, and art), but a certain discomfort (one again marked by James) with the dying body of the novelist, and what everyone senses as a certain impatience with the material of his fiction. But such a reading discounts the other effect death had on Dickens's novel. It is written with a new, weird, quite wonderful energy, as if he had survived death and could do *anything*: the speed of its plots, the rush of its conclusions, its bumpy energy and flashes of genius resist its own pull towards death. Indeed, those qualities can be read in two ways: the first, as the genius at his heights, writing what will be his version of *The Tempest* and meditating on his Prospero-like "arts";[17] the second, as the weary craftsman, reflecting on his "labor." The latter set of terms is that laid out by Henry James, who referred to this as the most labored of Dickens's novels, and it is worth returning to James's critique, to connect it again with the questions of female labor (of the labor of fiction; of laboring with women) in this novel. But we can take the discussion of labor still further: back into the questions of circulation, usury, and eccentricity. We can use Henry James's horror at the inhumanity of the late Dickens to open up once more the Dickens carnival – to ask again, what kind of "person" is the freakish daughter, and what kind of house can she inhabit?

The Old Curiosity Shop seemed to argue for the centrality of female eccentricity to narrative art; it featured female monsters, sphinxes, dragons, waxworks, curiosities of all sorts – and its chief curiosity, the good daughter, little Nell. This is the chief note sounded by Jenny Wren, who, though central to so many of the book's thematic concerns, makes her strongest impression through her internal *lack* of congruence: not just that she cannot be "typed" by other characters, or that even the narrator cannot explain her or explain her away, but that her very attraction lies in the oddities, the jagged quality of her character. After all, when "the charm was broken," "The person of the house . . . had become a little quaint shrew," "dragged down by hands that should have raised her up" (294). Her power is in those contrasts: her call to "come up and be dead" would not be so haunting if it were not sung in a "little sweet voice . . . musically repeating . . . in a silvery tone" (334–335); her excessively long, extraordinarily beautiful hair would not be so striking if it covered a "normal" body. As Dickens wrote to Marcus Stone, commenting on the frontispiece the artist was concluding, "The doll's dressmaker is immensely better than she was. I think she should now come extremely well. A weird sharpness not without beauty is the thing I want."[18] That sharpness (one stressed in the name Fanny Cleaver, as well as in her stabbing needle, her sharp and "cutting" words, her quick-wittedness) marks a powerful difference in this novel, as if the acidity allowed to minor women characters (*David Copperfield*'s Rosa Dartle and Miss Mowcher, to name only the most obvious) were brought back into the center of the books – brought back and eroticized, given beauty, made the artist's uncanny partner.

What I want to recapture here is some of the difference Dickensian eccentricity makes: and more, the difference it makes in the plot of what might otherwise seem quite conventional, renunciatory, domesticated femininity at the end of his career. Jenny Wren's presence is not like Miss Mowcher's narratorial interference, when the latter enters the plot abruptly to bring back the villainous manservant Littimer and make amends for Dickens's satire of the vertically challenged. Jenny Wren's difference is in her complete *inclusion* into the text's daughterly plots: not just her reinscription in an inappropriate love-match we are meant to admire (Sloppy is as questionably her equal as any heroine's intended, and poses the same problems of closure and domestic containment that Bella Wilfer's transformation into the "complete British family house-wife" did), but her possible inclusion as erotic presence as well as textual oddity. The eccentric not only includes the erotic, but has made itself central.

This might allow us to say something different finally about the role of eccentricity in Dickens, and the aspect that James feared: that you cannot have, as he expresses it, "a community of eccentrics"; that society is maintained by "natural sense and feeling," not by "exceptions." Dickens refuses to except the exceptional. This is not to say that the inclusion of the eccentric is a proof of Dickens's "humanity" and fellow feeling, that the Dickens carnival allows us all to play equally. In fact, what continues to please about Dickensian eccentricity is its lack of equality: Jenny Wren's powerful sense of her difference, her pain, her absence from the central plot is her strength, as a "character" and as a character. Instead, what I want to argue is that something attractively inhuman remains at the center of Dickens's fiction – that, as James had it, to put Dickens at the center of all novelists is to exile yourself from humanity. And why wouldn't you, to return to where this chapter began, if humanity (and its social formations) is to be represented by the conventional happy endings *Our Mutual Friend* puts forward.

The happy ending of *Our Mutual Friend* is about nothing so much as testing the limits of closure as a social and a narrative force. In the last chapter, Eugene's friend Mortimer Lightwood goes to test the extension of "society's" blessing to Eugene and Lizzie's marriage. In its parody version, this marriage is described by Lady Tippins as the wedding of a muscular boatwoman (a "horrid female waterman" who cannot be "graceful" [888]) to the proper young man, the destruction of "My respected father's" hopes of Eugene's uplifting (and socially upraising) marriage. All the other "social" characters join in. Only one, the muffled but honorable Mr. Twemlow, can imagine another solution. For the first time in the novel which has seen him perpetually confused, Twemlow sees his way clearly: he states definitively that Eugene's gentility necessarily extends itself over his "feelings," and over the "lady" in question. This successful trouncing of the annoying Tippins and Podsnaps by the meek Twemlow satisfies the readers, and makes "society" itself seem redeemable; but the reinvocation of Lizzie's difference at that moment (factory girl, waterman, penniless) marks the absolute limit of Dickens's social fantasy. It is, in that way, not so different from the last doll Jenny sends on its way, to the little "Miss Harmon," the child born into the redeemed Harmony Jail, the doll Sloppy will watch over (as we are led to believe he will watch Jenny herself) "with more care . . . than if she was a gold image" (883). A gold image (the redeemed golden dustman's daughter; Bella "the truest golden gold") is what the daughter's plot has produced, and the doll merely its double; something of *other* value has been lost.

But this is not the whole story, and I think the bringing together of the daughter, the dwarf, and the "it" suggests a different reward than James conceived when he asked, "what do we get in return for accepting Miss Jenny Wren as a possible person?"[19]. The novel's ability to keep the human and the inhuman in its gaze at once (to see in Jenny Wren at once the fantasist visionary, the pained and crippled little girl, and something weirdly inhuman and sharply alien) is its chief power, and is where Dickens has something of particular use for feminists. As in the realist/romance split the property plot participated in, and in the material world of the novel, where excrement stays excrement at the same time it turns to gold, the novel gets to have things both ways, and points up some of the fictionality of our own longing for proof and redemption – and our bitter knowledge that we live in a material world, one of (increasingly) limited possibilities, limited options for what it means to be "human."

The book's goodness comes out of its manipulations, the heroines' triumphs out of their bewilderment. Any sense of truth is wrung (with pain, and in doubt) from deceptions too multiple to record or account for. The book, at the end, can only ask us to stop counting, to believe in magic, to embrace poverty as the way to riches and deception as the way to clarity. It is Dickensian paradox, as much as Dickensian figuration, that is out of control in this novel. Audrey Jaffe has noted the ominousness of the words "mutual" and "friend" in this novel;[20] I have noted throughout that for all its urgent chumminess and bringing-together of plots, the novel suggests more powerfully a world of strangers, darkness, and loss: the world, as Bella expressed it early, where one is a spectacle, "the talk and the laugh of the town . . . made the property of strangers."

But the novel has a power that transcends that darkness – that suggests that Dickens himself came through the other side of the book, as he did through the train crash, carrying his characters, a little bruised and shaken, a little dusty, a little in need of restoration and restoratives, but capable of redemption, resurrection, revivification. "Who but Dickens could have written it? Who indeed?," asks Henry James in despair, irritation, and (perhaps) envy. "Seldom, we reflected, had we read a book so intensely *written*, so little seen, known, or felt."[21] *Our Mutual Friend* tries to stake its claim aggressively as a novel "about writing," a novel that resolutely pulls away the power of writing from anyone who might usurp it, and ends on its "master's" own note: "the end" written after his name. For the daughter, the writer and reader of and for the dead, little remains to be written, her bold signature canceled, her pen lost in her hair, only her "weird sharpness" left, "not without beauty." The Boffins, in their manuscript dress, were, Dickens tells us, "much soiled, but unhurt": doubtless, that is the best that can be asked for in this novel. But, like Pleasant Riderhood, lone seeker of Romance, with her name and character at war, figure and plot-function jockeying away from each other, perhaps the heroine might look up from the reeking streets, and ask for something more.

She might; and here is where Jenny Wren returns to claim something from us, to ask for her own house, in which she can be not a daughter but a person. This question hangs over Dickens's last novel, *The Mystery of Edwin Drood*. This unfinished novel has yet another pair of heroines, the fragile Rosa Budd and the aggressive Helena Landless, whose name echoes that of Ellen Lawless Ternan, Dickens's mistress. The two women come together, not unexpectedly, but they leave radically altered: Rosa leaves the cathedral town where she has been sheltered, and moves into rooms in London; Helena leaves the town as well, and, some readers have speculated, comes back disguised as a man. Rosa breaks off her engagement to the young man to whom she has been willed, Edwin Drood, and gives him back the ring that marked the betrothal; that ring seems (in a weird recapitulation of the ring-exchange at the end of *The Merchant of Venice*) to be the one clue that will enable the detection of Edwin Drood's murderer. Rosa Budd's ring is the single element for which the murderous John Jasper could not plan; the heroine's refusal of the romance plot will baffle death and illuminate the darkness.

Both of *Drood*'s heroines move towards rooms of their own; though Jenny Wren seems destined for the marriage plot with the improbable Sloppy, it is hard to imagine her not winning every property battle in sight, not retaining her own personage. (Sloppy, after all, has been saved from the poor house; possession does not seem a word in his emotional vocabulary.) The novel stops short of some absolute identity of female autonomy: Dickens could never imagine female enfranchisement; he wants to enclose every fair heroine in a golden bower; he never quite sheds the impulse David Copperfield expresses, to shield the damsel from everything she fears, even if it is just "mice, to which she had a great objection." But the weirdness of Jenny Wren, the necessary singularity of the heroine with the bad back and the queer legs, seems to offer some other account of property and persons for Dickens. In that alternate account, one in which the heroine has a house that is less bleak, and in which she can sign her name to her own (however antic and crooked) story, it is the heroine who gets to write after it, for herself, "the end."

Notes

INTRODUCTION

1 Michael Slater recounts that both daughters were at a disadvantage because of the scandal, and because they remained with their father and his wife's sister. Though they brazened it out, they were increasingly uncomfortable in society, forced to behave like *arrivistes* in one of their father's novels, calling on people for whom they formerly had contempt. In their eagerness, they even called on the people who were the models for the fictional Pecksniffs – who snubbed them instantly. See M. Slater, *Dickens and Women* (Stanford: Stanford University Press, 1983), p. 184.

2 Gladys Storey, *Dickens and Daughter* (London: Frederick Muller, 1939), p. 219.

3 The most compelling early account of this is George Gissing's, but it runs through many more contemporary reviews than one might expect. For useful samples, see the summaries of *Bleak House* reviews in *Bleak House*, edited by George Ford and Sylvère Monod (New York: Norton, 1977) and A. E. Dyson's fine "casebook," *Bleak House* (Nashville: Aurora Publishers, 1970). A sharp modern account of this is John Carey's in *Here Comes Dickens* (New York: Schocken Books, 1974), pp. 154–174.

4 "Nurse's Stories" in *Selected Short Fiction*, edited by Deborah A. Thomas (Harmondsworth: Penguin Books, 1976), pp. 221–223.

5 See Slater, *Dickens and Women*, p. 191; he is quoting Mamie's letter to Annie Fields from Adrian Arthur's *Georgina Hogarth and the Dickens Circle* (London: Oxford University Press, 1957), p. 158.

6 Among important discussions of law and narrative, see Jacques Derrida, "The Law of Genre," in *On Narrative*, edited by W. J. T. Mitchell (Chicago: University of Chicago Press, 1980, 1981) and "Devant la Loi," in *Kafka and the Contemporary Critical Performance*, edited by Alan Udoff (Bloomington: Indiana University Press, 1987). For an expansion of these ideas, see Judith Butler, *Gender Trouble: Feminism and the Subversion of Identity* (New York: Routledge, 1990) and Caren Kaplan, "Resisting Autobiography: Out-Law Genres and Transnational Feminist Subjects," in *The Politics of Gender in Women's Autobiography*, edited by Sidonie Smith and Julia Watson (Minneapolis: University of Minnesota Press, 1992), pp. 115–138.

7 See, for a useful discussion of similar issues, Lorna Hutson, *The Usurer's*

208

Daughter (London: Routledge, 1994). For a fine study of writing and property that treats many of the same issues I raise, see Jeff Nunokawa, *The Afterlife of Property: Domestic Security and the Victorian Novel* (Princeton: Princeton University Press, 1994).

8 Blackstone, *Commentaries on the Laws of England*, edited by Joseph Chitty (London: William Walker, 1826), Vol. 1, p. 449.

9 Michael Ragussis's fine book, *Figures of Conversion: "The Jewish Question" and English National Identity* (Durham, NC and London: Duke University Press, 1995) isolates the story of the Jewish daughter (from Shylock and Jessica through Sir Walter Scott) as a central story of the formation of national and racial identity in the English consciousness; he does not, however, discuss Blackstone's eccentric isolation of such a narrative. For an important discussion of women and the transmission of meaning from a different literary perspective, see Margaret Homans, *Bearing the Word: Language and Female Experience in Nineteenth-Century Women's Writing* (Chicago: University of Chicago Press, 1986).

10 Alison Milbank, *Daughters of the House: Modes of the Gothic in Victorian Fiction* (New York: St. Martin's Press, 1992), p. 17; the passage she quotes from Ousby is in *Bloodhounds of Heaven: The Detective in English Fiction from Godwin to Doyle* (Cambridge, MA: Harvard University Press, 1976).

11 The best discussion of the Married Women's Property Act and the debate in the 1850s remains Lee Holcombe, *Wives and Property: Reform of the Married Women's Property Law in Nineteenth-Century England* (Toronto: University of Toronto Press, 1983).

12 Stewart, *Crimes of Writing: Problems in the Containment of Representation* (Durham, NC: Duke University Press, 1994), p. 3.

13 See in particular Raymond Williams's discussion of "family" and "private" in *Keywords: A Vocabulary of Culture and Society* (New York: Oxford University Press, 1976, 1983).

14 *David Copperfield*, edited by Trevor Blount (Harmondsworth: Penguin, 1966), p. 937. All subsequent page references are included in the text.

15 Criticism along these lines has its origin in Edmund Wilson, "The Two Scrooges" in *The Wound and the Bow* (London: Methuen, 1961). For other important discussions of this fragment, see Steven Marcus, "Who is Fagin," in *Dickens from Pickwick to Dombey* (New York: Norton, 1965); Robert Newsom, "The Hero's Shame," *Dickens Studies Annual* 11, 1983, pp. 1–24; Albert D. Hutter, "Reconstructive Autobiography: The Experience at Warren's Blacking," *Dickens Studies Annual*, 6, 1977, pp. 1–14.

16 See Miller, "Secret Subjects, Open Secrets," *Dickens Studies Annual*, 14, 1985; reprinted in Miller's *The Novel and the Police* (Berkeley: University of California Press, 1988).

17 Poovey, "The Man-of-Letters Hero: *David Copperfield* and the Professional Writer," in *Uneven Developments: The Ideological Work of Gender in Mid-Victorian England* (Chicago: University of Chicago Press, 1988); Welsh, *From Copyright to Copperfield: The Identity of Dickens* (Cambridge, MA: Harvard University

Press, 1988). My reading of *Copperfield* owes much to Welsh, and to his earlier and equally brilliant reading of the novel in *The City of Dickens* (Cambridge, MA: Harvard University Press, 1971).

18 Gwendolyn B. Needham, "The Undisciplined Heart of David Copperfield," *Nineteenth Century Fiction*, 9 1954, pp. 81–107.

19 See Welsh, *The City of Dickens*, pp. 180–195.

20 See Sylvia Manning's discussion of this paragraph, and the problem of retrospection in *David Copperfield*, in "*David Copperfield* and Scheherazada: The Necessity of Narrative," in *Studies in the Novel*, Vol. 14, Number 2, Winter 1982, pp. 327–336.

21 John O. Jordan has discussed the centrality of the word "station" to these questions of retrospection and self-fictionalizing in a fine essay, "The Social Sub-Text of *David Copperfield*," in *Dickens Studies Annual*, 14, 1985, pp. 61–92.

22 For a similar argument about women, writing, and authority in Dickens, and his rivalry with women writers like Charlotte Brontë, see Robert Newsom, "Authorizing Women: *Villette* and *Bleak House*," *Nineteenth Century Literature*, Vol. 46, No 1, June 1991, pp. 54–81. For a general discussion of the relationship between female subjectivity and novelistic (and ideological) authority, see Nancy Armstrong, *Desire and Domestic Fiction: A Political History of the Novel* (New York: Oxford University Press, 1987).

23 For an account of the differences between the male and female progress to sexual maturity, and the difficulties Freud has in accounting for them, see Sarah Kofman, *The Enigma of Woman: Woman in Freud's Writing*, translated by Catherine Porter (Ithaca: Cornell University Press, 1985), pp. 124–225 in particular. See also Jane Gallop, *Feminism and Psychoanalysis: The Daughter's Seduction* (London: Macmillan Press, 1982).

24 For Freud, writing and women are always connected to houses and homelessness. This is not unexpected, since his writings from the *General Introduction to Psychoanalysis* link not only rooms and consciousness, but in particular, houses and women, which are alike in "being the space which encloses human beings" (*The General Introduction to Psychoanalysis* in *The Standard Edition of the Complete Psychological Works of Sigmund Freud*, edited by James Strachey, [London: Hogarth Press, 1953–74]. Vol. XV, p. 163). Robert Newsom has usefully expanded on Freud's idea of the essential uncanniness of homes and houses in his reading of *Bleak House*, observing that, for Dickens as well, stories of homes and homelessness are stories of identity, not only of individuals but of their parents, their history, their place within the social; for all their material importance, they continue to suggest the power of animation within the inanimate; of something beyond "realistic," immediate perception (Newsom, *Dickens on the Romantic Side of Familiar Things: Bleak House and the Novel Tradition* [New York: Columbia University Press, 1977], pp. 104–5 in particular). But as the quotation suggests, when Freud returned to houses late in his career, in *Civilization and its Discontents*, it was with a different sense of the world beyond realist perception (*Civilization and its Discontents*, in *The Standard Edition*, Vol. XXI, p. 91.) My reading of

homes and consciousness has been influenced by the work of Kristina Deffenbacher in "Housing Wandering Minds" (unpublished dissertation: University of Southern California, 1998), a study of consciousness and social work in the Victorian novel.

25 See Meisel, "Dickens' Roman Daughter," in *Realizations: Narrative, Pictorial, and Theatrical Arts in Nineteenth-Century England* (Princeton, NJ: Princeton University Press, 1983), pp. 302–321.

26 Welsh, *The City of Dickens*, p. 223.

27 My sense of the law's female "silhouette" is enhanced by Derrida's reading of it in "Devant la Loi," where being before the law is a "paradox or enigma," and the law itself is "frightening and fantastic"; it is "an apparition of the Law, and it is a feminine 'silhouette'" (pp. 131, 138, 142).

1 THE UNCANNY DAUGHTER: *OLIVER TWIST, NICHOLAS NICKLEBY* AND THE PROGRESS OF LITTLE NELL

1 *Oliver Twist*, edited by Peter Fairclough (Harmondsworth, Middlesex: Penguin Books, 1966), p. 36. All subsequent page references are included in the text.

2 *The Old Curiosity Shop*, edited by Angus Easson (Harmondsworth, Middlesex: Penguin Books, 1972), p. 42. All subsequent page references are included in the text.

3 See James Kincaid, in *Dickens and the Rhetoric of Laughter* (Oxford: Clarendon, 1966), pp. 50–75, for a discussion of Fagin and the Artful Dodger as other axes of readerly interest.

4 For two fine accounts of the composition and generic incoherences of *Oliver Twist*, see Burton Wheeler, "The Text and Plan of *Oliver Twist*', *Dickens Studies Annual*, 12, 1983, pp. 41–61 and William T. Lankford, "'The Parish Boy's Progress': The Evolving Form of *Oliver Twist*," *PMLA*, Vol. 93, No. 1 1978, pp. 20–39. For more general accounts of the creation of the novel, see Kathleen Tillotson, Introduction, *Oliver Twist* (Oxford: Clarendon Press, 1966), Kathryn Chittick, *Dickens and the 1830s* (Cambridge: Cambridge University Press, 1990), and Ian Duncan, *Modern Romance and the Transformation of the Novel: The Gothic, Scott, Dickens* (Cambridge: Cambridge University Press, 1992).

5 See Alexander Welsh, *The City of Dickens* (Cambridge, MA: Harvard University Press, 1971), pp. 141–163, for the classic discussion of Dickens's Angels of the Hearth.

6 See Garrett Stewart, *Dickens and the Trials of Imagination* (Cambridge, MA: Harvard University Press, 1974), pp. 160–170, for a discussion of fire-gazers and their power; interestingly, Stewart omits Nancy from his list.

7 Marcus, *Dickens from Pickwick to Dombey* (New York: Norton, 1965), pp. 54–67 in particular.

8 My reading of the Dickens's performance is generally dependent on Philip Collins, *Sikes and Nancy and Other Public Readings* (Oxford: Oxford University

Press, 1975), pp. 229–231. Collins draws heavily on Charles Kent, *Charles Dickens as a Reader* (1872, reprint New York: Haskell House Publishers, 1973).

9 It seems important to stress here the differences between conventions of imprisoned lovers (love is a jail; my lover is my keeper) and the specifics of Victorian representations of prison life. Dickens's fascination with prisons was hardly as biographical as criticism suggests. His tour of American prisons was not exceptional, and the early Victorian debates over prisons, like so many of the debates that marked the bureaucratizing of discipline in Victorian England, focused on questions of identity very similar to those the novel (and particularly the "Preface") asks: what is human nature; what in nature can be transformed; does evil exist, and can it (as *Oliver Twist* so firmly asserts) be altered only by death?

The tensions between what I am loosely calling "realism" and "romance" (or criminality and masochism, plots of social determinism and of transformative love) could be seen as sides of this social debate – but it is important to note that for Dickens, female masochism, blind love, devoted victimization, offered a way *out* of this debate. Somehow, Nancy's sacrifice will eradicate Bill's villainy, in a way nothing but death could; it is guilt over Nancy's death that brings Bill to an appropriate death-by-hanging, one the state then does not have to inflict. But of course, Nancy's masochism also *permits* Bill's violence, as female devotion and blindness always seem to encourage, even incite crime in the story Dickens tells. And of course, the move towards the disciplining of the heart is precisely the move noted by historians like Michel Foucault and Michael Ignatieff in the movement to reform the prison: to quote a central passage cited in Ignatieff's *A Just Measure of Pain: The Penitentiary in the Industrial Revolution* (New York: Pantheon Books, 1978), "there are cords of love as well as fetters of iron" (74–75). That reformer, John Brewster, went on to argue that those who would not bend before the "passion of fear" might be won over by "More tender impressions" – as Ignatieff sums this thought up, "by cords of love, Brewster meant the reformative and utilitarian justifications of punishment that would persuade the offender to accept his sufferings and face his own guilt." The story of female devotion Dickens tells offers the same "cords," and the same discipline.

While it is true, as Philip Collins has persuasively demonstrated, that Dickens grew increasingly severe in his attitudes towards crime and his hopelessness about reformation, it is important to recognize that even his earlier, "softer" writings on crime involve the forced reformation of "offenders." In this instance, the reformation comes through the recognition of the (bodily) suffering of (loving) women, a recognition that will bind the offender over more completely than would any discipline enforced from the outside. Ignatieff draws heavily, as do I, on the work of Michel Foucault, particularly *Discipline and Punish: The Birth of the Prison* (New York: Vintage, 1979). For the best treatment of the internalized monitoring of the "disciplined heart," see D. A. Miller's *The Novel and the Police* (Berkeley: University of California Press, 1988). Collins's *Dickens and Crime* (London: Macmillan,

1965), offers a fascinating discussion of the bitterness of the late Dickens, particularly his response to penal reforms, in which he resembles no one so much as Josiah Bounderby.

10 Audrey Jaffe has argued, convincingly, that no one in the novel ever looks at Nell; if I have focused on the scenes of spectacle in which she is stared at intensely, I would still argue that the primary visual mode of the novel is disavowal, and that Nell must be looked-away-from for the plot to work (her grandfather does not see her bleeding feet; people dismiss her pain as her angelic nature, etc.). See Jaffe, " 'Never be Safe but in Hiding': Omniscience and Curiosity in *The Old Curiosity Shop*," *Vanishing Points: Dickens, Narrative, and the Subject of Omniscience* (Berkeley: University of California Press, 1991).

11 This rape is foreshadowed by his constant physical abuse of his wife, whose "arms . . . were seldom free from impressions of his fingers in black and blue colours" (156). When Quilp keeps his wife awake all night by staring fixedly at her, as when he instructs his wife to "worm yourself into her secrets" (96) (or, indeed, when she hints at his sexual voracity by insisting any one of her friends would marry him at her death) the novel insists on sexualizing (though not, I would argue, eroticizing) its violence.

12 Quilp is, of course, the central exhibit of the novel, but there seems much *less* curiosity about him exhibited by the characters (or even the narrator) than we might expect. In some ways, he has no story, no origins; he simply "is" Quilp.

13 The more curious version of this comes when Nell (like Frankenstein's monster) follows the sweet Miss Edwards and her visiting sister, hoping to catch as if by influence their sisterly affections, much as she thinks "if she had such a friend as that to whom to tell her griefs, how much lighter her heart would be" (315).

14 The notorious Miss Biffin, with no legs and arms, was a favorite figure of his; she looks forward to her fictional counterpart Miss Mowcher, the dwarf in *David Copperfield*, and further still to Jenny Wren, introduced as "a child – a dwarf – a girl – a something."

15 Even the constable, near the end of the novel, stares at Miss Brass "as if in some doubt whether she might not be a griffin or other fabulous monster" (546).

16 That this may be a clue to Quilp's sexual taste is suggested late in the novel by the resemblance of his odd fetish (which he imagines to resemble his nemesis, Kit) to "the authentic portrait of a distinguished merman, or great sea-monster" (564).

17 Stewart, *On Longing: Narratives of the Miniature, the Gigantic, the Souvenir, the Collection* (Baltimore, MD: Johns Hopkins University Press, 1984).

18 See Musselwhite's extremely interesting *Partings Welded Together* (London: Methuen, 1987) which makes the case for the superiority of the early, unnovelistic "Boz" over the late, interfering, hegemonic "Dickens."

19 G. H. Wilson, *The Eccentric Mirror* (London, 1807) and *Wonderful Characters* (London, 1821, 1842).

20 Henry Morley, *Memoirs of Bartholemew Fair* (London, 1880, reprinted Detroit,

Singing Tree Press 1968, p. 189) quoted in Richard Altick, *The Shows of London* (Cambridge, MA: Harvard University Press, 1978) p. 36.

21 This and the following extract are from Altick, *The Shows of London*, p. 257.

22 After her death, Crachami was exhibited – in skeleton form – at the Royal College of Surgeons. She is there still, along with "the Fairy's tiny slippers, stockings, and death mask"; alongside her are two "giant" skeletons, to make her tininess even frailer – and to suggest she could never "shrink" quite far enough. (Altick, *The Shows of London*, p. 260).

23 *Nicholas Nickleby*, edited by Michael Slater (Harmondsworth, Middlesex: Penguin Books, 1978), p. 365. All subsequent page references are included in the text.

24 *Little Dorritt* (Harmondsworth: Penguin, 1967), p. 121.

25 Ruskin, *Fiction, Fair and Foul, Works*, edited by E. T. Cook and Alexander Wedderburn (1903), XXXIV, 275n, quoted in *Dickens: The Critical Heritage*, edited by Philip Collins (London: Routledge & Kegan Paul, 1971), p. 100.

26 Stewart, *On Longing*, pp. 108, xii.

27 Welsh, *The City of Dickens*, p. 158.

28 Alexander Welsh noted this as well in an early article, "King Lear, Père Goriot, and Nell's Grandfather" in *Literary Theory and Criticism: A Collection of Essays in Honor of Rene Wellek*, edited by Joseph P. Strelka (Bern: Peter Lang, 1984), pp. 1405–1425.

29 Altick, *The Shows of London*, pp. 43–44.

30 Wilson, *The Eccentric Mirror*, Vol. III.

31 Ruskin, *Fors Clavigera*, Letter 90, May 1883. *Works*, xxix, 424–425, quoted in *Dickens: The Critical Heritage* p. 101.

32 It is the novel in which Dickens most compulsively imagines himself as heir to Shakespeare and English literature – curiously, again in one of the dithering maternal fantasies of Mrs. Nickleby, truly a "stage mother."

2 *DOMBEY AND SON*: THE DAUGHTER'S NOTHING

1 For another discussion of family in *Dombey and Son*, see Robert Clark, "Riddling the Family Firm: The Sexual Economy in *Dombey and Son*" *ELH* No. 41, 1984, pp. 69–84.

2 *Dombey and Son*, edited by Peter Fairclough (Harmondsworth, Middlesex: Penguin Books, 1970); the phrase appears at the end of Chapter 16 (p. 298) and again at the end of the novel, p. 941. The first appearance was omitted from all editions of the novel after 1858; it is usually restored in modern editions to justify Miss Tox's second use of the phrase at the book's happy ending. All subsequent page references to the novel are included in the text.

3 Julian Moynahan, "Dealings with the Firm of Dombey and Son: Firmness *versus* Wetness," in *Dickens and the Twentieth Century*, edited by John Gross and Gabriel Pearson (Toronto: University of Toronto Press, 1962), p. 130; for a fine rereading of Dombey père and the problem of "firmness" see Robert Newsom, "Embodying *Dombey*: Whole and in Part," *Dickens Studies Annual*,

Vol. 18, 1990, pp. 197–219. For other essays that treat "Dombey and daughter," see Nina Auerbach, "Dickens and Dombey: A Daughter After All," *Dickens Studies Annual*, Vol. 5, 1976, pp. 95–114; Lynda Zwinger, "The Fear of the Father: Dombey and Daughter," *Nineteenth Century Fiction* 39, 1985, pp. 420–440; and Helene Moglen, "Theorizing Fiction/Fictionalizing Theory: The Case of *Dombey and Son*," *Victorian Studies*, Vol. 35, No. 2, 1992, pp. 159–84.

4 For two of the more interesting such essays, see Steven Marcus, "The Changing World," in *Dickens from Pickwick to Dombey* (New York: Norton, 1965), and John Lucas, "Dickens and *Dombey and Son*: Past and Present Imperfect," in *Tradition and Tolerance in Nineteenth-Century Fiction*, edited by David Howard, John Lucas, and John Goode (New York: Barnes and Noble, 1967).

5 "Nothing" is the most powerful of the links between *Dombey* and *King Lear*, in which the daughter's "nothing" prompts the paternal response, "nothing will come of nothing." As a number of critics have argued, Cordelia's "nothing" is the true gift of love – and, of course, her claim that she cannot speak her love (cannot "heave [her] heart into her mouth") prompts several powerful and persuasive speeches. But the "nothing" also suggests the nothing of female genitalia it always suggests for Shakespeare; the daughter, lacking the phallus, cannot own herself, and yet, somehow, remains invulnerable to the powers of patriarchy. Among the discussions of *Lear*, daughters, nothing, and love, see Sigurd Burckhardt, "*King Lear*: The Quality of Nothing" in *Shakespearean Meanings* (Princeton, NJ: Princeton University Press, 1968), pp. 237–259; Stanley Cavell, "The Avoidance of Love: A Reading of *King Lear*, in *Must We Mean What We Say?* (New York: Scribners, 1969), pp. 267–353; David Willbern, "Shakespeare's Nothing" in *Representing Shakespeare: New Psychoanalytic Essays*, edited by Murray M. Schwartz and Coppelia Kahn (Baltimore, MD: Johns Hopkins University Press, 1980), pp. 244–263; and Coppelia Kahn, "The Absent Mother in *King Lear*" in *Rewriting the Renaissance*, edited by Margaret W. Ferguson, Maureen Quilligan, and Nancy J. Vickers (Chicago: University of Chicago Press, 1986), pp. 33–49. Kahn's reading in particular is compatible with (and influential upon) this chapter. My reading is further influenced by William Empson's brilliant and moving "Fool in Lear," in *The Structure of Complex Words* (Totow, NJ: Rowman and Littlefield, 1979).

6 Samuel Richardson, *Clarissa* (Harmondsworth, Middlesex: Penguin Books, 1985), p. 77 (Letter 13).

7 Sadoff, *Monsters of Affection: Dickens, Eliot and Bronte on Fatherhood* (Baltimore, MD: Johns Hopkins Press, 1982), p. 63.

8 Moynahan, "Dealing with the Firms of Dombey and Son."

9 Moynahan, *ibid.*

10 Audrey Jaffe, *Vanishing Points: Dickens, Narrative, and the Subject of Omniscience* (Berkeley: University of California Press, 1991), pp. 74, 84.

11 For the most sophisticated discussion of melodrama and signification, see

Peter Brooks, *The Melodramatic Imagination: Balzac, Henry James, Melodrama, and the Mode of Excess* (New York: Columbia University Press, 1985).

12 In this way Edith moves out of the melodramatic register, which demands a speaking silence – what Florence offers throughout. Edith's gesture, if anything, is an Iago-like refusal of the *comforts* of discourse.

13 Horton, *The Reader in the Dickens World* (Pittsburgh, PA: University of Pittsburgh Press, 1981).

14 The last chapter of any Dickens novel has a similar feeling of enmirement, as all the characters we thought we had left behind rise perkily up, becoming wholly and annoyingly themselves again, in one last display of that repetitive quirkiness that novels call "character," and Freudians call neurosis.

15 For readings of *Dombey* and *King Lear*, see Newsom ("Embodying *Dombey*," who, following and amplifying Kathleen Tillotson and Alexander Welsh, sees in Dombey's cry a revision of Lear's "Reason not the need!" (Tillotson, in *Novels of the Eighteen Forties* [Oxford: Clarendon Press/Oxford University Press, 1954], p. 170; Welsh, in *Copyright to Copperfield: The Identity of Dickens* [Cambridge, MA: Harvard University Press, 1988]). These essays do not link Florence's redemptive move directly to Cordelia's dilemma of "heaving" her heart into her mouth, but any attempt to read the good daughter's silence as expressive poses again the problem of how much love would be enough – and how the daughter is, as in the powerful initial scene of *King Lear*, both to appease her father's devouring need for love and still win for herself a husband. Needless to say, Cordelia has no mother to offer her models of daughterly double-talk – or to tear her away from the loyalty she owes to her father – but her crisis of *staging* her love takes us back to the spectacle Florence constantly and inadvertently must make of her dumbness. John Carey has argued about *The Old Curiosity Shop* that "we are invited to regard Nell as an improved Victorian version of Cordelia, without Cordelia's regrettable impoliteness in the first Act" (*Here Comes Dickens* [New York: Schocken Books, 1974], p. 140), and we might be tempted to make this argument about Florence as well; Lisa Jardine, however, has noted that *King Lear* opens with Cordelia's "culpable silence," and that it is Lear's misreading that is the "moral mistake": "To her father, Cordelia's silence is not a mark of virtue, but a denial of filial affection"; this gives birth to "disorder, gives place to *misrule*" (Jardine, *Still Harping on Daughters* [Sussex: Harvester Press, 1983], pp. 108–109; emphasis in the original). As Alexander Welsh has argued in *The City of Dickens*, "like Cordelia, Nell's only dower is truth" (p. 170).

3 *HARD TIMES* AND *A TALE OF TWO CITIES*: THE SOCIAL INHERITANCE OF ADULTERY

1 *David Copperfield* (Harmondsworth, Middlesex: Penguin Books, 1966), pp. 685, 335.

2 The importance of what David "sees" when he thinks he sees her adultery connects with the narrator's repetition of Aunt Betsey's quiet refrain "blind, blind, blind," the sign of his misunderstanding of his own "mistaken impulses" and "undisciplined heart," all of which lead him to marry Dora rather than Agnes; Annie Strong's speech is crucial to David's coming to clearer (for which, read adult) erotic sight. See Gwendolyn Needham, "The Undisciplined Heart of David Copperfield" (*Nineteenth-Century Fiction*, 9, 1954, pp. 81–107) for the classic exposition of these questions; see my Introduction for further discussion.

3 Alexander Welsh, in *Copyright to Copperfield: Dickens and Identity* (Cambridge, MA: Harvard University Press, 1988) makes this connection between the child's names. For accounts of the breakdown of Dickens's marriage, see, among others, Michael Slater, *Dickens and Women* (Stanford, CA: Stanford University Press, 1983).

4 There are several studies that attempt to connect various "personal" plots to political structures; see in particular Catherine Gallagher, "Relationship Remembered against Relationship Forgot," in *The Industrial Reformation of English Fiction: Social Discourse and Narrative Form 1832–1867* (Chicago: The University of Chicago Press, 1985). Several of these studies raise questions of imagination and wonder; few connect them explicitly to sexual adventures.

5 *Hard Times*, edited by George Ford and Sylvère Monod (New York: Norton, 1990), p. 78.

6 At many points in the novel, Dickens seems to suggest industrialism might go on as it is, and only be softened by the relaxation of play-days: the "attributes" of Coketown that produce the "comforts of life" that make their way "all over the world" can continue; those aspects "which are voluntary" should be changed, to give some "physical relief" and "recognized holiday" to the workers, lest their craving for relief "inevitably go wrong" (pp. 22, 24). For a wonderful analysis of Dickens's "industrial" prose, see Nicholas Coles, "The Politics of *Hard Times*: Dickens the Novelist versus Dickens the Reformer," *Dickens Studies Annual*, Vol. 15, 1986, pp. 145–179; my favorite critique of the "let them have circuses" argument remains John Holloway's, in *Hard Times: A History and a Criticism*, edited by John Gross and Gabriel Pearson (Toronto: University of Toronto Press, 1962). Holloway takes on squarely the chief defense of the novel's "moral fable," that of F. R. Leavis (in *Dickens the Novelist* [New York: Pantheon, 1970]) and argues for Mrs. Sparsit's pursuit of Louisa as the liveliest part of the novel: The "passages in *Hard Times* where Dickens most shows his genius," he argues, come when he is least involved with what Leavis terms the "peculiarly insistent moral intention" (p. 174).

7 For a compelling feminist reading of the "Bluebeard" scene and *Mrs. Gradgrind*, see Jean Ferguson Carr, "Writing as a Woman: Dickens, *Hard Times* and Feminine Discourses," *Dickens Studies Annual*, Vol. 18, 1989, pp. 161–178.

8 Stephen uses this phrase so often that characters within the novel tease him for it – Rachael (54) and Bounderby (113) in particular. It is not really possible, given the inter-textual mockery, to believe that Dickens thought Stephen had an adequate response to the complexities of industrialism.

9 The passage appears in manuscript and in the corrected proof, where it is not cancelled, yet it did not appear in the *Household Words* publication of *Hard Times* or subsequent editions. See *Hard Times* (Norton Critical Edition), p. 247.

10 Nonetheless, the quiescence of both plots remains hard to accept – and it is interesting in that light that only Louisa escapes the worst of her fate. My colleague Barry Glassner has suggested to me that the difficulty in aligning the Louisa/Stephen plots lies in the absence of a specific political program for the working class in the 1850s; while Louisa's plot can be read through the debates over the married women's property laws, despite the widespread interest in the Preston Lockout, there was no comparable political debate in the 1850s over increased workers' representation.

11 Douglas, *Purity and Danger: An Analysis of the Concepts of Pollution and Taboo* (London: Routledge and Kegan Paul, 1966), p. 40.

12 Robert Newsom has noted that the "problem of identity" is "absent in any sustained way from *Hard Times*," but it seems to me where it comes up most powerfully is in Louisa's attempt to make the connection between her legal identity *as* Mrs. Bounderby, and her psychic identity as both Tom Gradgrind's daughter and her own, self-possessed self. That the parody of the quest for identity is Bounderby's repetition of himself in a multiplicity of renamed orphans comments again on the relationship between individual identity and legal, marital, reproductive identity. See Newsom, "'To Scatter Dust': Fancy and Authenticity in *Our Mutual Friend*," *Dickens Studies Annual*, Vol. 8, 1980, pp. 39–60.

13 There is a powerful body of work connecting the French Revolution to sexual anxiety: See in particular Neil Hertz, "Medusa's Head: Male Hysteria under Political Pressure" (*Representations* 4, 1983, reprinted in *The End of the Line: Essays on Psychoanalysis and the Sublime*, New York: Columbia University Press, 1985, 161–191)' Catherine Gallagher's response in the same volume (pp. 194–196) suggestively relocates the site of anxiety, as I have tried to do, from male castration to female generativity. For further work along these lines, see Dorinda Outram, *The Body and the French Revolution: Sex, Class and Political Culture* (New Haven, CT: Yale University Press, 1989), and *The Family Romance of the French Revolution* (Berkeley: University of California Press, 1992); for general discussions of problems of representation and revolution, in particular the power of spectacle, see Lynn Hunt, *Politics, Culture, and Class in the French Revolution* (Berkeley: University of California Press, 1984).

14 Thomas Carlyle, *The French Revolution* (London: Everyman's Library, 1906, 1973), Vol. 1, p. 115. For a fine essay on doubling in *A Tale of Two Cities*, see Catherine Gallagher, "The Duplicity of Doubling in *A Tale of Two Cities*," in *Dickens Studies Annual*, Vol. 12, 1983, pp. 125–145.

15 The second of the novel's "Books" is called "The Golden Thread," suggesting the almost organic work that Lucie (or her symbolic embodiment, her hair) must do. This organicism is another of the things that links the novel to the historical work of Thomas Carlyle, to whose researches and thematic exposition Dickens was profoundly indebted in writing *A Tale of Two Cities*. This debt to Carlyle is too extensive to be explored here; Andrew Sanders has offered a compelling account of the more specific borrowings in " 'Cartloads of Books': Some Sources for *A Tale of Two Cities*" in *Dickens and other Victorians: Essays in Honor of Philip Collins*, edited by Joanne Shattock (New York: St Martin's Press, 1988), pp. 37–52. Obviously, Carlyle's influence extends throughout the historical and social novels of the 1850s, as the dedication and the section titles for *Hard Times* ("Sowing," "Reaping," "Garnering") suggest; where it enters the adultery plot is both in the spectacularizing of the revolution in both novels, and in the faith in spiritual growth that centers both Louisa and Sydney Carton's "Dawn of knowledge of [their] immaterial self," to quote the working plans for *Hard Times*.

16 *A Tale of Two Cities*, edited by George Woodcock (Harmondsworth: Penguin, 1970), p. 121; all subsequent page references to the novel are included in the text.

17 Hunt, *Politics, Culture and Class*, p. 56. See her discussion of public life, pp. 33–46.

18 Carlyle, *The French Revolution*, ibid.

19 Daniel Gerould, in *Guillotine: Its Legends and Lore* (New York: Blast Books, 1992), p. 153.

20 Jacques Barzun, *Berlioz and the Romantic Century*, quoted in Gerould, *Guillotine* p. 85.

21 Robespierre, *Oeuvres completes*, X, p. 353 (February 5, 1794); quoted in Daniel Arasse, *The Guillotine and the Terror*, translated by Christopher Miller (London: Allen Lane The Penguin Press, 1989), p. 81.

22 Arasse, *The Guillotine and the Terror*, p. 83.

23 The passage from Marat reads in full: "It is essential that every justified denunciation should entitle the informer to public respect. Each unfounded denunciation, if made from patriotic motives, should not expose the informer to any penalty." Marat, *L'Ami du Peuple*, quoted in Peter Vansittart, *Voices of the Revolution* (London: Collins, 1989), p. 228. Vansittart also quoted a decree from the Paris Commune that no certificate of citizenship shall be issued to "those who, while in no ways hostile to the Revolution, have lifted no finger on behalf of it" (250); in *A Tale of Two Cities*, "Five were to be tried together, next, as enemies of the Republic, forasmuch as they had not assisted it by word or deed" (314); they are condemned before Darnay, who has been temporarily freed, has time to leave the building.

  The count of dead Girondins comes from Arasse, *The Guillotine and the Terror*, p. 83; the tanning of aristocrats is given by Carlyle, as described by Montgaillard: "The skins of the men, he remarks, was superior in toughness (*consistance*) and quality to shamoy; that of the women was good for almost nothing, being so soft in texture!" (Carlyle, *French Revolution*, II: 328.)

Gerould describes Frenchman appearing in Haiti with wallets of human skin; I have not found this detail elsewhere. The description of perukes is also Carlyle's: "O Reader, they are made from the Heads of Guillotined women! The locks of a Duchess, in this way, may come to cover the scalp of a Cordwainer; her blond German Frankism his black Gaelic poll, if it be bald. Or they may be worn affectionately, as relics; rendering one Suspect? Citizens use them, not without mockery, or rather a cannibal sort." (*The French Revolution*, II:327).

24 Gerould, *Guillotine*, p. 5.

25 For a brilliant reading of rape and revolutionary politics as "generational" conflict, see Albert D. Hutter, "Nation and Generation in *A Tale of Two Cities*," *PMLA*, 93, 1978, pp. 448–462.

26 Carol Delaney, "Seeds of Honor, Fields of Shame," in *Honor and Shame and the Concept of Mediterranean Unity*, edited by David Gilmore (Washington, D.C.: American Anthropological Society, 1987), pp. 35–48; extract p. 40.

27 Delaney, ibid, p. 41.

28 Dickens first conceived the hero's sacrificial plot in writing *The Frozen Deep* with Wilkie Collins; in initial performances, Dickens played the Carton figure, ending with his death, as the tears of the actress playing the heroine fell on his face. The sister of that actress was Ellen Ternan, herself a minor player in the drama, with whom Dickens was to carry on an affair for the rest of his life. Among the other details that link *Tale of Two Cities* to Dickens's adulterous passion, Michael Slater has noted that he gave Lucie Manette the wrinkled and expressive forehead of Ellen Ternan (Slater, *Dickens and Women*, pp. 210–11). In general, the novel's theatricality provides a continuing connection to Dickens's theatrical self-presentation and the end of his marriage.

29 Garrett Stewart gives a beautiful reading of this scene in *Death Sentences: Styles of Dying in British Fiction* (Cambridge, MA: Harvard University Press, 1984), pp. 83–97. But he reads Carton's last vision as "prophetically remembered," and seems to accept its veracity in ways I cannot.

4 *BLEAK HOUSE* AND THE DEAD MOTHER'S PROPERTY

1 Under the laws that governed married women's separate property, what few rights women had over their property (particularly over land) could be maintained in equity courts: this is in keeping with the original design of the Chancery court, to allow exceptions for individual in the face of the harshness of Common Law. As George Ford and Sylvère Monod note in their edition of *Bleak House* (New York: Norton, 1977), "By Dickens' time, however, what had once been a humane and flexible institution had developed rigidities of its own" (p. xvii; all subsequent page references to this edition are included in the text). The Court of Chancery had undergone some reformation in the 1850s – though not as much as Dickens's critics claimed it had. Interestingly, just as Chancery courts were married women's

allies in property disputes, so Caroline Norton claimed Dickens as an ally in her fight for women's rights: she begins her "defense," *English Laws for Women in the Nineteenth Century* (1854; reprinted Chicago: Academy Chicago Press, 1982), with the following quotation from *Bleak House*: "It won't do to have TRUTH AND JUSTICE on our side; we must have LAW AND LAWYERS." Calling that quotation her "text," Norton expands on it: "I write in the hope that the law may be amended; and that those who are at present so ill-provided as to have only "Truth and Justice" on their side, may hereafter have the benefit of "LAW and LAWYERS." What was irony for Dickens is power for Norton: the chance to claim a subject position before the law.

2 My reading of the uncanniness of these early chapters, and of the centrality of the "Bleak House question," ("what connexion can there be?") is dependent on Robert Newsom's definitive reading of *Bleak House*'s beginnings, its circles and circumlocutions, and of the "Bleak House effect." See Newsom, *Dickens on the Romantic Side of Familiar Things: Bleak House and the Novel Tradition* (New York: Columbia, 1977).

3 For a reading of naming, paternity, and nobody, see Michael Ragussis, *Acts of Naming: The Family Plot in Fiction* (New York: Oxford University Press, 1986), pp. 87–109, and Katherine Cummings, *Telling Tales: The Hysteric's Seduction in Fiction and Theory* (Stanford, CA: Stanford University Press, 1991), pp. 191–229.

4 The other only person I know to have noted this is Susan Shatto, in "Lady Dedlock and the Plot of *Bleak House*" in *Dickens Quarterly*, Vol. 5, No. 4, 1988, pp. 185–191. For other interesting essays on Esther, Lady Dedlock, and the will plot, see F. S. Schwarzbach, "'Deadly Stains': Lady Dedlock's Death," *Dickens Quarterly*, Vol. 4, 1987, pp. 160–165; Michele S. Ware, "'True Legitimacy': The Myth of the Foundling in *Bleak House*," *Studies in the Novel*, Vol. 22, 1990, pp. 1–9; David Holbrook, "Some Plot Inconsistencies in *Bleak House*," *English: The Journal of the English Association*, 39, 1990, pp. 209–214, and Gillian West, "The 'Glaring Fault' in the Structure of *Bleak House*," in *The Dickensian*, Vol. 89, 1993, pp. 36–38. Timothy Peltason, in a fine essay entitled "Esther's Will" (*ELH*, Vol. 59, 1992, pp. 671–691) connects Esther's absence from the suit and her "compulsive self-denial" (671) to a larger problem of will in Dickens's fiction; these issues will return in my chapter on *Little Dorrit*.

5 Among the many significant readings of Esther's narration, see in particular Alex Zwerdling, "Esther Summerson Rehabilitated," in *Charles Dickens: New Perspectives*, edited by Wendell Stacy Johnson (Englewood Cliffs, NJ: Prentice Hall, 1982), pp. 94–113, and Suzanne Graver, "Writing in a 'Womanly' Way and the Double Vision of *Bleak House*," *Dickens Quarterly*, 4, 1987, pp. 3–15; see also Cummings, *The Hysteric's Seduction*.

6 As Miller notes, Esther has an "absolute refusal to be touched by the suit and [it is] the constitution of Bleak House that her refusal enables." "Discipline in Different Voices: Bureaucracy, Police, Family, and *Bleak*

House" in *The Novel and the Police* (Berkeley: University of California Press, 1988), p. 76.

7 Tulkinghorn brings her attention back to this "start" when he tells her story to Honoria, Sir Leicester, and Volumnia: "a train of circumstances with which I need not trouble you, led to discovery. As I received the story, they began in an imprudence on her part one day, when she was taken by surprise; which shows how difficult it is for the firmest of us (she was very firm) to be always guarded" (506). As Audrey Jaffe notes, "by revealing that she knows something, she endangers what she knows." Jaffe further notes that this is the "novel's originating moment," but that if "surprise operates as both beginning and ending" it begins "what must be a retrospective account" (Jaffe, *Vanishing Points: Dickens, Narrative and the Subject of Omniscience* [Berkeley: University of California Press, 1991], pp. 152–153)

8 W. Blackstone, *Commentaries on the Laws of England* (London: William Walker, 1826), pp. 454–59. See also Barbara Bodichon, *A Brief Summary in Plain Language of the Most Important Laws Concerning Women; Together with a Few Observations Thereon* (London: John Chapman, 1854).

9 Jacques Derrida, *Spectres of Marx* (New York: Routledge Press, 1994).

10 My reading of the politics of maternal gothic has been shaped deeply by Terry Castle's essays in *The Female Thermometer: 18th-Century Culture and the Invention of the Uncanny* (New York: Oxford University Press, 1995) and *The Apparitional Lesbian: Female Homosexuality and Modern Culture* (New York: Columbia University Press, 1993). See in particular her essays on "Phantasmagoria and the Metaphorics of Modern Reverie" and "Spectral Politics: Apparition Belief and the Romantic Imagination" in *The Female Thermometer* (pp. 140–189). For a fine reading of *Bleak House* and the dead mother, see Carolyn Dever, *Death and the Mother From Dickens to Freud* (Cambridge, UK: Cambridge University Press, 1998).

11 The still definitive account of this chaos is J. Hillis Miller's in his introduction to the Penguin edition of *Bleak House* (Harmondsworth, Middlesex: Penguin 1971), pp. 11–34; the definitive response to it is D. A. Miller's. I would place my argument between theirs not in following D. A. Miller's lead in *The Novel and the Police* and reading the linguistic excess as further policing, but in seeing Dickens's linguistic tricks (or Esther's, as deceptive narrator) as leading our eyes away from a serious plot of property, one that underwrites the extravagance of the documentary wars we witness.

12 The phrase is D. A. Miller's (*Novel and the Police*, p. 67).

13 Robert Newsom has suggested to me that the scene also holds out the possibility that if Lady Dedlock is the Lord Chancellor's wife, Esther must be his daughter – an interesting version of "wards of the court," and Chancery's power to unmake as well as make orphans.

14 The confusion cannot be explained away in purely verisimilar terms: I think Dickens both wanted "Barbary" to be Esther's mother, and knew it couldn't be, if John Jarndyce was to be unaware of Esther's familial connections. Or, put another way, it was so important to Dickens to get the name Barbary into the mock-Chancery of Krook's warehouse, and so before

Esther's eyes, that he sacrificed "realism" – in part, I would argue, so that we can watch her suppress any knowledge of her "own" name.

15 The letter is from George Rouncewell to Esther, apologizing for offering a sample of Captain Hawdon's handwriting to Tulkinghorn to pay off the debt Rouncewell owes Smallweed. The sample he had offered came from a letter to George asking him to forward letters to a beautiful young lady then in England – obviously, the letters to Honoria. (Smallweed, in keeping with the love-debt connection, has copies of Hawdon's handwriting only on unredeemed promissory notes.) The letter to Esther is written in the "other narrative": she never receives it in hers.

16 The phrase "dear one" is repeated, oddly enough, by Allan Woodcourt, when he proposes to Esther and is rejected: he claims the memory of the "dear one" will consecrate him to a new life, but he will not press her to change her mind. It seems to me a sign of how much she loves him at this moment, that she hears her mother's endearment in his voice.

17 See Newsom, *Dickens on the Romantic Side*, p. 87.

18 There are ways of reading Esther's repressed desire in the novel, particularly in her coy mentions of Allan throughout. These can also, of course, be read as the "reality checks" of the impoverished and unendowed heroine who cannot expect to win any love in a marriage market – or the more pleasurable coyness of the heroine who retrospectively celebrates the love she in fact *did* win (won and held on to, a feat not accomplished by her beloved and quite miserable Ada) and who teases the reader by pretending not to know her own happy ending. It is also possible to read in these admissions and repressions of desire a sexual desire that even now cannot be written freely, for the Esther who writes *Bleak House* is still proving her worthiness to inhabit it by being certain of exactly nothing.

19 Portion might also take us back to "part," and narrative parts – both Dickens's tendency towards self-reflexive joking about his serialized narratives, and the novel's interest in parts and wholes – again a recurrent motif in Dickens's novels, and one I have been noting throughout.

20 As D. A. Miller has noted, "Other closural moments in *Bleak House* similarly end by producing a corpse" (*The Novel and the Police*, 96).

21 One of the few comes in the last chapter, when Esther is "looking up from my desk as I write, early in the morning at my summer window" (768). The summer, of course, conjures up her own name, and her repetition of others' admonitions: that there could be no shadows where 'someone' was.

22 D. A. Miller, *Bringing Out Roland Barthes* (Berkeley: University of California Press, 1992), p. 53.

23 In "Discipline in Different Voices," p. 105.

5 AMY DORRIT'S PRISON NOTEBOOKS

1 Trilling, "Little Dorrit," in *The Opposing Self* (New York: Harcourt Brace Jovanovich, 1955), p. 46.

2 What I read as compression, Sylvia Manning reads as ideological incoher-

ence; it should be clear that these readings are not mutually exclusive. See Manning, "Social Criticism and Textual Subversion in *Little Dorrit*," *Dickens Studies Annual*, Vol. 20, 1991, pp. 127–147.

3 Jeff Nunokawa, in *The Afterlife of Property: Domestic Security and the Victorian Novel* (Princeton, NJ: Princeton University Press, 1994) offers a fascinating reading of *Little Dorrit* that follows many of the same lines my argument offers; he reads the daughter's property as, finally, sexual and contained in ways I do not, but we share a skepticism about the limits the novel places on circulation of persons and property.

4 *Little Dorrit*, edited by John Holloway (Harmondsworth, Middlesex: Penguin Books, 1967), p. 49. All subsequent page references are included in the text.

5 The book's title was extremely ambiguous: Elizabeth Gaskell spent time trying to read the book over someone's shoulder on a train, guessing that "Little Dorrit" was the daughter of the prison keeper in Marseilles. John Butt and Kathleen Tillotson in *Dickens at Work* (London: Methuen, 1957) assume that if Dickens had chosen the novel's name earlier (see note 9 below), he would have made Amy's name more prominent in Chapter 3, and would have led up more clearly to the first appearance of the name. I do not agree; as I read the novel, the point of Amy's introduction is that she is almost not there at all – that, as Affery says, "Oh! *She's* nothing; she's a whim of hers" (80). The title usefully recalled Little Nell; and its oddity was similarly useful in arousing curiosity. As one critic remarked, "For, let us say at once, that 'Little Dorrit' is not a broom, not a village, not a ship, – as has been variously surmised at various tea-tables, – where the book in the green cover is as eagerly expected as the news of the last battle, – but a live flesh and blood little girl" (*The Athenaeum*, 1 Dec 1855). Butt and Tillotson, in *Dickens at Work* suggest the title's evocativeness is echoed in Flora's "and of all the strangest names I ever heard the strangest, like a place down in the country with a turnpike, or a favourite pony or a puppy or a bird or something from a seed-shop to be put in a garden or a flower-pot and come up speckled" (316–317) – and again "though why that strangest of denominations at any time I never did myself." (466). But strictly speaking, we cannot say the novel is eponymous, any more than if *Great Expectations* were called "Boy" Pirrip, or *David Copperfield* "Trotwood." I have made an effort throughout to use "Amy" to signify the character, and "Little Dorrit" the collective fantasy that gathers around her, and that is summed up reductively by Mr Meagles as the personification of "Duty" – what Lionel Trilling refers to as the "Paraclete in female form" (*The Opposing Self*, p. 57). My reading, nonetheless, is not as far from Trilling's as this nominal distinction pretends.

6 As Nancy Metz has pointed out, Little Dorrit's story violates most of the laws of story-telling; in conventional terms, it lacks not only details, precision, chronology, but that essential Dickensian element, sympathy. See Metz, "The Blighted Tree and the Book of Fate: Female Models of Storytelling in *Little Dorrit*," in *Dickens Studies Annual*, 18, 1989, pp. 221–241.

See also the discussions of Amy's story in Elaine Showalter, "Guilt, Authority and the Shadows of *Little Dorrit*," *Nineteenth Century Fiction*, 34, June 1979, pp. 20–40, and Janice Carlisle, "*Little Dorrit*: Necessary Fictions," *Studies in the Novel*, 7, Summer 1975, pp. 195–214.

7 Audrey Jaffe has written that what is striking about this passage is on one hand, "its resemblance to an authorial point of view and, on the other, its hostility"; the way the narrator's relation to the characters involves "a demonstration of knowledge and an element of aggression." It is interesting, however, that Dickens places that hostility in the words of a relatively unreliable narrator – his own narratorial knowledge, he might be suggesting, is both more partial and less dictatorial. Jaffe, *Vanishing Points: Dickens, Narrative, and the Subject of Omniscience* (Berkeley: University of California Press, 1991), p. 13.

8 Here as elsewhere, Miss Wade explicitly echoes Esther Summerson, whose "aunt" (not grandmother) lies to her about her birth, and whose sight is destroyed by the possibility of self-revelation.

9 "Nobody" has a difficult history in *Little Dorrit*; the novel's original title was "Nobody's Fault" (Butt and Tillotson claim it was "Nobody's Fault" for at least five months, through the writing of the first eleven chapters [Butt and Tillotson, *Dickens at Work*, p. 223]), which in the novel means variously that no one is taking responsibility for anything; that orphan/bastard children are being abandoned (Miss Wade, Tattycoram, and Maggy being only the most visibly so stigmatized), and that Arthur and Amy, who pride themselves on not occupying too large a role, in their own lives can use "nobody" as a figure to disavow their own pain. "Nobody," I will argue, returns as the novel's "vanishing point"; for a brilliant reading of "nobody" as a figure for female authorship see Catherine Gallagher, *Nobody's Story: The Vanishing Acts of Women Writers in the Marketplace 1670–1820* (Berkeley: University of California Press, 1994).

10 I use the terms "prolepsis" and "analepsis" as Gérard Genette does, to look backwards and forwards within narrative, and I invoke them to suggest the peculiar displacements and hauntings that the narration of *Little Dorrit*, particularly in its constant interruptions through female narrators, stages in its attempt to present what is usually dismissed as a tiresomely conventional will plot. Again, the point is the always Gothic nature of female property – and the narrative (and afterlife) it conjures up. See Genette, *Narrative Discourse: An Essay in Method* (Ithaca, NY: Cornell University Press, 1980), p. 40.

11 "Tattycoram" is named, Oliver Twist-like, by the orphanage; she is called "Harriet Beadle," but the name so horrifies the Meagles that they rename her after Thomas Coram, the father of the institution, and diminutize her first name. But none of these names offers any "authentic" naming, for which, I think, Dickens always means us to supply the name given by a loving mother.

12 This point of view is well articulated in an essay by Sarah Winter, "Domestic

Fictions: Feminine Deference and Maternal Shadow Labor in Dickens's
Little Dorrit" (*Dickens Studies Annual*, Vol. 18, 1989 pp. 243–254), which follows
Arlie Hochschild's treatment of "the managed heart" in seeing Amy's labor
as emotional work – work which, rather than providing an exit from the
book's labyrinths, becomes another form of "circumlocution" (Hochschild,
The Managed Heart, Berkeley; University of California Press, 1983).

13 Walter Benn Michaels, "The Phenomenology of Contract," in *The Gold
Standard and the Logic of Naturalism* (Berkeley: University of California Press,
1987), pp. 124, 133.

14 Michaels, "Phenomenology of Contract," p. 118, quoting Richard von
Krafft-Ebing, *Psychopathia Sexualis* (1902, translation New York: Pióneer
Publications, 1943), p. 199.

15 Quoted in Mary Poovey, *Uneven Developments: The Ideological Work of Gender in
Mid-Victorian England* (Chicago: University of Chicago Press, 1988), p. 74.

16 Rotman, *Signifying Nothing: The Semiotics of Zero* (New York: St. Martin's Press,
1987), p. 5.

17 Alexander Welsh has noted that this reversal of order "is peculiar," and is
one of the images of Little Dorrit "as dead or as one untroubled by death"
(*The City of Dickens* [Cambridge, MA: Harvard University Press, 1971], p.
207); Janice M. Carlisle has called it "a final self-conscious reference to
[Dickens's] own literary form," an "obvious parody of the conventional
narrative pattern" (Carlisle, "*Little Dorrit*," p. 195).

6 IN THE SHADOW OF SATIS HOUSE: THE WOMAN'S STORY IN
GREAT EXPECTATIONS

1 *Great Expectations*, edited by Angus Calder (Harmondsworth: Penguin Books,
1965), pp. 90, 329. All subsequent page references are included in the text.

2 The best discussion of this problem in the novel remains Peter Brooks's, in
Reading for the Plot: Design and Intention in Narrative (New York: Alfred A. Knopf,
1984). See also Edward Said's important discussion of the novel in
Beginnings: Intention and Method (Baltimore, MD: Johns Hopkins Press, 1975)
and Max Byrd's fine essay, "Reading in *Great Expectations*," *PMLA*, No. 91,
1976, pp. 259–265.

3 This process is one best read, I believe, through the dynamics of Freud and
Hegel; for a splendid account of these issues, see Jessica Benjamin's *The
Bonds of Love: Psychoanalysis, Feminism, and the Problem of Domination* (New York:
Pantheon Books, 1988).

4 For a brilliant reading of the uses of violence in this and other Dickens
novels, see John Kucich, *Excess and Restraint in the Novels of Charles Dickens*
(Athens: University of Georgia Press, 1981).

5 Freud, *Civilization and its Discontents*, in *The Standard Edition of the Complete
Psychological Works of Sigmund Freud*, edited by James Strachey (London:
Hogarth Press, 1953–74), Vol. XX, p. 66.

6 Jacobus, "Is there a Woman in This Text?" in *Reading Woman: Essays in*

Feminist Criticism (New York: Columbia University Press, 1986), p. 105; her discussion is dependent, as is my own, on Sarah Kofman's *The Enigma of Woman: Woman in Freud's Writings*, trans. Catherine Porter (Ithaca, NY and London: Cornell University Press, 1985).

7 Freud, "On Narcissism: An Introduction," in *The Standard Edition*, Vol. XIV, pp. 73–102; quotation is from pp. 88–89.

8 For recent essays that attempt to reread Miss Havisham's story along different lines, see Linda Raphael, "A Re-vision of Miss Havisham: Her Expectations and Our Responses" *Studies in the Novel*, 21, 4, 1989, pp. 400–412, and Susan Walsh, "Bodies of Capital: *Great Expectations* and the Climacteric Economy" *Victorian Studies*, Vol. 31, 1, Autumn 1993, pp. 73–96.

9 It would be small comfort to her to hear that Joe tells Pip, as well, that he married her for the sake of the small child. The only attempt I know of to see anything sympathetic in Mrs. Joe's character is Richard Barickman, Susan MacDonald, and Myra Stark, *Corrupt Relations: Dickens, Thackeray, Trollope, Collins, and the Victorian Sexual System* (New York: Columbia University Press, 1982), pp. 66–75. They, too, focus on the violence of the novel; they do not note in such detail the traces of an earlier, happier life for Mrs. Joe.

10 For a discussion of "making" and its counterpart in the novel, "forging," see John Jordan's fine essay, "The Medium of *Great Expectations*," *Dickens Studies Annual*, No. 11, 1983, pp. 73–88.

11 Robert Polhemus's beautiful reading of the novel, "The Fixation of Love: Charles Dickens's *Great Expectations*" in *Erotic Faith: Being in Love from Jane Austen to D.H. Lawrence* (Chicago: University of Chicago Press, 1990, pp. 137–167), opens with a reading of Pip's confession at Magwitch's deathbed, and its movement from heavenly comfort to erotic devotion. Estella, of course, is not allowed near her father's deathbed – and of course, there is no suggestion that she (any more than Pip did initially) would welcome this, but she is not allowed the possibility of moral redemption that caring for Magwitch quite beautifully offers Pip. It is important to stress, however, that she has parents: like Oliver and Esther (to whom she is linguistically linked) and *unlike* "real" abandoned infants (Miss Wade, Tattycoram) she is not the daughter of "nobody" after all. Unlike them, she never learns this.

12 The still classic treatment of the question of these hulking and menacing doubles is Julian Moynahan's "The Hero's Guilt," in *Essays in Criticism*, 10 January 1960, reprinted in *Critical Essays on Charles Dickens's Great Expectation*, edited by Michael Cotsell (Boston: G. K. Hall, 1990), pp. 73–87.

13 See Polhemus "The Fixation of Love" for a fine and suggestive reading of these scenes.

14 For a compelling discussion of such violence, see Anna Clark, *Women's Silence, Men's Violence: Sexual Assault in England 1770–1845* (London: Pandora Press, 1987).

15 A discussion of this "doubling" of the ending that parallels and nicely balances mine is D.A. Miller's in *Narrative and its Discontents: Problems of Closure in*

the Traditional Novel (Princeton: Princeton University Press, 1981, pp. 273–77);
Miller is the only other critic I know of to have noticed that Pip and Estella
do not share an ending.

7 *OUR MUTUAL FRIEND* AND THE DAUGHTER'S BOOK OF THE DEAD

1 *Our Mutual Friend*, edited by Stephen Gill (Harmondsworth: Penguin Books,
   1971), p. 43; all subsequent page references are to this edition.
2 James Kincaid has noted that the novel reduces Bella's critique of poverty
   to "a tiresome and frivolous attraction to baubles," in *Dickens and the Rhetoric
   of Laughter* (Oxford: Clarendon Press, 1971), p. 244.
3 As John Romano expresses it, "[Miss Peecher's] exemplus is bittersweet."
   "A good and harmless creature," as he terms her, "she nonetheless suffers
   from an addiction to rules and forms." See *Dickens and Reality* (New York:
   Columbia University Press, 1978), p. 66.
4 Marc Shell, "The Wether and the Ewe: Verbal Usury in *The Merchant of
   Venice*" in *Money, Language, and Thought* (Baltimore, MD: Johns Hopkins
   University Press, 1982), pp. 47–83, extract from p. 68.
5 Davis cites H. J. Nieboer ("the fact, that one man is the property or posses-
   sion of another beyond the limits of the family proper", *Slavery as an
   Industrial System* [the Hague, 1900] and Edward Westermarck (*The Origin and
   Development of the Moral Ideas* [London, 1906]). Davis, *The Problem of Slavery in
   Western Culture* (Ithaca, NY: Cornell University Press,1966), pp. 31–32.
6 Shell, "The Wether and the Ewe," p. 68.
7 For a revealing account of the novel's view of bankruptcy, see Michael
   Cotsell's wonderful essay, "The Book of Insolvent Fates: Financial
   Speculation in *Our Mutual Friend*," in *Dickens Studies Annual*, 13, 1985, pp.
   125–142. Mary Poovey has drawn on this material to good effect in "Reading
   History in Literature: Speculation and Virtue in *Our Mutual Friend*," in
   Historical Criticism and the Challenge of Theory, edited by Janet Levarie Smart
   (Urbana: University of Illinois Press, 1993).
8 This reading of Pleasant Riderhood depends in part on Garrett Stewart's
   stunning reading of Jenny Wren; I will return to the latter at the end of the
   chapter. See Stewart, "The Golden Bower of *Our Mutual Friend*" in *Dickens
   and the Trials of Imagination* (Cambridge, MA: Harvard University Press,
   1974).
9 Among the important treatments of this problem, see Edwin Eigner,
   "Shakespeare, Milton, Dickens, and the Morality of the Pious Fraud," in
   Dickens Studies Annual, Vol. 21, 1992, pp. 1–5; Robert Newsom, "To Scatter
   Dust: Fancy and Authenticity in *Our Mutual Friend*," *Dickens Studies Annual*,
   No. 8, 1980, pp. 39–60, and J. Hillis Miller in *Charles Dickens: The World of His
   Novels* (Cambridge, MA: Harvard University Press, 1958). For a critique of
   omniscience and trickery, see Audrey Jaffe, "Taking the Reader by
   Surprise," in *Vanishing Points: Dickens, Narrative, and the Subject of Omniscience*
   (Berkeley, University of California Press, 1991), pp. 150–166.

10 Al Hutter has memorably examined the culture of articulation in "Dismemberment and Articulation in *Our Mutual Friend*," in *Dickens Studies Annual*, Vol. 11, 1983, pp. 135–175. My discussion of dismemberment and alienation is dependent on Catherine Gallagher's brilliant essay, "The Bio-Economics of *Our Mutual Friend*" in *Fragments For a Human Body: Part Three* (Cambridge, MA: Zone Books, MIT Press, 1989) which lays out the central questions of value, property, and the human in the novel. Among other related discussions, see Nancy Aycock Metz's fine "The Artistic Reclamation of Waste in *Our Mutual Friend*," in *Nineteenth Century Fiction*, 34, 1979, pp. 59–73, and Andrew Sanders "'Come Back and Be Alive': Living and Dying in *Our Mutual Friend*," *The Dickensian*, 74, 1978, pp. 131–143.

11 For an extended argument about usury along these lines, see Benjamin Nelson, *The Idea of Usury: From Tribal Brotherhood to Universal Otherhood* (Chicago: University of Chicago Press, 1969).

12 Henry James, review in *The Nation* December 21 1865, reprinted in James's *Views and Reviews* (Boston: Ball Publishing Co., 1908, reprinted Freeport, NY: Books for Libraries Press), 153–161. Quotations are from pp. 155, 156, 159, 160.

13 James's dislike of Jenny Wren is all the more pointed because of Jenny's resemblance to James's own Rose Muniment, the sickly and quite weird sister of Paul Muniment in *The Princess Cassamassima*, who bears more than a passing resemblance to Alice James (whose sickness and weirdness gave her a remarkable amount of power) and who quite terrifies, as well as fascinates, Hyacinth Robinson. James's disavowal of this figure suggests some of his own anxieties about fiction, power, and the female body.

14 See Stewart's reading in "The Golden Bower of *Our Mutual Friend*,"; for a very moving reading of Jenny that stresses some of the same points of tension and pain that mine does, see James Kincaid's fine chapter in *Dickens and the Rhetoric of Laughter*.

15 I was reminded of this connection by Stewart's discussion of the passage, "The Golden Bowers," p. 206.

16 *The Pickwick Papers*, edited by Robert Patten (Harmondsworth: Penguin Books, 1972), p. 898.

17 Edwin Eigner makes some of these connections to *The Tempest* clearer in *The Metaphysical Novel in England and America* (Berkeley: University of California Press, 1978), pp. 202–203.

18 Letter of 12 September, 1864 to Marcus Stone.

19 James, review, p. 155.

20 Jaffe, "Taking the Reader by Surprise," pp. 162–163.

21 James, review, pp. 153–154.

Index

CAMBRIDGE STUDIES IN NINETEENTH-CENTURY
LITERATURE AND CULTURE

General editor
Gillian Beer, *University of Cambridge*

Titles published